MYSTICAL THEOLOGIAN

THE WORK OF
VLADIMIR LOSSKY

Mystical Theologian

The Work of
Vladimir Lossky

Aidan Nichols OP

Gracewing

First published in England in 2017
by
Gracewing
2 Southern Avenue
Leominster
Herefordshire HR6 0QF
United Kingdom
www.gracewing.co.uk

No part of this publication may be reproduced, stored in a retrieval system, or transmitted in any form or by any means, electronic, mechanical, photocopying, recording or otherwise, without the written permission of the publisher.

The right of Aidan Nichols to be identified as the author of this work has been asserted in accordance with the Copyright, Designs and Patents Act 1988.

© 2017 Aidan Nichols

ISBN 978 085244 904 2

Cover design by Bernardita Peña Hurtado

Image, Leonid Alexandrovich Ouspensky (1902–1987), *Virgin of the Sign*

Typeset by Word and Page, Chester, UK

CONTENTS

Preface	vii
1. Lossky's Life	1
2. Apophaticism and the Quest for the Vision of God	23
3. The Latin Master: On the Apophatic Eckhart	59
4. A Fundamental Theology	95
5. The Trinity and Creation	113
6. A Christology, and the Life of the Incarnate Word	137
7. Pneumatology and Sanctification	167
8. Theological Anthropology	187
9. The Mother of God and the Saints	205
10. The Church and her Mysteries	223
11. The Pattern of Salvation	237
Conclusion	249
Bibliography of the Writings of Vladimir Lossky	255

PREFACE

This book should really have been written by Archbishop Rowan Williams (now Lord Williams of Oystermouth), the peerless master of its subject-matter. But though permitting his simply outstanding Oxford D.Phil. thesis on Vladimir Lossky to be translated into Russian and published in the Russian Federation (for the Russian Orthodox in their homeland, prevented from any major publishing activity for decades by the Soviet State, there is an acute need to catch up with their own classics, especially those of the early-twentieth-century Diaspora), he has not been willing to let it appear as a book in its original form. Scholarly perfectionist as he is, it would require (he tells me) too much new work.[1] The present author belongs to the Chestertonian school of thought for which if a thing is worth doing, it is worth doing badly.

That is the spirit in which I offer this study of a writer who is not only a major figure in twentieth-century European theological history but also one of those who can inspire a serious Christian life. In contrast to Rowan Williams, I have not been so preoccupied by placing Lossky within the world of patristic scholarship or the history of Russian religious thought, though there are elements of that here, especially in what concerns his rough treatment of his older contemporary, Father Sergeĭ[2] Bulgakov, about whom I have written elsewhere in a largely (but by no

---

1 The Bodleian Library has, however, put on-line a scanned version of the original typescript, doubtless owing to interest in its author as much as in its subject. There is an article length study by this author which covers part, only, of the ground traversed by the thesis: 'The Via Negativa and the Foundations of Theology: An Introduction to the Thought of V. N. Lossky', in Stephen Sykes and Derek Holmes (ed.), *New Studies in Theology* (London: Duckworth, 1980), pp. 95–117.

2 For the punctilious, the proper post-ordination priestly spelling of his name is 'Sergiĭ'.

means unreservedly) sympathetic way.³ My chief focus is, rather, on Lossky's substantial spiritual teaching—and, accordingly, that of the teachers, especially ancient and mediaeval, he commended. The title I have chosen for this study, *Mystical Theologian*, is meant to imply as much. It might be regarded as a title with a 'New Age' ring to it, so I need to point out that, with Lossky, spirituality is never detached from doctrine. My title echoes Lossky's own in his best-known book, *The Mystical Theology of the Eastern Church*, a work chock-a-block with doctrinal reflection. Even so, I give, if anything, more weight to his final, posthumously published, lecture course, *Théologie dogmatique*, where I reference the French original, since an especially complete edition, from the hands of Olivier Clément and Michel Stavrou, postdates the American translation of an earlier version.

To go deep into Lossky, cordial concern for the spiritual and intellectual concern for the propositional must walk hand in hand. The consequent initiation into the depths of divine revelation Lossky can supply will, I think, be likely to profit in both heart and mind anyone who hears his message and seeks in coherent fashion to put it into effect.

I have, in this book, a subsidiary aim—secondary, that is, to the principal intention of communicating Lossky's teaching. That additional aim is subterranean for much of my text, but it surfaces at key points, and notably in regard to what Lossky has to say about Meister Eckhart, the German Dominican mystic, in Chapter Three, and in connexion with Lossky's references to another 'sophiological' Russian thinker, Pavel Florensky, in my Conclusion. This other aim is to encourage the taking further of a process on which, in the latter years of his life (if report can be trusted) Vladimir Lossky was embarked.⁴ That process is a re-evaluation by the Orthodox of the theology (and the person) of Sergeĭ Bulgakov in terms of his completed life work, some-

---

3 *Wisdom from Above. A Primer in the Theology of Father Sergei Bulgakov* (Leominster: Gracewing, 2005).

4 Olivier Clément, *Orient-Occident. Deux passeurs. Vladimir Lossky, Paul Evdokimov* (Geneva: Labor et Fides, 1985), p. 93.

Preface

thing impossible at the time when the sophiological controversy (to be explained below) exploded on the Church. Lossky was, it should be stressed, by no means Bulgakov's only critic. Yet if, in the view of many Orthodox, deep shadow darkens Bulgakov's name, that state of affairs is, in significant part, a consequence of Lossky's admirable, yet excessive, youthful zeal. I call attention in my Conclusion to points where, contrary to expectation, the emphases of Lossky and Bulgakov if anything coincide rather than clash. In so doing, I hope to contribute, if in a small way, to the growing conviction of many Orthodox that the neo-patristic mode of practising theology, so indebted to another critic of Bulgakov, Georges Florovsky, and the philosophically inclined alternative manner, with which Bulgakov's name is forever linked, are in fact cousins german, and not at all total aliens, the one to the other.

Blackfriars, Cambridge
Great Saturday, 2016

✛ 1 ✛

Lossky's Life

VLADIMIR NIKOLAEVICH LOSSKY was born on 8 June 1903, not in Russia but in Wilhelmine in Germany. The reason was accidental enough. His father, a graduate of the University of St Petersburg, was at the time living with a family in Göttingen, the mediaeval university city to the south of Hanover, for the purposes of what we should now call 'postgraduate work'. It may seem odd to begin an account of a 'mystical theologian' by describing not the subject's own philosophy but that of his *father*. There is, however, method in my madness. It was by reaction against the philosophical world of discourse his father embodied that Vladimir Lossky set out on his own distinctive path, the path which this book will in due course describe.

Lossky's father, the professional philosopher

Nikolaï Onufrievich Lossky (1870–1965) was an original if by early-twenty-first-century standards unfashionable thinker who synthesized the philosophy of being of the German metaphysician Gottfried Wilhelm Leibniz (1646–1716)[1] with the theory of knowledge, often described as 'intuitionism', of the French epistemologist Henri Bergson (1859–1941), a Jew who towards the end of his life was seriously attracted to the Catholic Church.[2] The Christian Platonism of the rather unplaceable late-mediaeval theologian Nicholas of Cusa (1401–64) also played a part in this mix. It is worth paying attention, albeit briefly, to Nikolaï Lossky's philosophical thought — and not simply for the light it sheds on Vladimir's rigorously academic family background.

Nikolaï's thought was an example, though an unusual one, of the Western-derived, post-mediaeval philosophy so influential in nineteenth-century Russia for which Lossky *fils*, as he grew up, had absolutely no time. The younger Lossky, without any personal animosity against his father, defined himself nevertheless over against the elder Lossky's kind of work. The intellectual revolt of sons against fathers, while presumably commonplace in many cultures through a natural inter-generational tension, had been especially acute in the tense atmosphere of society and State in Russia's late-imperial period. The well-known novel *Fathers and Sons* by Ivan Sergeevich Turgenev (1818–83) sums it up.

So what did Nikolaï Lossky actually teach? For Lossky *père*, human knowledge is obtained through intuition, whether sensuous, intellectual, or mystical. Those three types of intuitive knowledge correspond to three kinds of ontological 'event' which in turn licence our speaking of *being* in three distinct ways. Firstly, events of a spatio-temporal character, such as those of history or everyday life, are 'real' being, as known by sensuous intuition. Secondly, those 'events' that have a non-spatio-temporal character, such as the relation between a quality and its bearer, are 'ideal' being, to be known by intellectual intuition. Thirdly, mystical intuition comes into play when the philosopher considers the 'Absolute'. This is the unique 'event' in the constitution of the universe that is totally unconditioned but itself conditions all else, and so can be considered 'being' in an unconditional—an *absolute*—sense. (The term is redolent of the broadly Idealist cast in the manner of the German philosophical tradition that this thinker gave his synthesis overall.)

In Nikolaï Lossky's judgement, the Absolute must be conceived as 'meta-logical': transcending the laws of identity, contradiction, and the excluded middle that are the ground rules of the logic of the conditioned.[3] To avoid a radical ontological pluralism that might endanger the intelligibility of the universe, he accorded the Absolute the key role in preserving the unity of being. For Lossky *père* the Absolute makes possible substantive agents (like ourselves) that are supra-temporal and supra-spatial, enjoying mutual interaction through intuition and possessing a freedom in which they can apprehend unconditional values and embody them in moral behaviour. This same Absolute can also be discovered through religious or devotional experience. In that context 'It' becomes 'He': the 'living God' of Scripture and Tradition.

Such a synthesis of mysticism with speculative philosophy from a modern rationalist or semi-rationalist background—baptized rather precipitately into Christianity—was just the sort of thing his son would come to deplore as an alien intruder in the world of the Church. It was, to Vladimir Lossky's mind, entirely out of place in the Orthodox context. Yet the elder Lossky believed he was precisely serving Christian thought and life. While like many in the later-nineteenth-century elite he had been alienated from the Church in his youth (in 1894 he was thrown out of the University of St Petersburg for disseminating anti-religious propaganda),[4] Nikolaï Lossky had become in adulthood a committed Orthodox Christian. Indeed, after the Second World War he taught for a while at New York's St Vladimir's Seminary, the priestly training-centre of the Russian metropolia in North America. Lossky *fils* would seek to replace such recourse to Orthodox variants on Rationalism and Idealism with an appeal to the philosophy and theology of the Fathers and the Byzantine doctors instead.

The Lossky home

Vladimir Lossky's childhood and adolescence nonetheless benefited (this at any rate is the view of the Orthodox lay theologian Olivier Clément (1921–2009), who knew him well) from the 'Socratic' presence of Nikolaï—even if he would come to judge his father woefully lacking in a sense of the tragic dimension of life.[5] The swingeing judgement of son on father might seem unfair inasmuch as one of the elder Lossky's works is entitled 'God and Cosmic Evil'. Evidently, Vladimir feared his father's 'theodicy' rendered evil providentially justified. Leibniz had exemplified that tendency, and Leibniz was an author the elder Lossky read with admiration.

The philosophical divergence did not, of course, appear immediately, nor did it occupy the whole of life. The Lossky home seems to have been a warm and loving one. A live-in French governess was an especially adored figure who played a major part in Vladimir Lossky's love-affair with France. Vladmir's son Nicolas, named for his grandfather and himself an eminent historical theologian, reports:

> It needs to be realized that for this Russian Orthodox theologian, who remained very authentically Russian in many respects, France was not, as it was for many émigrés, simply a 'land of exile'. Certainly it was that as well. But it was also a land of his most deliberate choice. His immense love for France goes back to his childhood.[6]

Study life — and the Revolution

That 'love' for France was also reflected in Vladimir's university studies. Enrolled in 1920 at the age of seventeen in the University of St Petersburg, where his father was then professor, he opted to study under a specialist in medieval French history, who was herself a pupil of the Sorbonne mediaevalist Ferdinand Lot (1866–1952).[7] When in 1924 the exiled Vladimir Lossky inscribed his name among the students of the Sorbonne, he was fulfilling a long-cherished ambition. But the price to be paid was the coming of another Vladimir — Vladimir Ilyich Ulyanov, otherwise 'Lenin' (1870–1924) — and his seizure of power.

In 1920, when Lossky's course of study began, the academic institution in St Petersburg was already overshadowed by the Bolshevik Revolution. But the purging of university teachers and the reconstruction of the curriculum was not yet a priority for the fledgling Soviet State. Lossky was able to profit by the lectures of the holder of the chair of mediaeval history there. The influence of Lev Platonovich Karsavin (1882–1952) on Lossky is apparent in the latter's choice of subject matter in later life, for Karsavin combined mediaeval, patristic, and wider philosophical interests. The Petersburg historian had made his name as a student of the mediaeval West; Lossky would write about St Bernard of Clairvaux (1090–1153) and subsequently, at vastly greater length, Meister Eckhart (c. 1260–1328). Vladimir's respectful interest in the positions of Western mediaeval writers is apparent too in his references to St Anselm (c. 1033–1109), Richard of

St Victor (d. 1173), and St Thomas Aquinas (*c.* 1225–74). These were approached, however, from a commitedly Orthodox standpoint. Karsavin's own deeply rooted Orthodoxy (his mother was the great-niece of the outstanding nineteenth-century Orthodox theologian and apologist Alexeĭ Stepanovich Khomyakov, 1804–60) explains his reaction to the Bolshevik revolution: he went out into the Petrograd parishes so as to preach Orthodox Christianity and found himself a new post at the city's seminary, a counter-cultural gesture if ever there was one! Expelled from Russia in 1922 on one of the notorious 'philosophy steamers' (a number of non-Marxist intellectuals were deported by the Bolshevik government in the years 1922–3),[8] a stay in Berlin where in 1925 Karsavin published a comprehensive introduction to philosophy, borrowing a title ('On Principles') from Origen of Alexandria (*c.* 185–*c.* 254),[9] was followed by resettlement in Paris, where his patristic interests surfaced the following year in an enthusiastic study, 'The Holy Fathers and Doctors of the Church'.[10] Vladimir Lossky would follow him here too, in the philosophically acute way he would read the Fathers—above all, those of the Greek East, though St Augustine (354–430) also cuts a figure. Nicolas Lossky, Vladimir's son, also mentions the inspiration of a lesser-known teacher, who was, however, important for the history of pedagogy in Russia. This was Ivan Mikhaĭlovich Grevs (1860–1941), who introduced Lossky to the Latin Fathers and may have sown the seed of his study of Eckhart.[11] Lossky was deeply in debt to the Fathers. But he was never a purely 'neo-patristic' thinker (if such a thing is possible). His writing would combine much of the pagan Greek inheritance, from Plato (427–347 BC) to Plotinus (*c.* 205–70), with emphases drawn from twentieth-century personalism and Existentialism.

The coming of exile

Like Karsavin, Lossky's family was among those expelled in the years 1922–3. Exposure to the first half-decade of Bolshevik rule included, for the still teenage Vladimir, one especially significant event: the trial, which he attended, of Metropolitan Benjamin of

Petrograd (Vasiliĭ Pavlovich Kazanskiĭ, 1874–1922). Benjamin was one of the first of the 'new martyrs' to be executed. The memory of the veneration shown to the condemned man by the people as he left the courtroom for prison was to stay with Lossky till the end of his life.[12]

On deportation, the family went first to Prague, where a Russian university-in-exile was in the process of creation. Not yet twenty, Lossky enrolled anew as a student, this time so as to follow the courses of the notable Byzantinist—specializing in art and archaeology—Nikodim Pavlovich Kondakov (1844–1925).[13] An early article in the Prague-based journal named, for Kondakov's contribution, *Seminarium Kondakovianum*, looked at the enormously influential Syrian Church Father, writing in Greek, Dionysius the Areopagite (*c.* 500).[14] Its topic was Dionysius' 'negative' or 'apophatic' theology—approaching God by rejecting positive or cataphatic claims about God as inadequate to God's mystery. Apophaticism would remain a permanent preoccupation, to the point of its being treated as the very litmus-test of Orthodoxy.

The making of a theologian

When in 1924 Lossky reached Paris, the Mecca of the Russian emigration, and began university life a third time, he discovered—happily for his cause—that his professor's wife, Myrrha Lot-Borodine (1882–1954), was not only Russian Orthodox but a theologian to boot.[15] From 1927 onwards, recommended, one might hazard, by Myrrha, Ferdinand Lot engaged Lossky to do work for the *Bulletin du Cange*, super-scholarly auxiliary to the lexical study of mediaeval Latin.[16] The work bore war-time fruit in his article, 'Étude sur la terminologie de saint Bernard'.[17]

Lossky's doctoral work, on Meister Eckhart, more important for his theology as a whole, would scarcely have been possible without this profound immersion in mediaeval Latinity. For the conceptual side of that work, Lossky's encounter with the premier historian of mediaeval philosophy, Étienne Gilson (1884–1978)—unlike Lot, a convinced Catholic who defined himself as a 'Christian philosopher'—was crucial. He would work under and with

Gilson until the outbreak of the Second World War, and then again, when the war had ended, until Gilson's departure for the Pontifical Institute of Mediaeval Studies in Ottawa. Gilson was undoubtedly the most important Catholic influence in Lossky's life; it is a pity that the authoritative biography of Gilson, by Laurence Shook, carries no reference to Lossky by name.[18]

Orthodoxy for the Gauls

Lossky's desire to become really rooted in his new *patrie* was pertinent to an unusual friendship, forged in the middle 1920s, with the priest Evgrafỳĭ Kovalevskiĭ (1905–70), a key figure in the creation of a cell of Western-rite Orthodoxy, later called L'Église catholique orthodoxe de France.[19] The subsequent history of this body has been chequered. Sponsored at first by the Moscow Patriarchate, to which Lossky belonged, it was later cast off, and adopted in turn by the Russian Orthodox Church outside Russia (whereupon Kovalevsky was ordained an 'Occidental Orthodox' bishop with the throne-name Jean-Nectaire) and the Romanian Patriarchate. Abandoned by the latter, it entered the limbo known as non-canonical Orthodoxy, where it languishes today. During these vicissitudes it continued (and continues) to run a small theological institute, the Institut Saint-Denis (founded in 1945), where Lossky would himself teach, eschewing as he did the larger and better-known Parisian Institut Saint-Serge, which was under the gentle authority of the exarch of the Patriarchate of Constantinople for Russian émigrés in Western Europe, Metropolitan Evlogiĭ (Vasiliĭ Semenovich Georgievskiĭ, 1868–1946). In a moment we shall see why.

In this context of a dogmatically firm yet culturally open Orthodoxy Lossky helped to create a 'brotherhood' (the idea, common also in the Latin Church in France in the period, was that of a 'new chivalry'), the Confrèrie de saint Photius le Confesseur. The choice for its patron fell on Photius of Constantinople (*c.* 820–91)—he of the short-lived yet, in the long term, disastrously influential conflict between the popes and the patriarchs of New Rome. This spoke eloquently of Lossky's historic ideals. He sought an Orthodoxy that would be utterly rigorous in its adherence to the dogmas. Yet he combined this with the desire for a Church that was flexible in all other matters. Kovalevsky's movement sponsored what, by the late twentieth century, would be termed 'inculturation', in the hope that Frenchmen would rally to a form of Orthodoxy that venerated the ancient French saints, and celebrated the former 'liturgy of the Gauls'.[20]

Moscow and Sophiology

That Lossky never taught at Saint-Serge stemmed in part from his decision not to sever ties with the Moscow Patriarchate—despite the way the *locum tenens* of the patriarchal throne had been made publicly to sign away the Church's independence to the Soviet State. During the Bolshevik persecution the Church of Russia had become, in its homelands, a martyr Church. Reluctance to cut himself off from the continuing story of the home Church (however regrettable the conduct of its chief hierarch under duress) was certainly a contributing factor. Rowan Williams has a characteristically complex and subtle discussion of the issues. Unlike the 'returning' Orthodox of the 'Russian Religious Renaissance',[21] Lossky was not in love with pre-Petrine Russia. He had no mystique of the 'Russian soul'. He showed no inclination to treat Russian Christianity as exceptionally favoured. He was not Moscow, that citadel on the way from the forests of the North to the Eurasian Steppe. He was St Petersburg, the window on the West. He was not an ideological Romantic, but an academically trained realist. Logically, then, he was open to post-imperial Russia, like—in that respect—the *locum tenens* of the patriarchal throne (who, however—and Williams does not make this point—had precious little choice in the matter).[22]

The late tsarist Russia he found so easy to abandon had been famed for its 'Silver Age' philosophy. Lossky was in fact alarmed by the continued influence at Saint-Serge of the current of later-nineteenth-century Russian religious philosophy known as 'Sophiology'. (He would have deemed sophiological dogmatics too defective to be termed 'theology' in the proper sense.) In this there may have been a continuing element of fighting an old battle with his father. Though Sophiology differed considerably from his father's philosophical system, there were also parallels—notably in the idea of the supra-temporal character of the finite self, and the dual functioning of the supra-mundane principle of the cosmos as both the Absolute and the living God.

The 'Sophiological Dispute' was an immensely divisive affair for the Russian émigré community in Paris, centring as it did on one of the latter's most revered figures, Father Sergeĭ Nikolaevich Bulgakov (1871–1944), who was dean, and effectively the founder, of Saint-Serge as well as the pastor of its parish. Bulgakov's mature Sophiology had long left behind the esoteric speculative or poetic visions inherited from Russia's Silver Age. But it still struck Lossky as damaged, not to say vitiated, by elements of the German Idealist philosophy which had once been popular in Russia and had served there as an important staging-post in the return of Silver Age intellectuals from atheism to the Church. In Lossky's judgement, those undesirably alien elements persisted subterraneously in Bulgakov's interpretation of the Wisdom of God as that theme is found in the Old and New Testaments, in the Fathers, and in the Liturgy and iconography of the Church. He considered Bulgakov to have blurred the dividing line between the uncreated and the created, between God and the world, introducing into the divine sphere an eternal 'Godmanhood' ontologically (and temporally) prior to the incarnation of the Word. There were difficulties too with Bulgakov's Christology (did it depart from Chalcedon in ascribing a single 'theanthropic' spiritual mind to the Word incarnate?), and with the possibly determinist bearings of Bulgakov's cosmic optimism (will all men—and fallen angels—ultimately be saved?).

Lossky's hostility to Sophiology, like his distance from the Russian Exarchate, did not increase his popularity in the émigré community, which was proud of these religious philosophers or creative theologians in their midst. Something of that pride comes over in a comment of the historian of the Russian emigration, Antoine Arjakovsky, whose family belonged to this same milieu.

> [I]n the emigration, the generation of Berdiaev and Bulgakov
> . . ., while continuing to differentiate itself from the Communist intelligentsia, made a strong claim to its own intellectual identity, affirming especially its affiliation in memory to the tradition which runs from Khomiakov to Solov'ëv and seeking to correct in so doing that tradition's ideological interpretation of the myth of the Kingdom of God on earth. It thus symbolizes in the history of Russian thought the reconciliation of a current of the intelligentsia with the Orthodox Church.[23]

Arjakovsky's words about the journal *Put'* may well be applied to this body of men (and women) as a whole. They saw themselves as called to 'pursue in the emigration the intellectual and spiritual revival of [Russia's] Silver Age'.[24] Lossky's option was, rather, for a new start—albeit one based in part on the excellent patristic scholarship of late tsarist Russia, and the 'philokalic' spirituality of the 'elders' or spiritual fathers of a number of its eighteenth and nineteenth-century monasteries.[25] The translation into Russian of the *Philokalia*, an anthology of Byzantine spirituality, in the late eighteenth century had been vital for the revival of *starchestvo*, or spiritual eldership, and gave a great impetus to interest in the Fathers.

Rumblings of discontent about Bulgakov's thought had been heard since the mid-1920s,[26] but the crisis over his work came to a head with the publication in 1933 of the first volume of his mature dogmatics, *Agnets Bozhiĭ* ('The Lamb of God'; as the title indicates, the book was centrally Christological). The Confrèrie de saint Photius composed a report on Bulgakov's work for the attention of the Moscow Patriarchate. Devastatingly, it elicited a formal condemnation (an *ukaz*) from the *locum tenens* of the patriarchal throne, Metropolitan Sergeĭ (Ivan Nikolaevich Stragorodskiĭ, 1867–1944). The text of the *ukaz* was published in Paris in the course of 1935, together with a response from Bulgakov and Metropolitan Evlogiĭ.[27] The latter was able to continue his support for Bulgakov since by this date he had become canonically independent of Moscow. In 1930 Metropolitan Sergeĭ had cast off his Parisian exarch, found 'guilty' of participation in an ecumenical gathering in London to protest against religious persecution in the USSR. The response of Evlogy, and the French parishes in his care, was to transfer their canonical allegiance to the Ecumenical Patriarchate, which they did in the following year.[28] Meanwhile, however, the *ukaz* was confirmed, albeit in somewhat different terms, by the third of the jurisdictions into which Russian Orthodoxy had become divided, the Yugoslav-based 'Synodal Church' or 'Russian Church in Exile'.[29] While repudiating the sophianic element in *Agnets Bozhii*, the latter found Bulgakov's 'kenotic' Christology in accord with tradition and had, apparently, no criticisms to make of his wider kenoticism.[30]

The principal bugbear for all the ecclesiastical critics was indeed Sophiology—understood by Arjakovsky as indebted 'in part to a traditional Christian concept of the Theanthropy, and in part to the Boehmian intuition of the inner life of God, of the abyss as foundation of Being'.[31] The reference is to the Lutheran visionary, Jakob Boehme (1575–1624), whose works were translated into Russian in the late seventeenth century; they influenced Vladimir Sergeevich Solov'ëv (1853–1900), the principal philosophical Sophiologist in Bulgakov's youth.[32] Solov'ëv's adherence to Orthodoxy had been fluctuating (in rather ambiguous circumstances he was—in some sense—reconciled to the Roman Catholic Church not long before his death). As to Boehme, the advent of his strange corpus of writings, a mixture of Lutheran Pietism and esoteric speculation drawn in part from the Jewish Kabbala, had set a whole series of hares running through the Russian countryside, or, more precisely, along the corridors of the palaces of the intellectually inclined aristocracy. Boehme was especially favoured in circles influenced by so-called 'higher-order' Freemasons.[33] It was no wonder that the Orthodox authorities sought to keep their distance from anything reminiscent of his work and not least from the Sophia concept, which (so far as its non-ecclesial origins are concerned) was especially associated with this figure.

Although the great Idealist teachers of late-eighteenth and early-nineteenth-century Germany were far more sober (as well as substantial) thinkers, Russians tended to assume that Friedrich Wilhelm Joseph Schelling (1775–1854), Georg Wilhelm Friedrich Hegel (1770–1831), and Johann Gottlieb Fichte (1770–1831) should be read against the background of Catholic and Lutheran religious writing from an earlier epoch.³⁴ This partly explains why Solov'ëv and his epigones thought a version of Idealist thought might be able to enter into combination with Orthodox dogmatics to mutual profit.

Lossky's role in the Bulgakov case

What exactly was Lossky's role in this crisis—for such it was, causing as it did bitter division in the émigré community in France? In the first place, as a leading member of the Confrèrie, Lossky was of course implicated in the original delation of Bulgakov to the patriarchal authorities in Russia even if in that context he was 'covered' by the group character of the Brotherhood's undertaking. Antoine Arjakovsky, however, has little doubt that Lossky's hand was guiding the pen that wrote (the other major contributor to the report Arjakovsky names as a former student at Saint-Serge, Alexeĭ Stavrovskiĭ).³⁵ But only in 1936 when Lossky published his own critique of Bulgakov—including a would-be demolition of Bulgakov's self-defence—did his position vis-à-vis many of the Russian émigrés in Paris deteriorate, and even become insupportable. This was *Spor o Sofii* ('The Debate about Sophia'), which must count as the first book-length work of this young scholar (he was thirty-three).³⁶

As the title suggests, much of the book is a critique of particular theses in Bulgakov's theological work. Lossky objected to the idea of Sophia itself;³⁷ he could accept for Wisdom only the status of one among many divine 'names' or attributes, not a Sophia that is a general principle of divine being.³⁸ As Rowan Williams points out in this context, Lossky found Bulgakov's 'mixture of intellectualism and mystagogy' only too reminiscent of Gnosticism, ancient and modern.³⁹ Lossky was equally opposed to Bulgakov's presentation of Godmanhood or 'Theanthropy',⁴⁰ based as this was on the thesis of the eternal affinity of the Word with humankind and thus the divine potential for an incarnation that constitutes the crown of creation. Lossky found here a distorted anthropocentrism in which the Incarnation is in effect a moral necessity for God and thus cannot be grace.⁴¹ Bulgakov's presentation of the Atonement also aroused Lossky's ire.⁴² The notion of 'the Cross in the Trinity', a kenotic Christ revealing an everlastingly kenotic Trinity, reduces Calvary to the status of a metaphysical process, ignoring the drama of divine and human freedom in the career of Jesus.⁴³ But this is only to be expected since, in Lossky's opinion, the Christ of Bulgakov is more or less Monophysite, his human will swallowed up by a 'theandric' will, englobing both his natures in one.⁴⁴ The whole critique is prefaced by a lacerating attack on the older man for his unwillingness to submit to due ecclesiastical authority.⁴⁵

The reader of the present study must await Chapter 10 of this book, on 'The Church and her Mysteries', to see why Lossky, a layman, laid so much more weight on canon law than did Bulgakov, a priest. It can at least be stated here that it concerns in some way the autonomous integrity of the Church vis-à-vis the world. And that coheres with Rowan Williams's divination of the ultimate ground of Lossky's acerbity. The latter was triggered by the 'individualistic assumption that the tradition is a repository of possibly useful and illuminating illustrations for an independently constructed metaphysical system'.⁴⁶ Nikolaĭ Lossky recounts in his memoirs the hostility to his son on the part not so much of Bulgakov himself—he was a famously generous spirit—but of Bulgakov's supporters, several of whom were intellectual leaders of the Russian community in exile (the metaphysician and theoretician of culture, Nikolaĭ Berdyaev (1874–1948), the historian of ancient Russia Georgiĭ Fedotov (1886–1951), and the literary critic Konstantin Mochulskiĭ (1892–1948)).⁴⁷ One feels for Lossky's father, who was unhappily placed, sympathetic to Bulgakov but under an obligation to defend his son's right to champion episcopal teaching—though, unusually, Sergeĭ had acted not synodically but, in the words of the comic librettist W. S. Gilbert, 'on his own recognizances'.

But which bishop (or bishops) should one follow? After a commission of enquiry set up at Saint-Serge by Evlogy had reported, essentially in Bulgakov's favour (though a minority report of two—one of whom was George Florovsky (1893–1979), later the doyen of neo-patristic theologians in the Orthodox world—was somewhat more severe), the Assembly of Orthodox Bishops of the Russian Churches in Western Europe (i.e. those under the *omophorion* of Constantinople) declared in a decree of 29 November 1937 that

> in concord with the Commission, the Assembly rejects this accusation heavy with heresy, not only because the works of Father Sergei Bulgakov have not yet been sufficiently studied or received authorized evaluations from the ecclesial magisterium, but also because the teaching of Father Sergei is not yet completed.[48]

Though their judgement expressed the desire that Bulgakov bring the Sophia concept into greater harmony with the customary teaching of Orthodox theology it was, overall, an exoneration of the thought as well as the man. In the circumstances, it is hardly surprising that, to the end of his life, not even when recognized as a star of the Russian emigration, Vladimir Lossky was never invited to speak at the Institut Saint-Serge.

Marriage and beyond

Turning to happier matters: Lossky was immensely fortunate in his choice of bride. He was married in 1928 to a woman of Jewish extraction, Madeleine Schapiro. The union would bring him a family of four, at least one of whom, named Nicolas for his grandfather, continued his theological work. Lossky could not have foreseen, five years before Hitler's coming to power, and twelve years before the invasion of France by the forces of the Third Reich, the political difficulties marriage to a Jewess could entail.

With the German occupation of northern France, Madeleine and their four children wisely uprooted themselves from the Île de France, migrating to the Midi, to what would soon become the territory of Marshal Pétain's Vichy regime. The head of this small household had taken up French citizenship in 1938. At the outbreak of hostilities with Germany Lossky at once applied for military service, but was rejected on the grounds that, in addition to suffering from a heart defect, he was also the father of a young family. But his patriotism would not let him rest. His war journal for June 1940 records not only his flight from Paris as the German forces closed in but also his attempts to find a gendarmerie willing to mobilize him for action in the home guard.

Lossky's journal provides a fascinating insight into how he understood the West—and above all the France—he had made his home. His journey, partly on foot, partly by train when the exceptional locomotive still ran, and partly in private vehicles when he could get a lift, prompted a series of diary entries later published, long after his death, under the title *Sept jours sur les routes de France*.[49] Here Lossky meditates on the issues of war and peace, culture and politics, and comes to see France as enjoying a favoured space for both humanity and Christianity—playing the kind of role, in fact, the writers of his father's generation had hoped might be the lot of Russia. His France was the France of the saints, but it was also the France of the *ancien régime*. Lossky's family delayed the publication of the book for forty years after his death, fearing that its disclosure of his royalism would undermine his reputation with both the Soviet authorities and the French intelligentsia.[50]

Inter alia, the book throws light on how he understood Kovalevsky's attempt at creating a Western-rite Orthodoxy in the land of the Gauls. 'Gaul', Lossky considered, has 'remained Gallican by instinct, in a certain measure up to our own day', citing a synod under Robert II (*c.* 970–1031) which reserved to councils the right to judge the decrees of the pope, 'if those decrees were contrary to those of the Fathers, to the Tradition of the Church'.[51] 'Gallicanism', at any rate in the broad meaning Lossky gives the word, is 'nothing other than the defence of the rights of a local church, autonomous in its inner life, faithful to its ancient traditions of piety and the Christian culture proper to it'.[52] A Western-rite Orthodoxy, Lossky is saying, is precisely what France had, and deserves to have again. Though praising France for its ability to absorb other ethnicities and cultures, he rejected the 'Latin' stream of influence, coming as it did, on his interpretation, in three waves—the Roman conquest, the Gregorian reform, and the classicism of the seventeenth century. The Latin spirit had left France a dubious legacy, a bureaucratic mind-set and a habit of philosophical abstraction, just as it bequeathed to the universal Church, in the name of a Latin-speaking (or at any rate Latin-writing) papacy, the attempted imposition of uniformity on the unity-in-diversity that is genuine catholicity.

The localism (not, insists his son, nationalism) of Lossky's devotion to France is reflected in his view of the just war. One should not fight for absolute values like 'freedom' or 'democracy', which, via 'hypostatized' or 'absolutized' concepts, function as idols that suck out identity from their worshippers: one should fight only for 'relative' values—specifically, for 'the soil, the earth, the fatherland'.[53] Lossky's model here was Joan of Arc, the 'Maid of Orleans' (c. 1412–31). Her military aims in the Hundred Years' War between England and France were restricted. She wanted to bring the Dauphin to be crowned at Rheims.

Devotion to the holy men and women of France, while focused on the patroness of Paris, St Geneviève (419/422–512), extended to such post-Schism figures as Maximin Giraud and Mélanie Calvat, peasant children who were vouchsafed a vision of the Mother of God at La Salette in the French Alps in 1846.[54] The war journal speaks eloquently of the tradition of chivalry, of the courage of the Crusaders, and the significance of the mediaeval literature inspired by the symbolism of the Holy Grail. For readers of Lossky's theological *œuvre* these are surprising enthusiasms, though they make more biographical sense when one reads of his family's conviction that the Losskys were originally Westerners, of noble stock.[55] Comparison with the poet and social philosopher Charles Péguy (1873–1914), casualty of the First World War, may come to the reader's mind as it did to Lossky's own:

> So long as the France of Péguy exists—simple and upright, with that human, peasant, uprightness that is the simplicity and rightness of the shepherds and kings of the cathedral of Chartres, we have nothing to fear from all the enemy invasions, since it is an eternal France, older perhaps than the Rome they call the eternal city.[56]

Endings

The decade or so of life left to Lossky after the end of the Second World War were very much a matter of light and shade. The withdrawal of the Institut Saint-Denis from the jurisdiction of the patriarch of Moscow in 1953 deprived him of his modest professional livelihood—and the prestige of the deanship of a small but high-quality institution. In 1956 the patriarchate did him the honour of inviting him to make a tour of Russian cities. The experience of the Stalinist context in which the Russian Church lived in its home territories was a painful one,[57] though he found the experience of the liturgical offices deeply moving. They were services 'at which one can assist for hours without noticing one's tiredness, without letting oneself be dispersed in futile thoughts'.[58]

At home he played a part in the Institut national pour la recherche scientifique and the École des hautes études, considering it vital to his role as interpreter of Orthodoxy to the West to find sympathetic points of entry into Western modernity (the Existentialist movement was pertinent in this context).[59] He cut a figure on the ecumenical scene, playing a similar role in the postwar years to that taken by Bulgakov in the inter-war period. In the summer of 1947 he spoke for the first time to the Fellowship of SS Alban and Sergius at its annual conference at High Leigh in Hertfordshire. In the autumn of that year he returned to England for an inter-denominational exchange on the Filioque. In 1954 he took part in the international congress of Augustinian studies held in Paris to mark the sixteenth centenary of St Augustine's birth,[60] and the following year spoke at the second of the legendary patristic congresses organized at Oxford by a canon of Christ Church, Frank Leslie Cross (1900–68).[61] But there was also a certain cooling in his relations with the great figures of the French Catholic movement of *ressourcement*. He had failed to heed their appeal to distance himself from certain anti-Catholic tirades of the patriarchate triggered by the Russian Council celebrating the fifth centenary of Moscow's autocephaly in 1948.[62] It did not help that only two years had elapsed since the Synod of Lvov, when the Ukrainian Catholic Church was forcibly incorporated into the patriarchate at Stalin's behest.

A number of major projects were either unfinished or not even begun.[63] He pondered the possibility of writing a complete Orthodox dogmatics, while also worrying about the danger of a systematics that claimed to say everything—even if saying it apophatically! More attractive was the idea of a comparative study of the Byzantine theologian of grace St Gregory Palamas (*c*. 1296–1359) and the Rhineland mystics, who were not only close contemporaries but (in Lossky's estimation) equally focused on the mystery of being and that commensurate other mystery, the human person. That at any rate is how his pupil and disciple Olivier Clément 'read' what would have been, if completed, a remarkable text, seeking to justify Eckhart not only to Catholics but to the Orthodox as well.[64] There were also suggestions of a new look at Bulgakov, less hasty in its reliance on excerpted passages rather than the underlying doctrinal intention, and leading to a possible rehabilitation (on the part, presumably, of the Moscow Patriarchate).[65]

But it was not to be. Death came, on 7 February 1958, in the shape of a cardiac failure stemming from a congenital deformity. The problem had been intensified, so Clément believed, by the 'hard winters of the Revolution and the civil war'.[66] The wintry hardness was not, of course, wholly climatological. A wider tragedy had engulfed his people. Though a lover of the little things that make life on earth bearable and even a joy, it is not surprising that the sights of this fervent believer were set elsewhere, on the vision of God.

Notes

1   Leibniz was a Lutheran rationalist, whose 'monadology' described the world as composed of essentially independent entities whose interrelations were divinely harmonized.

2   Vasiliĭ Zenkovsky in his survey of philosophical writing in Russia deals with Lossky under the general heading, 'Neo-Leibnizianism in Russian Philosophy', and is sceptical of the notion of a Bergsonian component: thus Vasilii Vasil'evich Zenkovsky, *A History of Russian Philosophy*, II (London: Routledge and Kegan Paul, 1953), pp. 657–75.

Lossky's Life

3   Louis J. Shein, 'Lossky, Nicholas Onufriyevich', in Paul Edwards (ed.), *The Encyclopedia of Philosophy*, V (New York and London: Macmillan, 1967), pp. 86–7.

4   Antoine Arjakovsky, *La Génération des penseurs religieux de l'émigration russe* (Kiev-Paris: L'Esprit et la Lettre, 2002), p. 61.

5   Clément, *Orient-Occident*, p. 95.

6   Nicolas Lossky, 'Préface', in Vladimir Lossky, *Sept jours sur les routes de France* (Paris: Cerf, 1998), p. 8.

7   *Ibid.*, p. 9. Nicolas Lossky gives her name as Ol'ga Antonova Dobyash-Rozhdestvenskaya.

8   Lesley Chamberlain, *The Philosophy Steamer. Lenin and the Exile of the Intelligentsia* (London: Atlantic Books, 2006).

9   Lev Platonovich Karsavin, *O nachalakh* (Berlin: Obelisk, 1925).

10   Lev Platonovich Karsavin, *Svyatỳe ottsy i uchiteli Tserkvi* (Paris: YMCA, 1926), described by a severe critic as 'not a particularly reliable or scholarly essay', but nevertheless 'of no small importance as adumbrating the patristic revival in twentieth-century Orthodox theology', Rowan Douglas Williams, 'The Theology of Vladimir Nikolayevich Lossky. An Exposition and a Critique', Oxford University D. Phil. thesis, 1975, p. 251.

11   Nicolas Lossky, 'Préface', in V. Lossky, *Sept jours sur les routes de France*, p. 9.

12   V. Lossky, *Sept jours sur les routes de France*, p. 79.

13   Ivan Foletti, *Da Bisanzio alla Santa Russia. Nikodim Kondakov (1844–1925) e la nascita della storia dell' arte in Russia* (Rome: Viella, 2011), pp. 73–84.

14   Vladimir Lossky, 'Otritsatel'noe bogoslovie v uchenii Dionisiya Areopagita', *Seminarium Kondakovianum* 3 (1929), pp. 133–44. By the date of actual publication, Lossky had left Prague; the journal's editors were able to update readers as to Lossky's subsequent work on unpublished manuscripts of Eckhart's writing, in Germany and France.

15   N. Lossky, 'Préface', in V. Lossky, *Sept jours sur les routes de France*, p. 9. See, on this figure, Marianne Mahn-Lot, 'Ma mère, Myrrha Lot-Borodine (1882–1945). Esquisse d'itinéraire spirituel', *Revue des sciences philosophiques et théologiques* 88 (2004), pp. 745–54.

16   Rowan Williams has pointed out that Lossky's care with words and terms, typical of a philologist, reaches back to an early period. His second published article, 'La Notion des "analogies" chez Denys le Pseudo-Aréopagite', *Archives d'histoire doctrinale et littéraire du Moyen-Âge* 5 (1931), pp. 279–309, carries some eighteen pages on the use of 'analogia' in Dionysius' corpus. See Williams, 'The Theology of Vladimir Nikolayevich Lossky', p. 7.

17 Vladimir Lossky, 'Étude sur la terminologie de saint Bernard', *Archivum Latinitatis Medii Aevi* (= Bulletin du Cange), 17 (1942), pp. 79–96.

18 Laurence K. Shook, *Étienne Gilson* (Toronto: Pontifical Institute of Medieval Studies, 1984).

19 See for an incisive picture of the man and his work Louis Bouyer, *Memoirs* (San Francisco: Ignatius, 2015), pp. 85–6.

20 Maxime Kovalesky, *Orthodoxie et Occident: renaissance d'une église locale* (Paris: L'Ancre, 1994).

21 Nicolas Zernov, *The Russian Religious Renaissance of the Twentieth Century* (London: Darton, Longman and Todd, 1963).

22 Williams, 'The Theology of Vladimir Nikolayevich Lossky', pp. 2, 9.

23 Arjakovsky, *La Génération des penseurs religieux de l'émigration russe*, p. 28.

24 *Ibid.*, p. 30.

25 See Vladimir Lossky and Nicolas Arseniev, *La Paternité spirituelle en Russie au XVIIIème et XIXème siècles* (Bellefontaine: Abbaye de Bellefontaine, 1977).

26 There is a good outline of its early stages in Arjakovsky, *La Génération des penseurs religieux de l'émigration russe*, pp. 126–8.

27 *O Sofii, premudrosti bozhii: ukaz Moskovskoi Patriarkhii i dokladnya zapiski Prof. Prot. S. Bulgakova i Mitropolita Evlogiya* ('On Sophia, the Wisdom of God: the Ukaz of the Moscow Patriarchate and Commentaries by Professor the Archpriest S. Bulgakov and Metropolitan Evlogii', Paris: YMCA, 1935).

28 Much later, Lossky would set out the grounds for his own 'Non possumus' to the renunciation of ties with Moscow in an article in the Russian Patriarchate's newly created post-War Western European journal: thus, Vladimir Lossky, 'Écueils ecclésiastiques', *Messager de l'Exarchat du Patriarche russe en Europe occidentale* 1 (1950), pp. 21–8.

29 Isaac Lambertsen (tr.), 'Decision of the Council of Bishops of the Russian Orthodox Church Outside of Russia , Dated 17/30 October 1935, On the New Doctrine of Archpriest Sergius Bulgakov concerning Sophia, the Wisdom of God', *Living Orthodoxy* 17 (1995), pp. 23–34.

30 Paul L. Gavrilyuk, 'The Kenotic Theology of Sergius Bulgakov', *Scottish Journal of Theology* 58 (2005), pp. 251–69, and here at p. 265, footnote 49.

31 Arjakovsky, *La Génération des penseurs religieux de l'émigration russe*, p. 98.

32 Zdenek V. David, 'The Influence of Jacob Boehme on Russian Religious Thought', *Slavic Review* 21 (1964), pp. 43–64.

33 James H. Billington, *The Icon and the Axe. An Interpretive History of Russian Culture* (London: Weidenfeld and Nicolson, 1966), pp. 310–11.

34 This assumption was by no means entirely foolish: see Ernst Benz, *The*

Mystical Sources of German Romantic Philosophy (Eugene, OR: Pickwick Publications, 1983).

35 Antoine Arjakovsky, *Essai sur le Père Serge Boulgakov* (Paris: Parole et Silence, 2006), p. 106.

36 Vladimir Lossky, *Spor o Sofii: 'Dokladnya zapiski' protopresbitera S. Bulgakova i smysl ukaza Moskovskoi Patriarkhii* ('The Debate about Sophia: The "Commentary" of Archpriest S. Bulgakov and the Meaning of the Ukaz of the Moscow Patriarchate', Paris: Confrèrie de saint Photius, 1936; reprinted Moscow: Izdatel'stvo Sviato-Vladimirskago Bratstva, 1996). It was a short book; Williams terms it, rather, a 'substantial pamphlet': Williams, 'The Theology of Vladimir Nikolayevich Lossky', p. 12.

37 Lossky, *Spor o Sofii*, pp. 23–46.

38 *Ibid.*, p. 27.

39 Williams, 'The Theology of Vladimir Nikolayevich Lossky', p. 50.

40 Lossky, *Spor o Sofii*, pp. 46–66.

41 *Ibid.*, pp. 53–4.

42 *Ibid.*, pp. 66–81.

43 *Ibid.*, pp. 71–3.

44 *Ibid.*, pp. 66, 70.

45 *Ibid.*, pp. 5–16.

46 Williams, 'The Theology of Vladimir Nikolayevich Lossky', p. 58.

47 *Ibid.*, p. 12, citing Nikolai Lossky, *Vospominanya: zhizn' i filosofskiĭ put'* ('Reminiscences: Life and the Philosophical Way', Munich: Fink, 1968), pp. 268–71.

48 Gennadyĭ Eĭkalovich, *Delo protopresbitera Sergiya Bulgakova* ('The Archpriest Sergii Bulgakov Affair', San Francisco: Globus, 1980), p. 35, cited by Arjakovsky, *Essai sur le Père Serge Boulgakov*, p. 47. And see Bryn Geffert, 'The Charges of Heresy against Sergii Bulgakov. The Majority and Minority Reports of Evlogii's Commission and the Final Report of the Bishops' Conference', *St Vladimir's Theological Quarterly* 49 (2005), pp. 47–66. Further enlightenment about the views of all the participants can be had from the richly documented article by Alexis Klimoff, 'Georges Florovsky and the Sophiological Controversy', *ibid.*, pp. 67–100.

49 Lossky, *Sept jours sur les routes de France*.

50 N. Lossky, 'Préface', *ibid.*, pp. 10–11.

51 *Ibid.*, pp. 38–9.

52 *Ibid.*, p. 53.

53 *Ibid.*, p. 22.

54 One wonders how on earth Lossky had come across La Salette. A clue may be found in Ralph McInerny, *The Very Rich Hours of Jacques Maritain. A Spiritual Life* (Notre Dame, IN: University of Notre Dame Press, 2003), pp. 35–42.

55 'Notice biographique', in Lossky, *Sept jours sur les routes de France*, p. 85,

56 *Ibid.*, p. 27.

57 Clément, *Orient-Occident. Deux passeurs*, p. 99.

58 Cited from a letter of 1956 to his father in Catherine Aslanoff, 'La Prière du théologien', in Lossky, *Septs jours sur les routes de France*, p. 80.

59 Williams, 'The Theology of Vladimir Nikolayevich Lossky', p. 27.

60 His offering was 'Les Éléments de "théologie négative" dans la pensée augustinienne', *Augustinus Magister I* (Paris: Editions des Études augustiniennes, 1954), pp. 575–81.

61 Lossky's paper appeared as 'Le Problème de la "Vision face-à-face' et la tradition patristique de Byzance', in K. Aland and F. L. Cross (eds.), *Studia patristica* II (Berlin: Akademie Verlag, 1957), pp. 231–54.

62 Williams, 'The Theology of Vladimir Nikolayevich Lossky', p. 26.

63 Clément, *Orient-Occident. Deux passeurs*, pp. 90–4.

64 *Ibid.*, p. 92.

65 *Ibid.*, pp. 92–4.

66 *Ibid.*, p. 99.

✣ 2 ✣

Apophaticism and the Quest for the Vision of God

LOSSKY'S OVERRIDING THEOLOGICAL, SPIRITUAL and — to use a term which entered parlance in his lifetime — 'existential' concern was with the vision of God. That is why he wanted to present theology in a 'mystical' manner. As he explains in the 1944 *Essai sur la théologie mystique de l'Église d'Orient*, the theologian must always be looking — with the Church — towards divine union which is the goal of revelation and the ultimate rationale of human life. While his best-known work is his classic statement of that crucial 'towardness', his fullest discussion of the arrival point, the beatific vision itself, must be sought in lectures on 'The Vision of God' given at the Sorbonne in the academic year 1945–6, where he presented the whole genesis of Byzantine spirituality in this perspective. Required reading, too, is a trio of essays from the years 1943 to 1953 brought together in the posthumous collection *In the Image and Likeness of God*. The sharp focus of those essays will best serve to introduce Lossky's account of 'Apophaticism and the Quest for the Vision of God'.

What is 'apophasis'?

In 'Apophaticism and Trinitarian Theology' Lossky provides a useful definition of what he takes the former to be.

> The negative way of the knowledge of God is an ascendant undertaking of the mind that progressively eliminates all positive attributes of the object it wishes to attain, in order finally in a kind of apprehension by supreme ignorance of him who cannot be an object of knowledge.[1]

Human understanding falters before the mystery of God. That can stand as a conceptual claim, but it can also serve as the vehicle of a supra-conceptual—indeed, Lossky would say supra-intellectual—mystical apprehension.

In this essay, originally published in 1953, Lossky draws an attractive comparison between iconography and an apophatically shaped theological understanding of God. Where visual images are concerned, the Old Testament was resoundingly 'apophatic', in the sense of following a negative path of denial of the 'imageability' of the divine. With the Incarnation, that aniconicism passed away, for God was now made known in his own elected image, Jesus Christ. Yet iconography, the authentic art-form of Christian sacrality, introduced a 'new negative element' into its canon.[2] Its 'sacred schematism' was 'a call to detachment, to purification of the senses, in order to contemplate the divine Person who has come in the flesh'.[3] Here Lossky was profiting from the recovery of the stylistic genius of the mediaeval Russian icon by both scholars and contemporary practitioners.[4] Yet iconography's hostility to naturalism is not iconoclasm.

Now compare with this the native condition of Christian theology. On the making of the New and Everlasting Covenant, whatever was 'negative and exclusive' about the monotheism of the Jews had to 'vanish' in the face of the 'necessity of recognizing in Christ a divine Person, consubstantial with the Father'.[5] And yet, as with sacred art, a new kind of negative quality entered into the thought of Christians about God. Lossky describes the latter as follows:

> [I]n order for Trinitarian theology to become possible, it was necessary for apophasis to preside at a divesting of the mind—for the mind to raise itself to the notion of a God who transcends all relation with created being, absolutely independent, in what He is, of the existence of creatures.[6]

Such an anti-rationalistic mode of thought is not 'gnosimachian', a word Lossky makes up from Greek components to stand for 'whatever is destructive of knowledge'. (Compare once again the asceticism of historic iconography and its difference from iconoclasm.) If apophasis were minded to *subvert* theological thought, declaring war on it, it would be untrue to the central fact of Christianity—the Incarnation—which is the foundation of both Christian art and Christian thinking about the triune God. (We shall see in the chapter of this book on 'The Trinity and Creation' that, for Lossky, the concepts of Incarnation and Trinity are inseparably intertwined.)

Lossky does not deny that the speculative procedures of the pagan Platonist schools (known technically as 'analysis') were pressed into service in this 'divesting' process. But that is not the essential thing.

> The existence of an apophatic attitude—of a going beyond everything that has a connection with created finitude— is implied in the paradox of the Christian revelation: the transcendent God becomes immanent in the world, but in the very immanence of His economy [God's saving self-involvement in history], which leads to the incarnation and to death on the cross, He reveals Himself as transcendent, as ontologically independent of all created being.[7]

I do not want at this stage to enter fully into Lossky's 'Triadology', but we cannot appreciate his apophaticism without some reference to the Holy Trinity and its 'economic outreach' to us. As he himself puts it:

> To the economy in which God reveals Himself in creating the world and in becoming incarnate, we must respond by theology, confessing the transcendent nature of the Trinity in an ascent of thought which necessarily has an apophatic thrust.[8]

Apophasis, then, for Lossky, belongs to *economic response*, to the attitude the saving self-disclosure of God in history properly evokes. If that response is to reach the true God as he is in himself, then it must learn not only how to speak of him aright in the saving economy but, more than this, how to speak of him 'outside of any cosmological link, outside of any engagement in the *oikonomia* vis-à-vis the created world'.[9] That is what Lossky means by saying that response to the divine economy should take the form of 'theology', that is the confession of God *as God is in himself*, in his very own life. (The contrast between 'economy' and 'theology' goes back to the Greek-speaking Fathers who had distinguished in this way between knowledge of God's works and knowledge of God in his own inner life.) And this is something that cannot be done unless we are willing to embrace an element of apophaticism.

> Every Trinitarian theology which wishes to be disengaged from cosmological implications in order to be able to ascribe some of its notions to the beyond, to God-in-Himself, ought to have recourse to apophasis.[10]

Looking to the Fathers

Having recourse to apophasis in the way suited to economic response is, however, easier said than done, as Lossky's investigations here of two patristic figures of note, Clement of Alexandria (c. 150–c. 215) and Dionysius the Areopagite, make plain. 'Looking to the Fathers' would become Lossky's rule of thumb in theology, so this is our initial exposure to a regularly recurring theme. The first of these ancient writers, Clement, applied his negative method in a manner only too conformable to a 'pre-Nicene' way of thinking about the Three. Writing before the First Council of Nicaea in 325 (which defined the 'consubstantiality' of the Father and the Son), Clement's mind was over-exposed to that 'subordinationism' for which just the Father—not the Son, much less the Holy Spirit—is fully God. Lossky's overall judgement on Clement as an apophatic practitioner is not dismissive. But it is severe. Clement's theology is

> conditioned by the triadological ambiguity which results from opposing the limitless Unbegotten to the 'limited' Person of the Begotten Son. After its first movement, that of analysis [i.e. the Platonist-type 'abstraction' of anything finite from the description of God], Clement's apophasis aims solely at the unknowability of the Father: the two other hypostases—the Son and 'Holiness' (the Holy Spirit, not distinguished from grace and rather eclipsed)—play the role of mystagogues, suppressing natural ignorance by the gnosis which they give of the transcendent being of the Father.[11]

Apophaticism

In order to place Clement on the spectrum of patristic doctrine, Lossky puts forward a distinction between 'triadic'—by which he means working with a threesome, which Clement certainly is—and 'triadological', a word he uses to signify having a sustainedly Trinitarian theology throughout. He explains:

> [Clement's] apophasis can be called triadic, since it does not go beyond the notion of the personal God in three hypostases, but it is not triadological, for, having as its object the transcendence of the Father-Pantokrator, this negative way does nothing to transpose Trinitarian notions into the beyond.[12]

Dionysius fares better—not difficult for he lived after the century of the great masters of Trinitarian thought and the early Ecumenical Councils which, with the assistance of those masters, taught (explicitly) the consubstantiality of the Son with the Father (Nicaea I) and (implicitly) that of the Holy Spirit with the Father and the Son (Constantinople I, in 381). Yet in Lossky's judgement Dionysius was in some danger of seeking the ultra-transcendent One *behind* the Holy Trinity (it was an issue with which Lossky was still struggling, in his massive doctoral thesis on Meister Eckhart, at the end of his life). Lossky's anxiety does not concern, then, whether Dionysius accepts that the three hypostases are divine in the full sense of the word. Dionysius plainly did—even if the treatise Dionysius says he wrote on the Triune God (assuming it was really written, which some have doubted) is now lost to us. The *dubium* in Dionysius' case turns, rather, on whether Dionysian apophasis 'transfers beyond the knowable the Trinity of divine persons'—which is what, in Trinitarian apophaticism, one would rightly expect, or whether, alternatively, by a disastrous exercise in crypto-Plotinianism, Dionysius' apophatic way

> goes beyond this in its negative rush toward a super-essential identity which, at the same time, would be a suprapersonal Unity.[13]

Lossky will have no truck with such supra-personalism. 'Person' is for him an absolutely non-negotiable term at all stages of the way towards the true God.

To Lossky's mind, the hundred-thousand-dollar question for interpreters of the Dionysian corpus is whether the unitive way, with its seemingly relentless assertion of the pre-eminence of negative expressions, leads ultimately to a 'One' (compare the Neo-Platonists) who lies beyond any merely triadic Henad—the 'Triunity' or, in simple English, the Trinity. Having looked into the matter, Lossky believes not—so Dionysius' orthodoxy is saved. As he concludes his essay:

> It is not the impersonal Monad but the 'super-essential and more-than-divine Triad' that the author of *Mystical Theology* invokes at the beginning of his treatise, in order that It direct 'even beyond unknowing' and towards the way of union with triune Divinity, the theologian in search of the God of Christian revelation, who transcends the opposition between the transcendent and the immanent, since He is beyond all affirmation and all negation.[14]

Darkness and Light

In 'Darkness and Light in the Knowledge of God' (originally from 1952) Lossky looks again at the dialectic of negation and affirmation, this time in terms of its principal biblical metaphor. Lossky's opening acknowledges the near-ubiquity of light imagery for knowledge of the divine. Having in mind, no doubt, the Taboric light of the Transfiguration episode (see Matthew 17:1–8, and parallels) and the later experience of Byzantine mystics, he remarks of divine 'light' that 'sometimes [it] is to be taken as a metaphor and sometimes is understood in a real sense as a datum of religious experience'.[15] Actually, there is not much in this study about either Mount Tabor (presumed site of the Transfiguration of Christ) or the Byzantine Hesychasts, but Lossky had already put on record his opinion of those matters, closely connected as they are for historical theology with the controversial fourteenth-century figure Gregory Palamas, whom he had taken some few years earlier as the centre-piece of the last of my trio of essays from *In the Image*.

This third essay (the original dates from 1945) Lossky entitled 'The Theology of Light in the Thought of St Gregory Palamas',

Apophaticism

on which more anon. But in 'Darkness and Light' it is, rather, authors of the patristic period Lossky has in mind.

Looking to the Fathers as was his wont, he can hardly *not* appeal to such 'authors of the patristic period'. But he insists we must not forget the primary source of all theology—including that of the Fathers and other ecclesiastical writers of the patristic age—namely, Holy Scripture. In the Bible, 'darkness' is frequently synonymous with the absence of God whether cognitively, morally, or ontologically. And yet, intriguingly, that is not universally so. One can think of Psalm texts for which 'darkness' is divinely positive. Psalm 17:11, in describing a theophany, is a case in point:

> He [the Lord] bade heaven stoop and came down to earth, with a dark cloud at his feet; he came, cherub-mounted, borne up on the wings of the wind, shrouded in darkness, canopied with black rain-storm and deep mist.

And then and above all—for it was influential on the Fathers—there is the Exodus account of the Sinai darkness where Moses met the Lord (Exodus 19–20).

Admittedly, Lossky has to select just which patristic readers of Scripture he will now proceed to highlight. That is made easier for him by the contours of the later patristic tradition, which gave more weight to, say, St Gregory of Nyssa (c. 330–c. 395) than to Clement of Alexandria—and as for Origen and his post-Nicene disciple Evagrius of Pontus (346–99, whom Lossky will also want to touch on), their memory would be positively excoriated by many in the Great Church.

In Clement, 'the image of the darkness of Sinai seems to stand less for the unknowability of the transcendent God than for the ignorance about God proper to human reason when left to its own natural resources',[16] while in Origen the 'terminology of night in relation to the knowledge of God is entirely absent'.[17] Lossky quotes approvingly the judgement of the French Jesuit patristic scholar Jean Daniélou (1905–74). Origen's is a 'mysticism of light', connected to an ideal of Christian *gnōsis*—'knowledge'—which Gregory of Nyssa (also studied at book length by Daniélou) will go beyond.[18] At the level of rhetoric the two 'mysticisms'—light and darkness—could perhaps be reconciled. Light may blind by its force and plenitude, and so become as dark. But Lossky finds something more sinister, or at any rate questionable, in the Origenistic tradition. The nature of his objection becomes obvious in his account of Evagrius.

> For Evagrius, the *nous* [the mind, or perhaps 'spiritual intellect'] need not go out of itself, beyond itself, because by its very nature the *nous* is a receiver of divine light. When once it has reached its pure state, the *nous* in seeing itself sees God, who fills it with His light. The receptivity of the *nous* in the contemplation of the Trinity is part of its nature: the *nous* is perfectly *nous* only in the measure in which it contemplates God.[19]

Quite apart from the lack of a doctrine of grace in this conception, the notion of a fundamental kinship between the human mind and the Divinity offends Lossky's sense of the abyss between creature and Creator. Certainly it is a far cry from what he admires in Gregory of Nyssa, 'for whom union with God is an infinite progress of the soul'.[20] This is the journey for which St Gregory borrowed from St Paul the word *epektasis*—literally, a 'stretching forward' (cf. Philippians 3:12–14).

And indeed St Gregory (along with Dionysius) is the hero of Lossky's 'Darkness and Light'. In the former's *Life of Moses* the dark encounter on the mountain summit is more significant than the radiant meeting at the Burning Bush below.

> If God appears first as light and then as darkness, this means for Gregory that of the divine essence there is no vision, and that union with God is a way surpassing vision or *theōria*, going beyond intelligence to where knowledge vanishes and only love remains—or, rather, to where gnosis becomes *agapē*.[21]

Gregory of Nyssa's reading of Exodus here was confirmed, as Lossky does not fail to mention, by his interpretation of a second Old Testament book, the Song of Songs, a paean to the love between the Lord and Israel, at least in rabbinic and post-rabbinic reading.

Mysticism or dogma in metaphor?

At this juncture in 'Darkness and Light' Lossky raises an important question. Those passages in Gregory of Nyssa's writing where the Cappadocian Father describes, in Lossky's summary, an 'infinite nocturnal course through which created being attains consciousness of the infinity of union with God':[22] are they articulating a mystical experience? Or are they simply giving metaphorical expression to a 'dogmatic fact'—more specifically, to the doctrine of the 'absolute transcendence of the divine nature', which can also be termed the 'radical unknowability of the divine essence'?[23] So far as St Gregory is concerned, Lossky leaves the question open, but when he turns from Gregory to Dionysius he seems to be in no doubt about the answer.

> It is enough to read the first *Letter* of Dionysius, an appendix to his treatise on *Mystical Theology*, in order to have to recognize that here we are concerned less with mystical experience of ecstasy than with dogmatic speculation about the conditions in which the knowledge of God is possible—speculation presented in the form of a dialectic of light and darkness, knowledge and ignorance, affirmation and negation.[24]

And if we ask just how this is so, Lossky replies on Dionysius' behalf:

> In that He manifests Himself and can be contemplated, God is light; and if divine darkness enters into Dionysius' line of thought concerning the conditions in which knowledge of God is possible, this is not in order to indicate a new mode of ecstatic experience which would necessitate the suppression of all mysticism of light, but rather to supply this mysticism of light with a necessary dogmatic corrective.[25]

The dual imagery enables Dionsyius to maintain divine immanence in light language and divine transcendence in darkness language. It also makes it possible for him, on Lossky's interpretation, to put forward the distinction between the unknowable—because necessarily hidden—divine substance or being (*ousia*) and the knowable—because economically epiphanic—divine 'energies' or powers which Gregory Palamas and the fourteenth-century Constantinopolitan councils often known by his name enshrine as (arguably) Orthodox dogma. Or at any rate, many—probably most—Orthodox spokesmen now consider the Palamite doctrine a constituent element of what Latin Christians are accustomed to calling the 'deposit of faith'.

Lossky insists, and it is typical of him, that this distinction must be seen in a personalist context, in terms of a 'synergy' or free collaboration between the divine invitation addressed to each human person and his or her response. This is a translation of Dionysius' idiom, not an echo of it, since for the Syrian monk believed to stand behind the *nom de plume* the central assertions of his doctrine concern, surely, the *ontology of being*, rather than the *meeting of persons*. In Lossky's frank summary: 'The Divinity is fully manifested and entirely present in the *dunameis* ["powers", Dionysius' equivalent of "energies"], but created beings participate therein according to the proportion or analogy proper to each'.[26] It will take some conceptual conjuring to make the Fathers into consistent personalists! (This is a motif to which we shall return.)

Lossky ends his essay by suggesting an explanation for the disappearance, more or less, of the 'darkness' metaphor in later Byzantine Christianity. It had served its purpose, he thinks, by acting as midwife to the essence–energies distinction. Henceforth, light mysticism, which was no metaphor but a 'real element in mystical experience', could reign unchallenged. The darkness of Sinai is replaced by the light of Tabor. Moses can at last see the 'glorious face of God incarnate'.[27] The way is open, in other words, for Gregory Palamas to come into the spotlight, from out of the wings.

Enter Gregory Palamas

In 'The Theology of Light in the Thought of St Gregory Palamas' Lossky had been less willing to consider the possibility that the essence–energies distinction arises not from mystical experience as such but from a dogmatic-speculative reflection on the conditions of the knowledge of God. That is because, in that final essay of my trio, he was concerned to defend the original claims of the

Hesychast monks as well as those of the subsequently defined Orthodox doctrine. And the monks were interested above all in contemplative experience, in prayerful God-awareness. It was their defenders who saw the need to take the fight onto the plane of theological epistemology.

As in *The Mystical Theology of the Eastern Church* which the 1943 essay on Gregory Palamas anticipates by a year, Lossky wishes to maintain *a.* the real connexion between mysticism and theology, *b.* the essence–energies distinction in which that connexion is wonderfully verified, *c.* the uncreated nature of the Taboric light which furnishes a New Testament foundation for the distinction in question, and *d.* the properly antinomic character of a theological approach for which apophaticism is not simply a corrective to excessive cataphaticism, much less at parity with cataphaticism in general, but actually exceeds it in importance. Only radical apophasis, with its transcending of a theology that is predominantly either conceptual or even empirical (for some had suggested that the 'light' of the Transfiguration, witnessed by three disciples, was a divinely arranged atmospheric effect), justifies in the last analysis the claims of the first three members of the list given above.

The Palamas essay sees Lossky at his most feisty, rumbustiously discontent with modern Latin readings of Gregory Palamas, and champion of the non-innovatory character of his doctrine when it is compared with the writings of the great Cappadocians (not only St Gregory of Nyssa but also St Gregory of Nazianzus, *c.* 329–*c.* 389, and St Basil the Great, *c.* 330–79), St Maximus the Confessor (*c.* 580–662), and St John of Damascus (*c.* 655–*c.* 750). It is important to notice that Lossky's apologia for Gregory Palamas sets out from the *Hagioritic Tome*, the defence of the claims of the Hesychast monks signed by a number of Athonite abbots and other monks, but compiled, in the late 1330s, by Gregory Palamas' disciple Philotheos Kokkinos (1300–79), later to be patriarch of Constantinople. As reported by Lossky, the *Tome* makes three basic claims. First, Old Testament prophecies foreshadow the 'dogmas' of the age of the Gospel. Secondly, those dogmas, because they are the anticipation of the future Kingdom, themselves appear as 'mysteries'. Thirdly, those 'mysteries' can be experienced by holy men and women in the Church, those who 'live in perfect union with God, transformed by grace and belonging rather to the future life than to our earthly life'.[28] The importance for theological history of taking as departure-point the *Tome* (and not, say, exegesis of the patristic texts relevant to the essence–energies distinction) is that it obliged Gregory Palamas, in defending the monks, to face a question wider than one point of doctrine: what form should Christian theology take if the claims of the *Hagioritic Tome* are true?

The question could open up a rich vein of 'fundamental' theology, to use a later Roman Catholic word. But in effect Lossky confines himself to the single aspect with which Gregory Palamas' name has become for ever identified. How, on this scheme, might one approach the issue of knowing God as he is in himself? Contrasting, in stripped-down terms, a Thomist approach with one better suited to the *Hagioritic Tome*, Lossky rules out the notion of a theology for which God is utterly simple, his attributes identical with himself, and his essence, whilst surpassing our understanding, knowable in part by means of analogies. And he rules in the notion of a theology which holds the divine essence to be absolutely unknowable ('one would sooner affirm that God cannot be termed a simple essence than allow His absolute unknowability to be weakened'[29]) and yet antinomically—by a pairing of seemingly opposed statements—also affirms the possibility of contemplating divine mysteries and thus of knowing God. The antinomy concerned is no regrettable necessity, suspect to logic but the best we can do in the situation. It is, says Lossky, the very lever which 'raises the spirit from the realm of concepts to the concrete data of Revelation'.[30]

Now the particular antinomy in question fits perfectly with the Dionysian manner we have already studied above. It is 'the antinomy of two theological ways, the positive and the negative, established by Dionysius the Areopagite'.[31] Lossky is well aware that for St Thomas and his school—whom he pays the compliment of taking as Orthodoxy's most prestigious alternative—there is also a dual employment of the *via positiva* and the *via negativa* in matters of divinity. But, in his view, the attempt fully to reconcile the two by allowing them to generate a third 'way', the so called *via eminentiae* or 'way of eminence', is the Achilles' heel of the Thomist approach. (One cannot say of the 'Latin approach' *tout court* since Lossky regards the fifteenth-century theologian Nicholas of Cusa—and indeed the 'entire German school of mysticism'—as thoroughly Dionysian on the point.[32]) But where presumably Gregory Palamas differs from the mediaeval Germans is that he does not regard the antinomy as vital in the epistemological (or the spiritual) order alone. More than this, the antinomy has its foundation in the divine being itself. As with the comparable antinomy of oneness and threeness, which takes its foundation from the distinction in God between the nature and the Persons, so here too 'the antinomy of the two ways discloses to our spirit a mysterious distinction in God's very being'.[33] It is of course the essence–energies distinction which we at last arrive at from that — by now — argumentatively rather distant beginning in the *Tome*.

Lossky's exposition of the essence–energies distinction is lucid, and it does not seek to conceal the sometimes strange character of Gregory Palamas' vocabulary. He emphasizes that the divine energies will be misconstrued if we take them to be *effects* of divine action—and even if we allow, or insist, that the divine Agent is himself operative and thus present in his effects (which is, no doubt, how most Catholic theologians would understand the meaning of the patristic texts, from Basil the Great onwards, that Gregory Palamas cites). Lossky stresses that, had the world never come into being, God would still have existed in the energies, outside his own essence of which they are the overflow (for that overflow, Gregory Palamas—or possibly, if the text concerned be inauthentic, a later disciple—uses the unhappy formula, the 'inferior Divinity'[34]). But, says Lossky, this does not entail a schism in the divine being. 'He remains identical in these two modes of existence', the same God—if also different, because, giving himself *energetically*, he is nonetheless incommunicable *essentially*.[35] Lossky notes how in the latter respect Gregory prefers to the term *ousia* the more exotic, Dionysian word *hyperousiotēs*, 'super-essence', in order to make the point that God is always more-than-essence if he is the living God attested in the Scriptures.

This emphasis on the fullness of God in his energies is, in Lossky's opinion, necessary in order to safeguard the realism of revelation, of mystical experience, and ultimately of salvation itself. Were the energies a diminished version of divine being then it would be difficult to say that in these three realms, crucial as they are to the Christian faith and hope, it was in the proper sense God himself with whom we have to do. If, in another curious and readily misleading idiom, Gregory Palamas calls the energies 'divinities' in the plural it is because he wants to say that in them all three Trinitarian Persons are giving themselves in our regard. In the context of a theology of beauty, Lossky's pupil Olivier Clément illuminates this otherwise rebarbative usage when he remarks:

> Glory springs forth like a river of beauty from the Father, by the Word, in the Spirit who is the silence at the heart of speech, the incandescence at the heart of beauty. The plural unity designated by the biblical name of Elohim signals finely this expansion of the Trinitarian plenitude *ad extra*, a kind of ecstasy of God in beauty.[36]

The energies, flowing eternally from the super-essence of God, and communicated to us by the Spirit, 'make us participate in the life of the Holy Trinity, which the Gospels call the Kingdom of God'.[37]

The experiential realism involved is what, in Lossky's opinion, inclined Gregory Palamas ultimately to prefer to the term 'energies' the less 'abstract and philosophical' language of the divine Light.[38] This is the glorious Light ascribed to God in Scripture and the Liturgy, the Light glimpsed by the disciples at the Transfiguration of Christ, and in the subsequent experience of the mystics. Some twentieth-century Latin critics, like the learned Byzantinist Martin Jugie (1878–1954), judged as puerile the claim that holy monastics were seeing God with their bodily eyes.[39] Not so fast, cries Lossky, for St Gregory of Nazianzus, St Andrew of Crete (*c.* 660–740), and St John of Damascus also found that possible—not to mention, outside the conventional time-limit of the patristic era, the impressive figure of St Symeon the New Theologian (949–1022). The triune God, 'living in inaccessible Light and penetrating by His energies the created world', which means the world both of pure spirits and of physical beings, is 'equally far from and equally close to the intelligence as [it is respectively "from" and "to"] the senses'.[40] Eschatologically, human beings will see God 'in the fullness of their created nature', which is body and not just soul (or spirit).[41] Why, then, should not the experience of grace (i.e. of the energies and thus the divine Light) include already here and now some foretaste of what the body will enjoy hereafter?

Lossky judged Gregory Palamas's theology to be nothing less than the 'dogmatic expression of the foundation of the mystical life proper to Orthodoxy'.[42] This is why so much hangs on a vindication of Gregory's contribution. Lossky can spell out the implications for Orthodox spirituality for us. That spirituality is eschatological and ontological, 'directed towards the fullness of the life of the future age, which ought to begin here below by a change in created nature'.[43] It is also Christologically modelled.

> Like the divine Person of the Word who assumed human nature, human persons in whom union with God is being accomplished ought to unite in themselves the created and the uncreated, to become, so to speak, persons of two natures, with this difference, that Christ is a divine Person while deified men are and always will remain created persons.[44]

And furthermore, Orthodox spirituality is Pneumatological, for our deification is the work of the Holy Spirit even if it is only rarely that his grace appears manifest—one shining example being the celebrated 'Conversation' of St Serafim of Sarov (1759–1833) with Nicholas Motovilov 'Concerning the Aim of the Christian Life' (which Lossky also cites *in extenso* the following year in *The Mystical Theology of the Eastern Church*).[45] The 'inner warmth' of Orthodox piety would not survive the de-mythologization as mere rhetoric of the language of divine Light.[46]

The Divine Light

So much for the trio of essays. They do not stand alone, for the penultimate chapter of *The Mystical Theology of the Eastern Church* is entitled precisely 'The Divine Light'—and that is to leave aside as by now familiar terrain the earlier chapter, on the 'Uncreated Energies', which rehearses the Palamite doctrine just expounded.

What do we find in Lossky's account of the divine Light in the celebrated *Essai*? What strikes one most obviously in Lossky's opening words is the emphasis on *gnōsis*, understood now as 'awareness in the ways of the spiritual life'.[47] Lossky writes, 'The further a person advances in the way of union, the greater is his growth in consciousness'.[48] Whatever else apophaticism might mean for Lossky, it does not portend the occlusion of consciousness. Absence of spiritual awareness would signify the 'sleep of the soul'—a sleep Lossky is inclined to identify, when it is at its worst, with spiritual death (in fact, with hell). Lossky's signature tune in 'The Divine Light' chapter of the *Essai* is a verse of St Paul's from the Letter to the Ephesians, 'Awake, thou that sleepest, and arise from the dead and Christ shall give thee light' (5:14).

As the highest stage of spiritual awareness, *gnōsis*, so Lossky maintains, is, precisely, experience of the uncreated Light. It is both what one experiences and the medium in which one experiences. Here he can call to the witness stand mystical teachers of stature: the nameless yet revered author of the *Macarian Homilies* (fourth to fifth centuries), and St Symeon the New Theologian again, though the simplest and most persuasive illustration of his claim is a Psalm text: 'In thy light we see Light' (Psalm 36:9). We shall not be surprised by now to find that Lossky understands the 'light' in question by way of the Palamite doctrine of the energies, though excusing himself from further explication on the grounds that the topic was already pursued earlier in the *Essai*. He confines himself in fact to the 'light' aspect of the energies, stressing—in line with the *Hagioritic Tome*—that what they furnish to the soul (and body) is neither sensuous nor intellectual light but a light that transcends this distinction. He makes much of patristic and mediaeval Byzantine discussion of the Transfiguration episode, and the prospect it opens on the eschatological experience of the uncreated Light, i.e. that Light as made available in heaven. Such future, eschatological experience cannot be purely spiritual, in the sense of non-bodily, since otherwise the Resurrection of the body would be useless to it.

Apophaticism

In *The Mystical Theology of the Eastern Church* Lossky seeks to distance himself from the 'dark-night' mysticism of the West, claiming that dryness and darkness can only be highly transient on the way of union, if indeed they are not signs, respectively, of spiritual tedium (what the mediaeval English spiritual writers call 'accidie') and, even more seriously, 'the sorrow of a tragic separation from God'.[49] For the Eastern tradition, grace will always 'make itself known as joy, peace, inner warmth and light'.[50] In a footnote, he admits, however, that St Tikhon Zadonskiĭ (1724–83), bishop and spiritual writer, has a teaching much like that of the 'dark night' of the Carmelite doctor St John of the Cross (1542–91), while St Bernard, hardly an eccentric figure in the Western tradition, is—like typical Orientals—a mystic of sweetness and light. And once again, the transfiguration episode in the life of St Serafim of Sarov is appealed to, as better able to make us understand than 'any number of theological expositions' what the consciousness of union with God is like.[51]

If we find Serafim too simple, the idea of seeing God too concrete, it is because our minds have been invaded by Kantianism and we instinctively feel, wrongly, that only phenomena, not 'noumena'—the realities behind phemomena—are within our grasp. That does not mean to say, though, that the simple experience of Serafim and his disciple and chronicler Motovilov can be readily described.

> Once again we find ourselves in the apophatic realm where we commenced our study of Eastern tradition. But instead of the divine darkness there is now light, instead of forgetfulness of self, the full flowering of personal consciousness in grace. What is at issue here is a perfection which has been acquired, a nature which has been transformed by union with grace, a nature which itself has become light.[52]

Where the apophatic dimension appears plainly in these otherwise seemingly cataphatic assertions is in Lossky's statement that the anticipatory experience of the realities of the Age to Come 'cannot be dogmatically defined', for the fullness of *gnōsis* cannot be expressed before the 'eighth day', the 'day' of the Parousia of the Lord.[53]

That does not mean, however, that Lossky holds back from all further theological reflection on that Parousia. Hints in Scripture and convictions of the Tradition enable one to say more than just 'This will be eschatological fullness'. Nevertheless, as I now note, his verdict is an ambivalent one. Following his interpretation of St Symeon, Lossky holds that by the moment of the Parousia the divine Light will already have illumined those who are to be saved, whether they are at that moment dead or alive. For the rest, the Light's rays will still strike and enter them—but 'from the outside', that is, against their will, by way of judgement to condemnation, and this not withstanding the fact that the 'Light' (which after all is grace) is in itself an expression of divine love.[54] 'The love of God will be an intolerable torment for those who have not acquired it within themselves.'[55] In the General Resurrection, which accompanies the Parousia, the secrets of all will be laid bare since their bodies will allow their souls to become transparent, to—in some cases—grotesque effect.

That is hardly a reassuring message, yet Lossky goes on to make the further, seemingly incongruous, statement, 'In the parousia, and the eschatological fulfilment of history, the whole created universe will enter into perfect union with God'.[56] There is a tension here, for in these words Lossky sounds even more of a universalist than his old adversary Bulgakov. The note of brash optimism is muted when we hear him say that such union will take different forms in accordance with the manifold differences of persons in the way, and to the degree, they have 'acquired' the Holy Spirit. This statement is in accord with the personalism which we shall be investigating in the context, chiefly, of his theological anthropology.

But that still tells us only of the variety of unions successfully achieved. Is he certain that there are no failures, no tragic exceptions? His answer is to appeal to the unbounded divine mercy: 'the limits of the Church beyond death and the possibilities of salvation for those who have not known the light in this life, remain a mystery of the divine mercy for us, on which we dare not count but to which we cannot place any human bounds'.[57]

Apophaticism

The vision of God

In *The Vision of God*—his fullest statement of the goal of apophasis—the crucial issue of the face-to-face vision is once again raised. Lossky notes the need for, yet abstains from, a debate on the matter with the Latin Scholastics, for whom the question 'Is God's essence knowable in the Age to Come?' ought to be answered in the affirmative. Their query 'Is it possible for a created intellect to see God as God actually is?' is for Lossky a philosophical distraction.[58] (Here Lossky has in mind Gabriel Vasquez (1549–1604), a Spanish Jesuit writing towards the end of the 'Second Scholasticism', not Aquinas, for whom 'the faculty of seeing God does not belong to the created intellect naturally but is given to it by the light of glory, a gift that establishes deiformity'.[59]) More important is to concentrate on the positive doctrine, entirely theological in character as this is: a reading of Scripture in Tradition, much as the Byzantines found it in their ancient predecessors.

It is impossible, remarks Lossky, not to note the twofold—and seemingly contradictory—way in which the Bible treats the vision of God. (We note the parallel to the way he has earlier begun from conflicting biblical texts on darkness.)

> [A]longside passages from Holy Scripture in which there can be found a formal negation of any vision of God, who is invisible, unknowable, inaccessible to created beings, there are others which encourage us to seek the face of God and promise the vision of God as He is, evidently representing this vision as the ultimate felicity of man.[60]

One swathe of texts stresses the divine inaccessibility. Another promises that those who seek God's face will not be disappointed for ever.

There is no difficulty in finding Scriptural warrants for denial of the possibility of 'seeing' God. For the Old Testament, in the Book of Exodus, Moses is warned, 'You cannot see My face, for no man can see My face and live' (33:20). For the New Testament, in First Timothy, St Paul describes God as living in 'unapproachable light, whom no man has seen or can see' (6:16). The 'cloud' is a term common to both Testaments for the hiddenness of God; yet in both Testaments (Lossky provides a rich diet of biblical references) the 'cloud' is also—whatever we may make of this—a pointer to his presence.[61] The ambivalence of the symbol underlines the ambiguity of the scriptural evidence at large. For the Bible also speaks of (as it were) *achieved* face-to-face vision, not least with Moses (Exodus 33:11; Deuteronomy 34:10), while prayer for the light of the divine face to shine on one is heard more than once in the Psalter, the prayer book of the Jewish Temple. Then in the New Testament the First Letter of John is categorical: 'we shall be like him for we shall see him as he is' (3:2, even if the 'for' can be interpreted either causally or demonstratively: seeing him as he is will make us be like him, or, alternatively, seeing him as he is will show that we are his likenesses), while in Paul's first letter to the Church at Corinth we shall see him 'face to face', rather than, as now, in a mirror, enigmatically (I Corinthians 13:12). Nor does Lossky forget the macarism in the Sermon on the Mount, 'Blessed are the pure in heart for they shall see God' (Matthew 5:8).

Patristic *ressourcement*

Some way must be found to resolve this dilemma, and a neo-patristic theologian will of course hope that 'looking to the Fathers' is it. What follows in *The Vision of God* is the most sustained act of patristic *ressourcement*—going back to the sources—in Lossky's corpus, as Lossky looks at a select number of Greek and Syrian Fathers before homing in on the Byzantine masters.

In the age of the Apostolic Fathers, those writing immediately after the New Testament authors, St Theophilus of Antioch (late second century) teaches that vision of God is possible eschatologically, once the soul is reclothed with its body in the General Resurrection. That is the message of the opening book of his apologia, addressed to Autolycus. The much-better-known St Irenaeus of Lyons (*c*. 130–*c*. 200) had the same understanding in his far fuller treatise *Against the Heresies*.[62] Irenaeus' account is, observes Lossky, complex, structured as it is by his biblically based teaching on succeeding dispensations of the Father's outreach to man through his Word and Spirit and by the principle of gradualism in human accommodation to communion with God, which is typically Irenaeus' own. Lossky sums it up:

> By vision we participate in God just as we participate in light by seeing it. Now the invisible God is revealed in Christ transfigured by the light of the Father, the light in which man receives the incorruptible state of eternal life. The possibility of enjoying the deifying vision here on earth by receiving the light of the Father through the Incarnate Word is, for St Irenaeus, projected on to an eschatological plane—it signifies the millennial reign of the righteous. It would seem that the theme of mystical contemplation was not raised for him in any other way than a new historical epoch for mankind, in which the righteous will be gradually accustomed to perfect communion with God.[63]

Seeking to discover how the subsequent Greek and Syrian Fathers took further these first essays in interpretation, Lossky surveys a number of figures. Chief among them are the early Alexandrian school (Clement—predictably enough, Origen, and a short section on St Athanasius the Great (*c.* 296–373)), followed by the great Cappadocians. Next come the Syro-Palestinians—a slightly unconventional grouping, consisting of mainly St Cyril of Jerusalem (*c.* 315–87), Epiphanius of Salamis (*c.* 315–403), St John Chrysostom (*c.* 347–407), and Theodoret of Cyr (*c.* 393–*c.* 460), whereupon the spotlight moves on to Theodoret's arch-enemy, St Cyril of Alexandria (d. 444), and a gaggle of 'ascetics', notably Evagrius, 'Macarius', and Diadochus of Photike (mid-fifth century), together with a second appearance for the Cappadocian Gregorys, regarded now as spiritual masters and not just dogmatic teachers. It is on this basis that Lossky equips himself to deal with those he sees as Byzantine theologians in the proper sense: Dionysius (of course), Maximus, John of Damascus, and Symeon the New Theologian, with, as their culmination (in the perspective of thought about the vision of God), the high-mediaeval Gregory Palamas.

Throughout, Lossky is at pains to distinguish a biblical message from a Hellenistic vehicle, bearing in mind the onslaught launched by the Swedish Lutheran Anders Nygren (1890–1978) against the Fathers for conflating biblical *agapē* and pagan *erōs* for God, and the milder remonstrances against 'philosophical spirituality' in the patristic Church found in the writings of the French Dominican scholar of late antiquity André-Jean Festugière (1898–1982). However, despite Lossky's commitment to a full-blooded eschatology he rejects any attempt to limit the Christian vision of God to the final consummation. As he puts it, 'The problem of communion with God in contemplation ought to be raised in Christian experience'.[64]

This, then, is Lossky's verdict, as he takes his patristic interlocutors one by one in a masterly survey. By an over-intellectualistic approach to the Christian life Clement, as to a degree Origen later, seeks to anticipate in the personal contemplation of perfected Christians what Irenaeus would have reserved to the Age to Come. Though Clement lacks the notion of the *ousia* of the Trinity, he holds out the hope that the Christian gnostic in whom love raises faith to knowledge will succeed in seeing the 'Abyss' of the Father, which is his equivalent of the 'beatific vision' of the essence of God.[65] As to Origen, he teaches that the ultimate goal of the contemplation in which the human soul celebrates its mystic nuptials with the Logos incarnate is the divine nature itself. Its simplicity is represented by the Father, as perfected spirits, reconstituted in their primordial condition by union with the Son, can come to know that Father, their minds made one with God. While Origen is an ardent Christian who longed for martyrdom, he is also a speculative Greek who took the crucial ontological boundary to run between the intelligible realm, divine and non-divine, on the one hand, and the world of psyche and matter on the other, rather than between the Uncreated and the created.[66]

In the case of Athanasius, treated much more briefly by Lossky, contact with the desert monasticism of St Anthony of Egypt (*c.* 251–356) took him far from the echoes of Origen in such early writings as his *Against the Pagans*. Anthony's example and influence saved Athanasius, so Lossky implies, from the hyper-philosophical reading of Christianity in the Alexandrian school.

> It is precisely this [desert] environment which represents for St Athanasius the realization of the Christian ideal: i.e.

communion with God in the Incarnate Word, in Christ who has conquered sin and death by communicating to created nature the premises of incorruptibility and future deification.[67]

On the Cappadocians, Lossky makes much of the significance of their anti-Arianism, since even for an Origen-influenced Alexandrian like Didymus the Blind (c. 313–98), affirmation of the consubstantiality of the Persons must rule out any notion that the Godhead is in every sense simple, and to that degree comprehensible, at least with the help of grace. Lossky sees the Cappadocian theology of the divine mystery as the pearl produced by the grit in the oyster that was 'Anomoeanism'. This radicalized form of Arianism, for which the Son was essentially 'unlike' (*anomoios*) the Father—in more recent scholarship it is often referred to as 'Neo-Arianism'—had produced in its spokesman Eunomius (d. 394) a Christological heretic who was also a fervent opponent of any notion of the incomprehensibility of God. For Eunomius the proper name of God can readily be found. It is 'unbegotten', meaning 'from itself', or 'having itself as its foundation of being'. Once we have grasped this basic metaphysical fact we understand as much about God as God understands about himself: namely, everything! It was because the Son, according to the New Testament witness, was, by contrast, *begotten* that Anomoeans could declare him to be utterly unlike God. The Cappadocians had to refute Eunomius' gnoseology if they were efficaciously to defend the faith of the Church.

Both Basil and Gregory of Nyssa write critiques of Eunomius, arguing that even the being of finite realities is inexhaustible: *a fortiori* how much more that of God—above all, once it is affirmed that the divine *ousia* is that of a Trinity of Persons. To the celebration of Its mystery Gregory of Nazianzus, the last of the Cappadocian trio, brings the gifts of a poet as well as a philosopher. For Lossky, as a convinced Palamite, it is impossible to overlook in this connection the distinction between the divine *ousia* and the 'energies' or self-manifesting operations of God, flagged up in this controversy by Basil. For the latter, while we know God in his operations (compare energies), which reach us in salvation history, God nevertheless remains inaccessible in his essence.

Of scarcely less importance is Nyssa's teaching on the endless longing progression into the divine mystery which exceeds the grasp of the Seraphim but is participable when it is mirrored in the purified and sanctified soul.[68]

The Syro-Palestinians (Lossky's portmanteau term for very different figures) continue to underline the divine incomprehensibility. John Chrysostom supplies the language of *synkatabasis* ('condescension') for an economic self-disclosure of God in biblical revelation that leaves God's essential mystery intact. That economy of condescension has its climax in the Incarnation, when God makes himself visible in the humanity of his Son—which will also be the case in the Parousia when the medium of his humanity, now clothed in glory, will be how the face-to-face vision of the New Testament promise is actually realized. In the more Nestorian-leaning Antiochene writers Theodore of Mopsuestia (c. 350–428) and Theodoret of Cyr, who lack any concept of the *perikhōrēsis* or 'interchange' between the divine and human natures of Christ, it is far from evident how that eschatological vision of his humanity can be, precisely, a vision of God.[69]

This is where, for Lossky, Cyril of Alexandria comes to the rescue. For the great champion of Mary's divine motherhood, we are deified by the Son in the Holy Spirit in a process whose sacramental foundation in baptism and eucharist remains crucial throughout. In the Age to Come, our partial knowledge now will be eclipsed by illumination from Christ—not simply from his humanity but from the divinity which after the hypostatic union in Mary's womb remains inseparably fused with it in his single Person. Then, in the true face-to-face encounter, the beauty of the divine nature will transform us.[70]

Perusal of selected ascetic writers from Evagrius to Diadochus suggests, in Lossky's portrayal, a parallel development to what we find in theology proper from Clement of Alexandria to his fellow citizen St Cyril. There is a journey away from a markedly intellectualist mysticism of ascent to God to an understanding of union which is both more 'cordial', of the heart, as well as more obviously bound up with the Christological hope of the Church.

Apophaticism

The monastic teacher Evagrius of Pontus was closely connected to all three of the great Cappadocian Fathers, so, unsurprisingly, the life of prayer for him is a life of contemplation of the Trinity. If in this he differs from the doctrinally more primitive Clement, he shares Clement's (and Origen's) emphasis on the intellect (*nous*) as the true locus of divine presence. In knowing itself the mind knows itself to be the place of God, the 'receptacle of the light of the Trinity'.[71] This condition (over against Nyssa with his emphasis on unending progress) is utterly stable. It is also without images of any kind. Whether Evagrius understands it as a vision of the divine essence, as distinct from divine Light, Lossky does not feel able to say.

Evagrius' dislike of images, even Christological ones, in the context of the prayer of the deified *nous*, has been ascribed to a reaction against the contemporary movement known as Messalianism: a 'mystical materialism', in Lossky's phrase, for which visible theophanies in sensuous form make up the staple of the life of union with God.[72] The homilies of Pseudo-Macarius have sometimes been seen—wrongly, Lossky was sure—as Messalian, though possibly Messalianism might be regarded as an extreme version of the spiritual tendency they represent. The homilies look to the perceived experience of grace in the heart of man and the likelihood, for those advanced on the way of union, of visionary revelations of God. At the same time, they are profoundly Christological, taking Christ to be the 'good painter' who re-paints the soul with his own likeness in its transformation by grace, using the 'light' of the Holy Spirit as the source of his spectrum or palette of colours. 'Macarius' is not a protagonist of full-vision mysticism. He stresses that the Trinity dwells in the soul only in the manner and to the degree in which human beings can receive It, though he expects a far fuller divine self-conformation to man in the world to come.[73]

The mid-fifth-century Diadochus of Photike, Lossky's final ascetic writer, takes up a position mid-way between Evagrius and the author of the Macarian homilies. On the basis of Christian baptism, Diadochus expects union with God to come about through love in a prayer-life characterized by 'perpetual recollection', not least through 'uninterrupted invocation of the name of Jesus'.[74] But it will be a formless light with which God then illuminates the mind, its beauty stemming (as 'energies', adds Lossky, supplying a word not found in Diadochus' text) from the divine nature itself. Only in the Parousia will that beauty take form, in the epiphany of Christ at history's end. The combination of affective mysticism with intellectual makes Diadochus, for Lossky, a forerunner of Byzantine Hesychasm — and one would have thought Lossky might have added in this context a reference to Diadochus' emphasis on divine light and the repetition of the holy name: both features of Hesychast spirituality.

All this is by way of preparation for the Byzantine theology, which is Lossky's real centre of interest in *The Vision of God*. By the time of writing these lectures in the mid-1940s, Lossky was an old hand at Dionysius interpretation, which began with the *Seminarium Kondakovianum* piece, mentioned in my opening chapter, as early as 1929 — and presumably Lossky was working on the theme when he participated in Kondakov's 'Byzantine' seminar earlier still. His view shows no significant alteration over time. Dionysius has stolen the clothes of the Neo-Platonists to express an emerging conviction of the Greek Church. Thanks to the divine infinity, God is inaccessible to us in his inmost essence whereas in his energies (his 'powers') he opens himself to participation — these energies of his which enable us to name the attributes of his nature as well as to identify the economies in history of the Son and the Spirit. Just as negative theology is needed to indicate God's transcendence of all that can be said of him, so too in personal approach to God knowing him is not enough. The soul that participates in the energies must go beyond knowing into the dark cloud described by Gregory of Nyssa in his *Life of Moses*. So likewise in the Age to Come we shall be beatified not only by enjoying the visible theophany of God in Christ but by a union that is above intelligence, beyond the *nous*.[75]

As with his treatment of the earlier Greek Fathers and ecclesiastical authors, Lossky was able to profit by the patristic research of Catholic and Lutheran authors, as well as, to a lesser extent (owing, no doubt, to the limitations of the libraries available to

Apophaticism

him) of the pre-Revolutionary Russian scholars of Christian antiquity—the number of whom was quite considerable. Thus it is with Maximus the Confessor, Lossky's next port of call *en route* to Gregory Palamas, where Hans Urs von Balthasar's epoch-making study *Kosmische Liturgie* lay to hand.[76] In his concise summary, Lossky presents Maximus' thought as a reworking of both Evagrian and Dionysian elements on the basis of a thoroughgoing Chalcedonian Christology, the principles of which are applied analogously to the human case. In the divine person of Christ interpenetration takes place between the Uncreated and the created natures and their respective energies. Just so in created persons the divine energies and our human will so interact that, in deification, the human person transcends its own limits towards a vision of God beyond both senses and intellect.

> [The] distinction between God's unknoweable *ousia* and His manifestations (dynamic attributes, *dynameis* or energies) . . . instead of limiting the mystical flight by placing the human being before a closed door, opens up an infinite path beyond knowledge.[77]

For John of Damascus, the synthesizer of the earlier Eastern tradition who plays a comparable role in Oriental Christianity to Thomas Aquinas in Latin Christendom, the divine nature can only be indicated apophatically, cataphatic assertions being predicated of God's attributes, not his essence. Yet, as figured forth in the Transfiguration episode, there is 'vision-participation in [the energies of] the divinity in the divine glory' and, thanks to the hypostatic union, that glory is also the glory of the *humanity* of Christ.[78]

John of Damascus speaks to us of the objective base—in the energies, and in the Word incarnate—of our communion with God. He does not, however, furnish an account of the subjective foundation—the basis in what befalls our own faculties. For this a Pneumatological complement is required. Already indicated by Cyril of Alexandria, it is superlatively expressed in the rhapsodic writings of Symeon the New Theologian. Study of Symeon (at any rate in the West) was in its comparative infancy when Lossky was writing, but he felt able to say:

> In the experience of the divine light in St Symeon's writings there is no trace of the depersonalizing ecstatic state, where human consciousness is lost in the contemplation of an impersonal divinity. On the contrary it is precisely the communion with a personal God which renders the experience of His light inexpressible in human language.[79]

The Light is both blessing and judgement; it is also a foretaste of the Parousia, a 'departure out of time and space towards "the mystery of the eighth day"'.[80] The vision of God to which Symeon looked forward was not, however, a vision of the divine essence but one appropriate to what Lossky calls, semi-apologizing for the consciously modern language, an 'existential communion' with God.[81]

It remains to be seen how this tradition fared in the fourteenth-century doctrinal conflict over Hesychasm, espoused by monks who sought a communion with God to be expressed ultimately, in the Age to Come (and occasionally, by way of anticipation, now), in the vision, soul and body, of divine realities through the uncreated Light.

The Palamite controversy is a footnote for Western dogmatics. But in Lossky's Orthodox perspective, it ushers in a new age of doctrinal definition, the Pneumatological phase—following on the (patristic) Christological phase in the task of clarifying the faith of the Church. The 'New Theologian' was its harbinger but it only fully arrives when this dispute forced out of their hermitages monks who, for several centuries, had already been buoyed up in their Christian lives by the 'pneumatological current in Byzantine thought, carried away by the mystery of the Holy Spirit dwelling in us, a thought which does not seek to be externalized, like Christological theology, but rather is wrapped in silence, in *hesychia*'.[82] Lossky's arguments for Palamitism are, in effect, twofold. First, the doctrine of grace as uncreated energies is the authentic summation of the Greek patristic tradition in its overall development. But secondly, to oppose it, by insisting that there is only either God's essential existence or created grace, introduces a 'rationalistic doctrine of causality' into the Holy of Holies that is God's intimate communion with man. Driving those who can see no other possibility is, he thought, a theory of the divine simplicity which is more philosophical then theological in character — and thus out of place in Christian dogmatics, where philosophy should be a servant, not a master. To change the metaphor, using the concept of the simplicity of God to exclude the doctrine of the energies is an egregious example of the tail wagging the dog. Gregory Palamas confronted his critics with

> the following dilemma: either they must admit the distinction between essence and operation, but then their philosophical notion of simplicity would oblige them to reject the existence of the glory of God, grace and the light of the Transfiguration among creatures; or else they must categorically deny this distinction, which would oblige them to identify that which cannot be known with what can be known, the incommunicable with the communicable, essence and grace. In both cases the deification of created being and therefore all actual communion with God would be impossible.[83]

Anti-Palamites thought Palamites were sensuous Messalians for saying God could be seen as light; Palamites thought anti-Palamites were intellectual Messalians for saying the divine essence could be seen by a created intellect. But the 'Light' in question is the energies which 'appear to contemplation as an ineffable reality for which the most suitable name is light'.[84] They are the reality for which Symeon the New Theologian was providing a language. They are what appeared on Tabor, which was neither a meteorological light nor an intellectual light but a light different in kind from both, since uncreated. How is it perceived by the mystics? According to the *Hagioritic Tome*, 'That is known only by God and those who have had the experience of his grace'.[85] Lossky hugely approves of the overcoming of the physical–spiritual divide in the Palamite description:

> Precisely because God transcends created being, because He is in essence absolutely inaccessible, because there is no co-naturality (*syngenneia*) between the divine and the intelligible . . ., God makes Himself known to the whole man; were it not for this we could speak of a purely sensible or purely intellectual vision.[86]

'Orthodox spirituality', Lossky tells his readers, is 'equally opposed both to intellectual gnosis [the affirmation of the knowability of the divine essence] and to the sensible perception of the divine nature.'[87] Instead, we have a 'communion of the whole man with the uncreated One', in a way that anticipates the life of the Age to Come.[88] The Latin divines who criticized Gregory Palamas (Lossky has in view at this juncture the superlatively learned Jesuit historian of doctrine Denis Pétau (1583–1652))

> did not see—and this is the great paradox—that all of Palamas' theological work constitutes a defence of the immediate vision of God, and that the distinction between essence and energy, far from being a separation or division of God into two parts, communicable and incommunicable, is an inevitable theological postulate if we wish to maintain the real and not just the metaphorical character of deification, without suppressing created being within the divine essence.[89]

Lossky ends *The Vision of God* by reminding readers of the brief reference he made to the victory of the iconodules in his chapter on John of Damascus and Byzantine spirituality. As with the theology of the icon of Christ, where (see the iconophile doctrine of St Theodore of Studios, 759–826[90]) it is Christ's hypostasis and not the divine—or the human—nature of the Saviour that appears in his visual images, so in a similarly sound mystical theology the 'vision of the luminous face of God turned towards each man' is the 'vision of Christ transfigured'. It is this understanding which receives its 'theological structure' in Gregory Palamas's teaching and the doctrine of the fourteenth-century councils.[91] In any case all is summed up in advance by John the Theologian: 'No one has ever seen God. The Son alone, who is in the bosom of the Father, has manifested him to us' (John 1:18).

Conclusion

'Mystical theology', like 'apophaticism', is a term that receives at Lossky's hands a careful formulation. It is not to be understood as exclusive of experience but neither is it couched in terms of experience. So he would avoid the criticism mounted in a later generation by Professor Denys Turner, who, noting the persistence in modern spiritual discourse of the language of interiority, ascent, and entry into a light that is darkness, observes that 'Whereas we appear to have "psychologized" the metaphors, the Neoplatonic mediaeval writer used the metaphors in an "apophatic" spirit to play down the value of the "experiential".[92] The "hidden divinity" of the mediaeval English classic *The Cloud of Unknowing*, for instance, indebted as it is to Dionysius; work, appears to be "hidden" precisely from experience.'[93]

By 'Neoplatonic mediaeval writers' Turner should not be thought of as looking elsewhere than to Lossky's sources. Turner begins his account of various late patristic and mediaeval figures with none other than Gregory of Nyssa, and, at greater length, Dionysius, and this is where Lossky's *The Mystical Theology of the Eastern Church* starts out likewise. Turner notes that 'mystical theology in the West is in itself unintelligible except against the background of Denys' writings'.[94] Briefly put, Turner's thesis has it that, for the classic authors he discusses, a 'dialectical epistemology' ruled the use of these metaphors, while from (approximately) the nineteenth century onwards what governed them was modern writers' assumption of 'experientialism'. In a concomitant process highly pertinent to 'experientialism'—the psychological concentration on 'my experience'—he remarks that the 'self', which once had been left mysterious in an 'apophatic anthropology', now took centre stage, arrayed in the colourful clothing of cataphatic assertions. Of the lessons taught by Turner's book perhaps the most useful for readers of Lossky is the following:

> It is of the greatest consequence to see that negative language about God is no more apophatic in itself than is affirmative language. The apophatic is the linguistic strategy of somehow showing by means of language that which lies beyond language. It is not done, and cannot be done, by means of negative utterances alone which are no less bits of ordinary intelligible human discourse than are affirmations. Our negations, therefore, fail of God as much as do our affirmations.[95]

Turner also points out how Dionysius reiterates the claim that the Cause of all is beyond both assertion and denial: 'We make assertions and denials of what is next to it, but never of it, for it is both beyond every assertion . . . [and] also beyond every denial'.[96] And with an unwitting echo of Lossky's study of Eckhart, Turner writes, 'Our language of "similarity" and "dissimilarity" fails of God', from which he draws the conclusion that 'our language fails and is known to fail to an unutterable degree'.[97] For 'God transcends the difference between similarity and difference', and thus 'It is on the other side of both our affirmations and our denials that the silence of the transcendent is glimpsed, seen through the fissures opened up in our language by the dialectical strategy of self-subversion'.[98] Turner draws the uncomfortable conclusion that if our language of distinction between God and creatures fails, then our language of union between God and creatures must fail likewise. Yet this contemporary English Catholic lay theologian does not deny the reality of the union. The mind 'led by its own eros of knowing ['the passion and yearning for the vision of the One'], . . . passes through to the darkness of union with the light'.[99] With this may be compared the words of a contemporary Greek Orthodox theologian on the 'distinction, more implied than stated' in Lossky's writing between (mere) apophatic method and (full-blooded) apophatic theology.

> Apophatic method is the negation of all positive names of God based on the affirmation that God is beyond being and thus beyond all positive knowledge, which is inherently linked to being. Apophatic theology is the fruit of such an exercise in the form of an *ekstatic* union with God beyond affirmation or negative, beyond being itself.[100]

Here the adjective 'ecstatic' is deliberately spelt in a way suggestive of its original etymology, for in the movement towards God we are to 'stand outside' or 'go beyond' ourselves in a communion of life and love surpassing all understanding.

Notes

1 Vladimir Lossky, *In the Image and Likeness of God* (Crestwood, NY: St Vladimir's Seminary Press, 1974), p. 13.

2 *Ibid.*, p. 14.

3 *Ibid.*

4 See Olga Medvedkova, *Les Icônes en Russie* (Paris: Gallimard, 2010), pp. 10–27.

5 Lossky, *In the Image and Likeness of God*, p. 14.

6 *Ibid.*

7 *Ibid.*, pp. 14–15.

8 *Ibid.*, p. 15.

9 *Ibid.*, p. 16.

10 *Ibid.*, p. 17.

11 *Ibid.*, p. 23.

12 *Ibid.*

13 *Ibid.*, p. 24. Some would prefer the description 'crypto-Proclean' for Neo-Platonist elements in Dionysius' thought.

14 *Ibid.*, p. 29.

15 *Ibid.*, p. 31.

16 *Ibid.*, p. 33.

17 *Ibid.*, p. 35.

18 *Ibid.*, citing Jean Daniélou, *Origène* (Paris: La Table Ronde, 1948), p. 291; the Gregory of Nyssa book is *Platonisme et théologie mystique. Essai sur la doctrine spirituelle de S. Grégoire de Nysse* (Paris: Aubier, 1944).

19 Lossky, *In the Image and Likeness of God*, p. 36.

20 *Ibid.*, p. 36.

21 *Ibid.*, p. 37.

22 *Ibid.*, pp. 37–8.

23 *Ibid.*, p. 38.

24 *Ibid.*, pp. 38–9.

25 *Ibid.*, pp. 39–40.

26 *Ibid.*, p. 41.

27 *Ibid.*, p. 43.

28 *Ibid.*, p. 50.

29 Ibid., p. 51.

30 Ibid., p. 52.

31 Ibid.

32 Ibid., p. 53.

33 Ibid.

34 Lossky argues for inauthenticity in *The Mystical Theology of the Eastern Church* (London: James Clark, 1957), p. 81. A different view is taken, however, in Jacques Lison, *L'Ésprit répandu. La Pneumatologie de Grégoire Palamas* (Paris: Cerf, 1994), p. 98.

35 Lossky, *In the Image and Likeness of God*, pp. 55–6.

36 Olivier Clément, 'Quelques aperçus sur l'icône comme théologie de la beauté', in Sante Graciotti (ed.), *Il mondo e il sovra-mondo dell'icona* (Venice: Olschki, 1998), pp. 19–30, and here at p. 19.

37 Lossky, *In the Image and Likeness of God*, p. 57.

38 Ibid.

39 Lossky refers to Jugie's comprehensive articles 'Palamas' and 'Palamite' in *Dictionnaire de théologie catholique* II, cols. 1735–76 and 1777–1818 respectively, as well as to his 1930 study, 'Les Origines de la méthode d'oraison des hésychastes', *Echos d'Orient* 30 (1931), one of a number of contributions by Jugie to this subject in the journal of the Assumptionists of Kadiköy.

40 Lossky, *In the Image and Likeness of God*, p. 63.

41 Ibid.

42 Ibid., pp. 64–5.

43 Ibid., p. 66.

44 Ibid., p. 65.

45 See G. P. Fedotov (ed.), *A Treasury of Russian Spirituality* (London: Sheed and Ward, 1950), pp. 265–79.

46 Lossky, *In the Image and Likeness of God*, p. 69.

47 Lossky, *The Mystical Theology of the Eastern Church*, p. 217.

48 Ibid.

49 Ibid., p. 224.

50 Ibid., p. 225.

51 Ibid., p. 227.

52 Ibid., p. 231.

53 Ibid., p. 233.

54 Ibid., p. 234.

55 *Ibid.*

56 *Ibid.*, p. 235.

57 *Ibid.*

58 'We do not claim to be making a reply to the question raised by Vasquez. We will simply try to see how the question of the vision of God is posed for the theologians of Byzantium', Vladimir Lossky, *The Vision of God* (Crestwood, NY: St Vladimir's Seminary Press, 1963), p. 24.

59 Anna Williams, *The Ground of Union. Deification in Aquinas and Palamas* (New York and Oxford: Oxford University Press, 1999), p. 38, with particular reference to Thomas Aquinas, *Summa Theologiae*, Ia., question 12, articles 4–5.

60 Lossky, *The Vision of God*, p. 25.

61 Lossky notes that the 'glory' of God likewise both reveals yet hides in mystery, *ibid.*, p. 28: the great theme of Hans Urs von Balthasar's theological aesthetics, *The Glory of the Lord* (Edinburgh: T. & T. Clark, and San Francisco: Ignatius, 1982–91, 7 volumes).

62 Irenaeus, *Against the Heresies*, V. 8, 1.

63 Lossky, *The Vision of God*, p. 44.

64 *Ibid.*, p. 64.

65 Cf. *ibid.*, pp. 47–55.

66 *Ibid.*, pp. 55–69.

67 *Ibid.*, p. 71.

68 *Ibid.*, pp. 73–89.

69 *Ibid.*, pp. 94–7.

70 *Ibid.*, pp. 98–100.

71 *Ibid.*, p. 108.

72 *Ibid.*, p. 111.

73 *Ibid.*, pp. 112–16.

74 *Ibid.*, p. 119.

75 *Ibid.*, pp. 121–8.

76 Hans Urs von Balthasar, *Kosmische Liturgie. Höhe und Krise des griechischen Weltbilds bei Maximus Confessor* (Freiburg: Herder, 1941).

77 Lossky, *The Vision of God*, p. 135.

78 *Ibid.*, p. 139.

79 *Ibid.*, p. 147.

80 *Ibid.*, p. 150.

81 *Ibid.*, p. 151.

82 *Ibid.*, p. 153.

83 *Ibid.*, pp. 158–9.

84 *Ibid.*, p. 161.

85 Cited *ibid.*, p. 163.

86 *Ibid.*

87 *Ibid.*, p. 167.

88 *Ibid.*, p. 163.

89 *Ibid.*, p. 166.

90 Venance Grumel, 'L'Iconologie de S. Théodore Studite', *Echos d'Orient* 20 (1921), pp. 251–68.

91 Lossky, *The Vision of God*, p. 168.

92 Denys Turner, *The Darkness of God. Negativity in Christian Mysticism* (Cambridge: Cambridge University Press, 1998 [1995]), p. 4.

93 *Ibid.*

94 *Ibid.*, p. 13. 'Interiority' does not figure in the Eastern Christian sources discussed but it certainly does in Augustine, where the 'journey inward' is crucial. And Augustine's use of the metaphor parallels Denys's of the others mentioned in that 'The language of interiority is, as it were, self-subverting; the more "interior" we are the more our interiority opens out to that which is inaccessibly "above" and beyond it', *ibid.*, p. 69.

95 *Ibid.*, pp. 34–5.

96 Dionysius, *The Mystical Theology* 5, translation from *Pseudo-Dionysius, The Complete Works*, tr. Colm Luibheid (New Jersey: Paulist, 1987), p. 141.

97 Turner, *The Darkness of God*, p. 44.

98 *Ibid.*, p. 45.

99 *Ibid.*, p. 47.

100 Aristotle Papanikolaou, *Being with God. Trinity, Apophaticism and Divine-Human Communion* (Notre Dame, IN: University of Notre Dame Press, 2006), pp. 17–18.

✣ 3 ✣

The Latin Master: On the Apophatic Eckhart

THE MATTER IS TAKEN FURTHER by Lossky's great work on the fourteenth-century German Dominican friar Meister Eckhart. Submission of his Eckhart thesis to the Sorbonne for the doctorate in letters it both sought and richly merited was prevented by his premature death. Whatever its origins in his St Petersburg period (see Chapter One above) the mature Lossky's attraction to Eckhart was surely based on the latter's apophaticism. So much is already apparent from the title of the posthumously published book, *Théologie négative et connaissance de Dieu* ('Negative Theology and the Knowledge of God').

There are, so Lossky tells us as the work opens, 'innumerable' passages in Eckhart's writings, whether Latin or German, affirming the ineffability of God.[1] He chooses to begin from a comment in Eckhart's *First Exposition of Genesis*, probably because it allows him to make an initial comparative study of four key figures: Augustine, Dionysius, Thomas Aquinas, and Eckhart himself. That may sound complicated. But in fact it will give us a relatively painless *entrée* to this substantial and demanding book, on which Lossky's reputation as a scholar (and not simply a thinker) chiefly hangs.

The search for the Name

In the wrestling match between Jacob and the angel at the Ford of the Jabok, in reply to the Hebrew patriarch's question, 'Who are you?', the divine figure retorts: 'Why do you seek my name?' (Genesis 32:39). Eckhart feels justified in adding an extension to the reply, based on a similar exchange in the Book of Judges (13:18), this time between Manoah (Samson's father) and the angel of the Lord. 'Why do you seek my name, for it is wonderful [*mirabile*]?'[2] Grammatically, the reference could be taken in more than one way, and, following mediaeval scholastic practice, Eckhart explores the possibilities in turn.

Perhaps, he muses, in a first stab at interpretation, the phrase should be translated, 'Why do you seek my name because it is "The Admirable"?' This triggers a search through a concordance for texts from the Psalter and the Prophets where 'wonderful' is indeed a description offered for the divine.

Secondly, though, the phrase might mean, 'Why do you seek my admirable name?' The obvious candidate for such a 'name' would be 'The *Qui est*' or 'The *Ego qui sum*'—since these are the result of divine self-naming in yet another book from the Heptateuch (the first seven books of the Hebrew Bible), namely at Exodus 3:14. 'And God said to Moses, "I am the God who IS; Thou shalt tell the Israelites, 'THE GOD WHO IS has sent me to you'."'. Were Eckhart a close follower of the premier theologian of his Order, St Thomas Aquinas, this would have been an opportunity to develop an account of the 'metaphysics of Exodus': a phrase coined for Thomas's understanding of the *Qui est* by the director of Lossky's thesis, Étienne Gilson. But, as we shall see, Lossky's Eckhart is not a Gilsonian Thomist, and, more than that, does not fit comfortably in the specifically Thomist school at all (which is not to say he has failed to learn from Thomas in any respect).

And so we come to a third possible interpretation, which relates the texts from Genesis and Judges already quoted to St Paul's Letter to the Philippians: 'The name you are looking for is astonishing because, whilst being a name, it is nonetheless "above every name"' (Philippians 2:9).[3] This will give Eckhart his key oxymoron: the *nomen innominabile*, the 'unnameable Name'. Lossky points out that St Augustine had already stumbled on the paradox of the 'unnameable Name' in his treatise on the use of Scripture, the *De Doctrina Christiana* ('On Christian Teaching').[4] In that guide to the interpretation of the Bible Augustine writes that, whereas in theory 'ineffable' means 'that which cannot be said', still, in calling God 'the Ineffable' one does, in practice, 'say' Him. But the inference Augustine draws from this paradox is not Eckhart's. The lesson the paradox teaches Augustine is that we should refrain from using apophasis 'absolutely'; that is, unconditionally. We should use it, certainly, but only 'relatively'; that is, in a qualified way. We should regard God as ineffable in the restricted, though important, sense that nothing we can say about him ever measures up to the outstanding excellence of the divine nature. Lossky finds in this qualified apophaticism of Augustine's an anticipation of the high-mediaeval Scholasticism of St Thomas. In Lossky's words:

> It is a prudent limitation of apophasis which already [i.e. in the period of the Latin Fathers] directs us towards the *via eminentiae*, where negations, instead of excluding all positive notion of the divine nature, serve only to remove from God the imperfections proper to our mode of understanding.[5]

Lossky admits there are passages in Eckhart which emulate this Thomist conception. But he goes on to point out that, elsewhere, Eckhart is manifestly not content with anything less than an 'absolute', rather than a 'relative', apophaticism.

So much becomes apparent when Lossky turns to Eckhart's fourth possible explanation of the Old Testament starting-point of this entire discussion. Somewhat periphrastically, the text could mean: 'It is astonishing that you seek my name, for I am unnameable'. Referring now to the prophet Isaiah, Eckhart comments that one can hardly be expected to know the name of a reality whose nature it is to be hidden. Compare Isaiah 45:15: 'Truly, you are a God who hide yourself, O God of Israel, the Saviour' (Revised Standard Version translation) There are, says Eckhart, two ways of taking this remaining possibility.

The sacred writer might have in mind 'the name of Him whose nature it is to be hidden'. Alternatively, the prophet may be thinking of 'the name of Him whose nature is the Hidden Being'. Both are expressions of apophasis, but Lossky considers it is the last phrase, 'the Hidden Being' or, in Latin, *Esse absconditum*, that takes us to the true centre of Eckhartian ontology—while not suppressing the concept of the 'unnameable Name'. If God can justly be termed *Esse* it is only because He is (*pace* Isaiah) a hidden God whose Name altogether escapes us.

Eckhart and *esse*

Although Eckhart can hardly be called a 'Thomist of the strict observance', he will not want simply to surrender the language of *esse*—the house specialty of the school of Thomas—when speaking of the divine. Just how he may wish to use it becomes clear when he proceeds to a last comment on this well-selected text. What we are concerned with—and this will come as no surprise to those who have dipped into Eckhart's sermons—is an inward journey.

Once again, Eckhart's thinking is triggered by a text from Augustine, this time from the *De Vera Religione* ('On the True Religion'). 'Do not go outside', advises Augustine. Instead, 'Enter into yourself'.[6] Lossky comments:

> The way towards the unknown God takes a fresh direction by obliging the subject to enter into himself, for in the perspective of *esse* God is not external to the one who is seeking his name.[7]

The 'Hidden Being', *qua* being, precisely, is not alien to the searcher, who must henceforth enquire into the intimate presence of *esse* not in being generally but in the depths of the enquirer's own being. But, as in the back reference to the *De Doctrina Christiana*, so also here: whilst respecting Augustine's text, Eckhart does not preserve Augustine's authorial intention. In the advice to 'go within', Augustine's aim was for the reader to recognize how, right at the source of his or her own judgements about truth, an 'interior Master' of an altogether transcendent nature must be at work: the changeless Truth whence illumination comes to human minds as they formulate objective standards for truth-telling of any and every description. Eckhart's aim is quite different from Augustine's. It is not to show us that the truth-claims we make are metaphysically legitimated. It is to propel our movement towards the Bearer of the unnameable Name.

If we are to find a patristic authority for Eckhart's venture, it will not, then, be Augustine. It will be Dionysius instead. After all, as Lossky points out, 'Eckhart did not invent the oxymoron *nomen innominabile*; he found it in the first chapter of the *Divine Names* of Dionysius'.[8] Not, he thinks, in the Latin translations by John Scotus Eriugena (c. 810–77) or John Sarrazin (c. 1150), though it exists there, but in the *Commentary on the Divine Names* by his fellow Dominican, St Thomas.

Recap on Dionysius

Since the earliest period of his writing, when the family were still living in the then Czechoslovakia, Lossky had been absorbed by Dionysius' *œuvre*. Dionysius was to be, with Maximus, Symeon the New Theologian, Palamas, and Serafim of Sarov, the hero of *The Mystical Theology of the Eastern Church*. Lossky had to do no new research to discover that the theme of the 'unnameable Name' was introduced by the Syrian writer in the course of expounding the two ways of Christian theology, positive and negative. For Dionysius the 'super-essential Thearchy', God in himself, can be named—Dionysius is more inclined to write 'praised', a sign of the doxological character of his attitude as theologian—on the basis of his energetic manifestations, shown as these are in the 'effect' that is the created world. The many names for God in Scripture, including of course, 'I am who I am' or 'He who is', are thus available for our worshipful use. Other names too, such as 'Good', 'Beautiful', Wise', are serviceable in this context. But if we ask, 'What of God in himself?' the answer we receive is, 'Why do you ask about my name, for it is wonderful?' It is 'wonderful' because it is the-Name-above-every-name-that-can-be-named, which is precisely Eckhart's point.

To Eckhart's own terms—the 'polynymy' (or 'many-named-ness') of God and the 'anonymy' (or 'no-namedness') of God—there correspond the affirmative and negative ways to God in the Dionysian corpus. Of these two Dionysius rates the second—anonymy—the more highly. Anonymy envisages the unknowable nature, the 'unions' that prevail over the 'distinctions' that make possible the affirmative way with its many names. It is, therefore, the more perfect route. It takes one beyond the language of being, and the language of non-being as well. This was Denys Turner's point, to which the reader's attention was drawn in the conclusion of Chapter Two.

> The Cause of all beings insofar as he manifests himself and makes himself participable, God, according to his inaccessible nature, remains outside all that is; in this sense one can say that he 'is not', or rather that he is beyond all affirmation or negation, exalted above the opposition of being and non-being.[9]

For Dionysius, God in his absolute or 'super-essential' nature transcends even *esse*. Contrastingly, for Eckhart—and here his continuing allegiance to a feature of the Thomist tradition makes itself felt—*esse* does not mitigate the divine ineffability. Rather, *esse* constitutes the latter's foundation.[10]

In his *Commentary on the Divine Names* Thomas Aquinas had turned Dionysius' substantive 'The Unnameable' into an adjective qualifying the word 'being'. He thus made the language of *esse* foundational vis-à-vis divine ineffability. What is God? God is *esse innominabile*, 'Being unnameable'.[11] In Lossky's opinion, Thomas was quite consciously correcting Dionysius here. In the first part of his *Summa Theologiae*, Eckhart's elder contemporary insists that God is above every existent not because he is beyond existence (Thomas actually writes 'deprived of all existence'—hardly fairly if the aim was to capture Dionysius' meaning!) but because, rather, God is his own existing.[12] For Thomas, it is because God is sheer Existing that he exceeds all knowledge. And yet inasmuch as the 'existential line' in which God transcends all creatures also includes all creatures it is, in Lossky's words, possible to 'turn our understanding towards him by the way of analogy, a way which gives no intellection of the divine Being as such but makes of God-*Esse* the principle of intelligibility of all created beings, *esse* being ascribed primordially and most properly to the God who *is* through himself'.[13] Existential energy, 'inseparable' (as Lossky says in an excellent *resumé* of Thomas's metaphysics) from 'Him who is' and yet also 'really distinct from [God]', finds a name when it is limited by actualizing some essence. By contrast, the pure act of existing—God, an Act not distinct from but identical with its essence—cannot be itself named. Thus *Qui est* 'names, without determining, [the God] who is his own existing'.[14]

Eckhart and Thomism

Lossky is clear that, despite some borrowings and, more widely, the sheer volume of his references to Thomas Aquinas, Eckhart is no orthodox Thomist.[15] He is not even a would-be follower of Thomas whose aspirations were foiled by intellectual convolutedness and a temperamental tendency to rhetorical exaggeration. The occurrence of much of the same vocabulary notwithstanding, the caste of mind disclosed in Eckhart's thinking is not really that of Thomas Aquinas at all. As research since Lossky's time has shown beyond reasonable doubt, there was in the Middle Ages a distinctive German Dominican school which was far more 'Albertine' (named for Albert the Great (*c*. 1200–80), Thomas's teacher at Cologne), than it was 'Thomasian'. The Albertine school gave greater weight than did its Thomist rival to both Dionysius and Augustine, and therefore to the Christian Platonism on whose basic premises both of those Fathers took their stand.[16] Lossky was, of course, more committed to Dionysius than to Augustine. So he would have been delighted to read some words of an early-twenty-first-century historian: Eckhart's era witnessed nothing less than a 'Dionysian Renaissance'.[17] What, however, is peculiar to Eckhart is the will to combine the Thomasian and, via the Albertine, the Dionysian.[18] Lossky's genius enabled him to see this well before it became a settled conviction of Eckhart scholarship.

How, then, does Lossky think of the difference between Eckhart and Thomas on the themes they treat in common? He writes:

> With St Thomas, [Eckhart] seems to recognize that God, intimately present in all beings, creates thereby their existence; but instead of making of this a principle of Christian metaphysics which would allow unequivocal speaking of the transcendent God from the starting-point of his created effects, he subjectivizes this existential relation of creatures to the Creator and wants to seek the immanence of the divine

Ipsum Esse, an immanent *Deus absconditus*, in the intimate depths of personal consciousness.[19]

Looking for the Thomist God who is *Esse* in the Augustinian *abditum mentis*, Augustine's 'mental abyss', Eckhart departs from both the mediaeval doctor and the Latin Father. He departs from them in the ordinary philosophical and theological sense of their language because he wants to reunite them on a mystical level for which he will try to forge, unusually, a speculative expression. In a nutshell, that is Lossky's Eckhart.

Such is the cryptic character of Eckhart's writing that there are many other Eckharts, some of which, in relation to the context of his work, are quite bizarre.[20] The Welsh historian of mediaeval theology Oliver Davies opened his own Eckhart book by noting how 'One of the first things to strike anyone who is anxious to deepen their knowledge of Meister Eckhart is the bewildering array of theories that surround him'.[21] Of course, many thinkers have been exploited by later writers with agendas of their own. The peculiarity of Eckhart's case, as Gilson observed in the preface to Lossky's study, lies in the multiplicity of interpretations of the corpus that are textually well founded. That said, Davies, for his part, agrees with the main thrust of Lossky's approach. Eckhart's teaching is a version of Latin Christian theology, and the theology in question, while employing metaphysics, functions as 'an instrument for the articulation of what is essentially a mystical, and therefore experiential, vision'.[22] We have noted with Denys Turner that the inference from mystical to experiential may be a *non sequitur*. Davies has an answer to that. Since the Meister 'seems to have been received in his own time as a preacher with a spiritual message . . . the onus is upon those who would deny such an experiential basis to Eckhart's work to "prove" their case'.[23] The scare-quotes around the word 'prove' indicate Davies's evident belief that demonstration will be difficult. From what we have seen in Chapter Two of the character of Lossky's apophatic concern, it seems barely credible that the Russian thinker—whatever his interest in either the history of the Western Middle Ages or the parameters of dogmatic exposition—would have spent so long on the Eckhart case unless he had glimpsed in this 'Latin Master' not only a theological metaphysician but also, and inseparably, a Christian mystic too. In his own words in the *Essai*, speaking in the name of the Orthodox Church as a whole, 'she makes no sharp distinction between theology and mysticism, between the realm of the common faith and that of personal experience'.[24]

The secret being of God

The mystical, yet also ontological, 'intimacy' of Eckhart's account of the God–man relation is for Lossky a vital clue to his metaphysical doctrine. In the *Commentary on the Gospel of John*, Eckhart identifies the 'best wine' of John 2:10 — it was the wine the bridegroom had kept 'hidden' from the guests at the Marriage Feast of Cana — with the secret *esse* of God himself as the latter is found in the intimate reaches of the soul. This *intimum* or intimate indwelling can also be described as 'darkness', for the One who is hidden there is the 'unknowable God who must be sought with Moses, in the darkness of Sinai'.[25] The reader will inevitably recall the darkness mysticism in Moses' ascent into the cloud of divine presence in Gregory of Nyssa's *Life*, itself reflected in Dionysius' *Mystical Theology*. But Eckhart develops the allusion in a significantly different fashion.

His emphasis is not so much on man ascending as it is on God descending. In the Latin sermon 'May He who began the Good Work in You Perfect it for the Day of Jesus Christ', Eckhart explains that the 'good work' the Lord has 'begun' in us starts with a 'descent' of God. Owing to the determinations of created essences in all their limitedness, this divine descent is inevitably englobed in darkness. Yet, completing its course, God's good work does finish in ascent, an ascent into the radiance of *Ipsum Esse* in all Its blinding purity.

Now despite the language of a 'work begun', borrowed from St Paul in the citation which gives the sermon its starting-point (Philippians 1:6), there is for Eckhart no real 'beginning' of such work. God works in the *dies aeternitatis*, the 'day of eternity', and his operation is his being. For our part, the *intimum nobis* or 'interior man in us' is not really in time or in a place either. Our inner man is in eternity. This must surely have put Lossky in mind of the supra-temporal language Bulgakov used for the human spirit (not excluding the term 'uncreated'), which had so angered Metropolitan Sergeĭ.[26] And indeed, Lossky is more than a mite suspicious: 'It seems that the ineffability of the divine *Esse* extends ... to the existing of creatures, by forming a univocal region of *esse absconditum* behind created essences'.[27]

In Eckhart's Latin sermon 'Whose Image is This?' the preacher describes the *esse absconditum* as the 'closed gate of the House of God' mentioned by Ezekiel in his prophetic vision of the renewed Temple (Ezekiel 44:1). It is the doorway whereby the Glory of the Lord enters and which, on this account, remains shut to all else. Even if, comments Lossky, it would be premature to conclude that here the secret being of creatures is actually identical with the secret being of God himself, we can at least say that, in Eckhart's view, 'for a created existent, "be-ing" in the proper sense of the word is be-ing in God, and at the same time, it is in the secret interior of self, in the univocally ineffable region of the *esse absconditum*'.[28] Lossky spells out what he takes to be the implications: '[Eckhart] wants to think *esse* above all on a mystical level, where the natural and the supernatural, existence and grace, make up only one and the same divine operation in *abdito animae* [the abyss of the soul]'.[29] Lossky was writing at the time of a controversy among Catholic theologians in France, where Neo-Scholastics, faced with a patristic reading of Aquinas by the Jesuit historian of theology Henri de Lubac (1896–1991), feared an imminent collapsing of the nature/grace distinction in theological thought.[30] In *The Mystical Theology of the Eastern Church* Lossky gave it as his opinion that the natural/supernatural distinction had become exaggerated in Latin theology.[31] He might have noted its utility at this point. And as to the distinction between created and Uncreated, that is of even greater moment to orthodoxy, whether the word be spelt with a capital letter or with a lower case 'o'. When Eckhart tries to develop his mystical doctrine in terms of a speculative theology he is obliged to distinguish created and Uncreated. Yet he does so in what Lossky calls a 'play of contradictory positions'.³² That 'play' is reflected in the riddling counsel—cited from the German sermon 'A Certain Nobleman went into a Far Country', 'You must seek him in such a way as never to find him; if you do not seek him, you find him'.³³ Lossky thought it perfectly normal that a 'mystic' doubling up as a 'dialectician' would 'tend towards a "beyond the opposition" of Creator and creature'.³⁴ That seems a very strange position for the impassioned anti-sophiological author of *Spor o sofii* to embrace.

On the many divine names

Be that as it may, Lossky turns now from 'anonymy' to consider 'polynymy' (though without leaving 'anonymy' entirely behind). After all, both the modern Russian theologian and the mediaeval Dominican friar are far from denying all validity to Dionysius' complementary, if secondary, 'affirmative' or cataphatic way to God. That second way is based on what Dionysius called the 'manifesting processions' which issue from the Good, the all-creative Cause. Here too Lossky finds a text of Eckhart's that can stand for many more. In his *Commentary on Exodus* Eckhart takes a line from the Song of Moses at Exodus 15:3 which in the Latin Bible reads 'Omnipotent is his name', and he uses it to set out his own 'polynymic' doctrine. Lossky explains:

> The name 'all-powerful' for Master Eckhart must correspond to a principle which would allow the unnameable Divinity to shine forth in a multitude of names, just like the 'agathonymy' [naming God as good] of Dionysius.³⁵

As Lossky presents matters, the name 'omnipotent', in Eckhart's writing, represents the junction between apophasis and cataphasis.

> it can guide the apophatic search for the 'unnameable name', in pointing the way for the human spirit towards the divine ineffability, just as it can also serve as a point of departure for the opposite movement, that of cataphasis, since the first Cause, superior to all names, contains all his effects, which must then render him 'all-nameable'.³⁶

'Omnipotent', in other words, is a name that ascribes to God all that he can produce while signalling his transcendence vis-à-vis his effects.

Here, then, Eckhart's doctrine of naming God takes on a new coloration and the shade chosen is, this time, quite Thomasian in hue. As with St Thomas, Eckhart uses the *via remotionis*, the 'way of removal', to elide the mode of signifying that would be otherwise proper to concepts that have been formed in order to express creaturely perfections. This procedure is swiftly followed (as with Aquinas) by the use of the *via eminentiae*, 'the way of eminence', where 'negations no longer prevail over affirmations'. That is with a view to applying these same concepts, suitably purified, to the transcendent Cause of all.[37]

Eckhart's understanding of creation

Eckhart's metaphysical concept, in this context, of the 'disjoined being' of the Cause and its effects is clearly very different from his mystical idea of the *esse absconditum* which joins God and creatures-in-God. There is, however, a connexion. The discovery of the 'hidden [divine] being' in creatures already had to take into account the 'proper' being of creatures, sadly limited as this is, since in and of itself that proper being 'darkened' the divine operation taking place in them. That implied there is indeed a distinction to be made between *Esse*-Cause, and *esse*-effects, the very distinction Lossky now wishes to set forth on Eckhart's behalf.

Telling just when Eckhart is speaking of which—*Esse* with a capital 'E', or *esse* with a lower case initial—is not always going to be easy. But when Eckhart speaks of the being that God 'confers' and the creature has 'from without' we can be pretty sure it is to the creature-brought-from-nothing-by-the-Cause that he is referring.[38] Creation as 'the bestowal of being after non-being' is certainly part and parcel of Eckhart's belief-system. The Creeds, after all, open with an acknowledgement of the Creator. And yet, for Eckhart's system, creatures already exist *intellectualiter* in the First Cause. That indeed is their primary being, their *esse primum*. They exist in their uncreated *rationes*, in the 'ideas' that God has of them. For Eckhart, so Lossky explains, creatures only begin to exist in themselves when their Cause confers on them *esse formale*, producing them 'from without'—that is, 'from nothing', as the multitude of *entia*, the array of determinate individuals, in the world around us. And whatever else this latter state of affairs may be, it is certainly not the *esse absconditum*.

The primary being of things is much removed from their secondary being. Considered in terms of their uncreated rationales (which are primary), creatures are objects of a changeless knowledge on the part of God, whereas in their formal being (which is secondary) they are mutable, fluid, and appropriately imaged, thinks Eckhart, as the 'waters' that, for the first Genesis creation account, denote the created world (compare Genesis 1:2). The 'separation' of the waters (compare Genesis 1:6–8) into 'higher' and 'lower' suggests to Eckhart the twofold *esse* of the creature: both its stable being in its origins in the Word and also its being in the form it takes outside the *rationes* in the individuated kinds we know from the cosmic environment.[39]

It is owing to the primacy of the creature's being in its own origin that we are required to go beyond God *qua* simply Cause of effects. 'First being' (as Eckhart puts it) must be co-essential with the creative Cause.[40] And most importantly—if theology and preaching are ultimately based on Scripture and not on philosophy—St John the Evangelist's affirmation 'in [the Word] was life' (John 1:4) should also be taken into account here. A thing, it would seem, can exist both exteriorly as something made and also in the Word, where it enjoys being as a supremely vital reality.[41] The divine life which enables us really to live, comments Lossky, is

> an uncreated world, that of the interior creation or the pre-creational Wisdom, a world coming to birth spontaneously in the divine thought, independent of all exterior causality which can only be exercised on what is becoming, on the *fieri* and not on *esse* properly so called.'[42]

It is hard to suppose this did not strike Lossky as reminiscent of the 'protological' element in Bulgakov's wisdom cosmology.[43] But in Eckhart's case it fails to elicit, contrary to what readers of

'The Debate about Wisdom' might expect, anything in the way of adverse comment. In this sympathetic reading of Eckhart, Lossky seems to echo, despite his allergy to Sophiology, a judgement passed by his fellow émigré, the lay theologian Paul Evdokimov (1901–70). For the tradition represented by Eastern Christian writers, 'things do not possess their own existence, being is only defined by its relation to God, to his creative Wisdom which made all things participated similitudes and of their noumenal *ensembles* theophanic places'.[44]

The Word of God

What are the implications of these assertions for the Word itself? I mean, for the second Trinitarian Person who, according to the Johannine Prologue, as also in the faith of the entire later Church, became incarnate as Jesus Christ? For Eckhart, the 'silent' Word, resting in the unity of the Fatherly Intellect, contains the eternal reasons of things. But when this 'first' or primary being of creatures is externalized, the Word becomes audible in the world, at any rate 'in the measure that it is perceived by created hearing' on the basis of the *esse* that the creature receives from God's causally efficient action. The qualification 'in the measure that' draws our attention to how the Father's Word (his co-eternal Son) could remain unknown in the world when present 'under the property of being'. In that phrase Eckhart refers, thinks Lossky, not just to the 'operative power' of the Word in creating (after all, by definition atheists and agnostics fail to discern createdness), but also to Its Incarnation as Jesus Christ (after all, not each and every one of the Saviour's contemporaries became his disciple).[45]

Commenting on Eckhart's phrase in the *First Exposition of Genesis*, 'The Word without a word, or, better, above every word', Lossky asks 'Does this negative expression oblige us to ascribe to the Word the "Name above every name" which would designate the First Cause in his very principle *in divinis*?' That is, can the 'wonderful Name' be given to the Person of the Son? Or, alternatively, 'should this unique name which gathers all names be applied to the First Principle of all divine "production", at the common Source of the generation of the Son and the creation of the world?'[46] Should the 'wonderful Name', Lossky means, be reserved, rather, for the Person of the Father? The doubt in Lossky's mind raises the question of Eckhart's teaching on the Holy Trinity specifically as such.

So far, little has been said about the Trinitarian relationships. For his part, Lossky claims that 'causal notions are inapplicable' there. In the treatise later called *Against the Errors of the Greeks*, Thomas—so Lossky recalls—had remarked that, whereas Latins use the term *principium* ('principle'), Greeks use *archē* ('principle') and *aitia* ('cause') indifferently.[47] That may be imprudent of Orientals. Certainly Eckhart wants to say, as in his *Book of the Parables of Genesis*, that the Word and the Spirit proceeding from the Father are no kind of 'effect'. To call them the Father's effects would be to regard them, heretically, as mere creatures. As Lossky explains on Eckhart's behalf: 'The Son and the Holy Spirit are not produced outside the One to whom they are identical, since they remain in unity with the Father to whom Master Eckhart attributes the name of the One'.[48] Bolstered by argument from Neo-Platonist sources, this 'exaltation' of the One gives a philosophical justification to the Church's dogma of the consubstantiality with the Father of Spirit and Son. And this helps us to see why the language of causality is inappropriate. Extraneity of product, with its implications of division and number, is wholly out of place in the context of the One.[49] But at the same time the essential 'non-outsideness' of the produced Persons throws light on why, for Eckhart, there must be at least an element of the Fall about the very act of creation, when the latter is seen as the exteriorization of the *rationes* of things and so a distancing from perfect being.

God and nothing

One of the putatively heretical propositions ascribed to Eckhart was that he had said of creatures, 'In themselves they are "sheer nothing"'. Yet for Eckhart whereas God creates *ex nihilo*, 'out of nothing', he does not create *in nihilo*, 'in nothing'. The reason for saying so is that God creates *in principio*, 'in the Beginning'.

What is meant there is not a temporal beginning. What is meant is that God creates in himself, in his Word.[50] Lossky's discussion of Eckhart's doctrine of *nihil*, nothingness, which the German friar sees as immediately opposed to created being (only),[51] is of especial interest given Lossky's campaign against the representatives of Russian 'religious philosophy' in their Paris exile. In Nikolaĭ Berdyaev's metaphysics, the idea of Nothing could certainly be called, by contrast, primordial in character, for Berdyaev speaks of *le Néant*—in the shape, or rather non-shape, of 'meonic' freedom—as constituent of reality as such.[52] 'Out of the abyss, out of the Divine Nothing, is born the Trinitary God, and He is confronted with meonic freedom.'[53] This is at the Antipodes from Eckhart's view. Perhaps Lossky, then, had Berdyaev at the back of his mind when he wrote:

> One cannot [in Eckhart's case] speak of *nihil* as a primordial notion. It is a derived term, a notion concomitant to that of created being, posterior, so to speak, to the creation which implies, with the idea of alterity, of duality, the possibility of opposition.[54]

The point of 'nothing' language is its usefulness in counterposing the idea of a creature to the only fully authentic being, which is God.

> Every time one opposes the creature to God as something other than him, it appears in its ontological nullity, which renders impossible the juxtaposition of absolute Being with a created *aliquid*.[55]

Hence Eckhart's ability to say that, opposed to God, the creature is nothing—a point at issue in the doctrinal process against him. Among the twenty-eight articles condemned by Pope John XXII in the bull *In agro dominico* (1329) the twenty-sixth reads: 'All creatures are a pure nothing. I do not say that they are a modicum or a something, but that they are a pure nothing.' This was among the eleven articles found not actually heretical but nonetheless, in the words of the bull, 'ill-sounding, temerarious and suspect of heresy'.[56] But properly speaking, Eckhart would reply, only God is being. Lossky replies for him that in the 'I am who I am' formula (and its variants in Greek and Latin), the God of the Bible 'manifests himself as Being properly so called and this revelation renders ambiguous and improper all other acceptation of the words *esse* or *ens*'.[57] Many of Eckhart's paradoxical declarations judged 'monstrous, dubious, or false' by his ecclesial critics (especially in the German sermons) can be explained, thinks Lossky, when one disassociates the Eckhartian version of being *qua* being from the philosophy of Aristotle (384–322 BC) and indeed from the natural theology of Thomas. Probably Eckhart never wanted to pit himself against Aristotle in this way. But, in his 'desire to find everywhere an expression of the single Truth', he can sometimes only cite the Stagirite by wresting his texts from anything remotely resembling their natural sense.[58] For instance, little could be less Aristotelean – or Aristotelian-Thomist – than declaring the quiddity of things to be their first cause, their interior principle in whom their true 'reason' exists, yet in Eckhart's thinking real quiddities are uncreated. And because the quiddity is the proper root of the thing (it is not *ab alio*, 'from another', and in this respect is unlike existence), the quiddity will be where the metaphysician rightly concentrates. He or she will properly direct their attention to the 'realm of pure essentiality, transcending the exterior causality which opposes creatures to God'.[59] Here Eckhart renounces the 'existential line', the existence-based thinking typical of Thomas in general and Gilsonian Thomism in particular, and makes his own the essence-based thinking of so much non-Thomistic metaphysics. Off that 'existential line' as they are, Eckhart's notions of analogy are *sui generis*. Analogy must incorporate both equivocity (insofar as the creature *qua* creature is 'nothing') and univocity (insofar as in its essential Cause it is indistinguishable from the Word as spoken by God).[60] Hence Lossky's coining, 'dialectised analogy'.[61]

A further reflection is germane. Lossky's admiration for Eckhart's subtlety is well-placed. But one can only wonder at Lossky's vehemence against Sophiology when we hear him write, in Eckhart's defence, of his underlying ontology:

> For Meister Eckhart, the production of individual substances is creation in the Christian sense, since the forms and matter

have been produced from out of nothing by a divine all-powerful efficacy. If the quiddity is for him the first 'essential' or 'original' cause, that is because before being produced from without, before receiving *esse ab alio* under their proper forms, things live in God: they are there as the eternal reasons, or, rather, as the unique Reason—the Logos of the Father.[62]

'The One' or 'The Good'?

For Eckhart, the Word cannot be named insofar as he is consubstantial with the Father and thus identical in his essence with the One. The 'silent praise' that goes on within the One excludes all names—even that of the One. But with the exterior praise offered by creatures outside the One things are very different. Such creatures can use a multiplicity of names that ultimately, however, 'converge' in a unique name, which stands above all others. In his *Exposition of Genesis* Eckhart firmly declares that name to be 'The One'.[63] 'The One' is the *nomen omninominabile*, gathering all the other, lesser names, in its 'unified excellence'.[64] It is the principle of the procession of the divine Persons as of the interior production which is the 'preamble of creation', the *previa creationis*.[65] That makes a contrast with Dionysius, for whom the name 'The Good' plays precisely that crucial role: hence Lossky's coining for the specifically Dionysian doctrine, 'agathonymy'.

Lossky is at pains to point how that this does not make 'The One' the unnameable Name. If it did, unnameability would of course evaporate. We are speaking here only about 'polynymy', on the cataphatic way. Nevertheless, the contrast with the Areopagite's teaching gives Lossky pause. In Dionysius' writing, the title 'The Good' signals the gratuity of creation and the personal character of a God who is More-than-the-One. In the context of polynymy, the surpassing name must unite both Trinity and Unity in God.[66] While the 'unnameable Name' belongs to the Triune God in his absolute transcendence, the name 'the Good' is the supreme denominator of that same God in the immanence of his 'manifestations'.

So here it is Eckhart, not Dionysius, who is closer to the neo-Platonists. At Eckhart's hands, the One, identified with the Father, becomes the 'common principle of both theogony and cosmogony'.[67] And yet, declares Lossky in his hero's defence, 'By situating the One after the unnameable Being the German theologian has lent [being] a new sense, which it could not have in the purely Plotinian tradition'.[68] What Lossky means is that, in Eckhart's vision, it is God's determination as *Esse* and not as the One that is the real reason for apophasis. The One 'represents [simply] the aspect under which this *Deus absconditus* [the God of Hidden Being] makes himself known as Trinity of persons and the first principle of creation'.[69] Lossky can see why some people might think, accordingly, that Eckhart believed in a realm of pure Being beyond the Trinity. Yet to assert as much would be to put words into his mouth, to 'harden' his theological position.[70] What can be said is that, for him, the name 'The One' follows immediately the 'unnameable Name' of 'the Deity considered *sub ratione esse*': God in the perspective of being.[71]

The 'transcendentals' and the Trinity

It is from the One that the transcendental qualifications of being follow—in the famous trio of *unum, verum, bonum* (unity, truth, goodness), and these will eventually be used to give to the Trinitarian Persons various distinguishing marks.[72] This is a feature of Latin pre-Scholasticism rather than the tradition of the Greek Fathers, and in the event Lossky largely confines himself to *unum* as a name of the divine Father.

The title 'The One', so Lossky discovered, has for Eckhart two functions in relation to *Esse*. First, it functions as an exclusive identifier, 'affirming the purity of *Esse* by the elimination of all that is not absolute Being'.[73] And secondly, it functions as an inclusive identifier, in that it 'affirms the plenitude of *Esse* by absorbing into God all being, in the measure that it is'.[74] But where does this leave faith in God as Trinity? In a Hermetic treatise, 'The Book of the Twenty-Four Philosophers', Eckhart found a congenial philosophical formula capable of adaptation to Trinitarian use. 'God is Monad, generating (*gignens*) the Monad, reflecting his ardour in himself': language which, while esoteric in a Latin Christian context, would not have been so to late antique readers with a background in the Platonic Academy.[75] Eckhart understands those words in a Trinitarian sense that distinguishes his reading from that of a Neo-Platonist such as Proclus (*c*. 410–85). For the latter, the going forth of being is, in relation to the One (the 'Monad'), a declension needing to be made good by a restorative return. For Eckhart, contrastingly, the Trinitarian Father, who in his producing of being is identified with the One and does not, as in the Neo-Platonist schemes, follow upon the One, so acts in generating the Son and spirating the Holy Spirit that his action is 'intrinsic to [his] unity'.[76] The divine Persons whose existence Eckhart found mysteriously encoded in the pagan document before him 'remain immanent in the One in their very procession'.[77]

Despite that reference to pagan philosophical sources, Lossky has little anxiety on the score of Eckhart's Trinitarianism. Eckhart can also cite Lossky's much-revered John of Damascus on how the Word is never deprived of the Spirit.[78] And he can invoke St Augustine on how knowledge is always loved, even if its object is not—and so the Word conceived in the Father's thought is accompanied by Love, the Holy Spirit.[79] (Lossky had more time for Augustine than most Orthodox theologians did.[80])

As a convinced Monopatrist (see Chapter Five), it is, however, the remarkable prominence Eckhart accords the Person of the Father that most attracts Lossky's interest. 'As with the "monarchy of the Father" in Eastern Trinitarian doctrine, the immediate convertibility of the One, the first hypostasis, with Being-Essence must here assure the essential unity or consubstantiality of the divine persons.'[81] But Lossky also draws attention to the disparity between Eckhart's dogmatic framework and that found in the greatest of the Greek patristic theologians of the Trinity, St Gregory of Nazianzus: 'When a Gregory Nazianzen wishes to express in Plotinian terms the mystery of the hypostatic distinction of the consubstantial Three, he will speak of the monad which sets itself into movement so as to surpass the dyad and find its term in the triad'. And Lossky concludes a short exposition of Gregory of

Nazianzus' doctrine of the Holy Trinity: 'The "surpassing of the dyad" is not a folding back on itself in the third hypostatic term, but, on the contrary, the perfect deployment of the monad, his opening to the personal Tri-unity'.[82] If Eckhart found the language of the 'Twenty-four Sages' about the 'Monad' who 'generates' and then 'reflects on' his own 'ardour' a suitable stimulus for Trinitarian thinking, that must be owing to the influence on him of the Latin doctrine of the double procession of the Spirit. In the Latin Christian context, the Holy Spirit, as bond between the Father and the Son, 'resolves their dyadic opposition by signalling their essential unity'.[83]

That does not please Lossky, for whom the Nazianzen citation is very much a litmus-test of right thinking, where the processions of Son and Spirit are concerned. In the thinking Lossky shared with 'Gregory the Theologian', the procession of the Spirit does not, as it were, confirm the relations of the Dyad (Father and Son) so much as surpass what could be a closed relationship—a divine *égoisme-à-deux*—in the open horizon of a Third.

The same—to Lossky, questionable—'triadic circularity', seen as an expression of the identity of being, will recur in connexion not just with the Trinitarian life but also with the eternal *rationes* of things. Things 'spring up from the unity of the paternal Intellect in coinciding with the Word, the unique Ratio, and in their internal "effervescence" they return to themselves by remaining identical with the Essence'.[84] This passage has an after-taste of the 'Book of the Twenty-Four Philosophers', and the connotations of that word 'return' remain distasteful in Lossky's mouth.

Intelligere and grace

In Eckhart's view, the 'Pure Act of Existing' spoken of by St Thomas must be correlated with the divine 'Intellectual Act'—which is a more distinctively German-Dominican-school way of expressing the supreme actuality of God. In that eternal Act of the divine Mind

> the One, Principle of operation, returns on its own inoperant and unknowable Essence, through manifesting its absolute

identity with itself and with all that is. The *Ipsum esse* is therefore the *Ipsum intelligere*, the divine actuality in which things 'are what they are' [and are so] virtually, according to their *esse primum*.[85]

God is *Intelligere*. He is understanding. Eckhart goes so far as to say that '[God's] intellection is the foundation of his being',[86] though Lossky counsels against overinterpreting this statement. It is not a remote prophecy of the German Idealist philosophy, which was nearly six centuries distant in Eckhart's time. To say 'since God understands, God exists' should be considered, rather, a striking way of 'signalling a negative aspect of the universal Cause', the Cause that, 'considered in its "purity" is infinitely unlike its exterior effects'.[87] Far more central to Eckhart's thinking is the notion that God's understanding is interchangeable with his being. God's existence and his understanding are convertible terms.

If so, it it is hardly surprising to find that, in Eckhart's doctrine, 'being one with God' pertains to a creature 'in the measure in which it shares in intellect or intellectuality'.[88]

> Identical with itself and with God only in the divine *Intelligere*, a created *ens* is not so in its own nature inasmuch as it is outside the Intellect.[89]

That 'inasmuch as' tells us that for Eckhart (rational) creatures can be within the divine Intellect (compare their 'primary' being), as well as outside that Intellect (compare their 'formal' or secondary being). Endowed with a dynamic principle of unity which enables them to surpass themselves and attain union with God, such creatures have in their composition what it seems we must call an 'uncreated' as well as a 'created' element. Lossky admits that Eckhart does ascribe *increabilitas* in this way to the human mind. He claims, however, that Eckhart's use of the word is saved from heterodoxy by its ambiguity. It should not be taken literally: taken, in the French expression that came easily to Lossky's pen, 'au pied de la lettre'.[90] (The same issue surfaces with a number of Western mediaeval mystical writers, such as the Englishwoman Julian of Norwich (c. 1343–c. 1426).[91])

The Latin Master

The twentieth-century German historian of mediaeval thought Martin Grabmann (1875–1949) had judged otherwise. He believed Eckhart had indeed committed himself to a doctrine of the properly uncreated character of the human mind.[92] The twenty-seventh of the twenty-eight articles drawn from Eckhart's work and condemned in John XXIII's bull ran, 'Something is in the soul that is uncreated and non-creatable; if every soul were such it would be uncreated and non-creatable, and that intellect is'.[93] Lossky would reply that *increabilitas* has, in Eckhart's Latin, a fundamentally negative meaning. It corresponds, in Eckhart's German texts, to the word *Abgeschiedenheit*. And the latter clearly signifies the abandonment of determined being at the (mystical) 'going out from this world and from oneself'.[94] 'Uncreatedness' belongs to Eckhart's discourse about mystical union.

Yet undeniably, as Lossky admits, there is a metaphysical aspect to the word. As *ens*, a particularized intellectual nature belongs to the *omnia* that form the universe. But by its *intellectus*, finding no place in the 'all', it detaches itself and goes out from the universe insofar as it is rejoins in the union with God the identity of the *omnia* with the One.

Though this is, to a degree, worrying, Eckhart does acknowledge that *intelligere* here has to involve grace. To know God other than by his created effects, the human intellectual faculty cannot manage without the grace of God. Grace is the effect of an interior operation of God who remains hidden 'in the abyss of the soul', in its essence, closer to it than all the rational soul's own powers or faculties. That is how grace can confer on man 'life in God and with God'.[95]

Whatever view one takes of the scope of the language of the 'supernatural', to have here below the experience of the unique being that is God there must supervene on human powers, by divine mercy, the influx of the light of grace. It is grace that makes possible an ecstatic knowledge *per speculum et in lumine*—'through a mirror and in light'—as Eckhart remarks in his Paris sermon for the feast of St Augustine. To speak of grace in the language of 'light' was a lesson Eckhart could easily learn from the writings of Thomas Aquinas, but the words fall gladly nonetheless on

Lossky's Palamite ears. In Eckhart's evocation of the consciousness of grace, this 'ecstasy of the mind' produces a 'wisdom, a kind of tasting knowledge' (*sapientia, quasi sapida scientia*), which arouses in the human subject a 'great affection', giving him or her a 'foretaste of the divine sweetness'.[96] Without such grace, the intellect cannot make progress on the way of return to 'being-one with God'.[97] Lossky's exposition will remind readers of the *Essai* of his account of the 'Way of Union', which I shall be investigating under the heading of 'Lossky's Pneumatology' in Chapter Seven.

For Eckhart, so Lossky explains (and once again Eckhart departs from the Thomasian script), grace is identical with glory. Or at any rate if there is a distinction between the two it is only owing to our imperfection. That is why *in via*, inasmuch as there is exteriority (what I have called on Lossky's behalf 'secondary being'), God presents himself in grace as our final Cause, enflaming the will with love. Grace makes us strive for assimilation to God. Yet final beatitude 'does not reside in the action of the will but in the passion of the intellect'.[98] Glory or beatitude, says Eckhart audaciously, is the same state in God and in him who receives. It comes about *active in Deo, passive in anima*, 'actively in God, passively in the soul'.[99] In the secret region where it gives *esse divinum*—that is, in the essence of the soul—grace exercises, strictly speaking, no operation, since, where only God can enter as *Esse* or Form, grace is simply beatitude, the union which transcends assimilation.

Meanwhile, however, there is a process to be undergone, which in *The Mystical Theology of the Eastern Church* Lossky will describe as 'penitence, purification, and perfection'.[100] In acting by grace as final Cause (rather than as Form), God re-establishes powers which in the natural order were destroyed by sin. That means for us a new *habitus*, a novel habitual disposition, under which created aspect grace is an effect of our justification, whereas uncreated grace is *esse unum cum Deo*, 'being one with God', in the assimilation-transcending union.

Lossky would have us recall how for Eckhart the 'interior man' who lives from God alone belongs entirely to eternity.[101] Though aware of the danger of anachronism in imposing on a mediaeval thinker a terminology not his own, Lossky thinks Eckhart distinguishes between person and individual in something of the way that he himself, and his Catholic interlocutor the Neo-Thomist philosopher Jacques Maritain (1882–1973), were accustomed to do.[102] In the *Essai* Lossky had written:

> A person who asserts himself as an individual, and shuts himself up in the limits of his particular nature, far from realizing himself fully becomes impoverished ... In giving up its own special good [the person] expands infinitely, and is enriched by everything that belongs to all.[103]

(This same person/individual distinction can also be found, incidentally, in one of the few modern Russian writers Lossky quotes approvingly, Evgenỳi Trubetskoĭ.[104]) The twentieth-century person–individual distinction is already implied, for Lossky, in Eckhart's distinction between the interior and the exterior man.

> Since the dignity of an intellectual (=supernatural) being created to God's image belongs to the 'interior man', the latter cannot be a person in the same sense in which the 'exterior man' is an individual of the common nature. The person-image could not be reduced to the closed individuality of the person-*suppositum*, individual part as this is of the cosmic 'whole'. That appears clearly when the deified state is in question: if the exterior man is an individual who finds his place among the *omnia* of his species, the interior man united to God ... contains not only all the individuals of the human species, but also the angels and all creatures.[105]

Thus the human person in his deification is like the divine Person of the Son in his Incarnation, for the latter assumed human nature and not a human individuality—a *suppositum*. It fits with this that Eckhart understands the 'Communion of Saints' to mean that, in heaven, each person gathers in himself all the grace and merits of the rest.

To know God thus 'through a mirror and in light' the human mind begins an ascent where it must abandon concepts, even that of being, so as to attain God beyond all that can be the object of knowledge and love, 'stripped of Goodness, Being, and every name'.[106] It is because such stripping can be total for the mind (which it cannot possibly be for the will) that one ought not to be a voluntarist, someone who puts will first. And here the journey is endless. Lossky makes the comparison, inevitable for a student of the Greek Fathers, with St Gregory of Nyssa.[107] Every likeness must be surpassed. One must 'search for God so as never to find him' (the meaning of the German sermon on 'A Certain Nobleman' is now plainer)[108] in the region of infinite unlikeness.

> [I]f the apophatic ascent of the intellect in via can only be limitless, it is not 'unknowing' which will find God in the eternal beatitude or the mystical experience of the 'catching up to the third heaven': as we shall see, the final exigence of the negative theology of Eckhart will oblige him to suppress the search for the Unfindable, by reversing the perspective of the ascent of the human intellect in God.[109]

The birth of the Son in us

So we come finally to Eckhart's theology of the deifying transformation. Because man is created 'in the image', and not just 'to the likeness' of God, when he is called to union he must transcend the exemplary relation that founds his quiddity in the Word and his nature in the universe, where the human species receives a determinate place in the hierarchy of *entia*. The Christian must look for a more eminent formation than that which determines his nature in the created context, a transformation that presses beyond the 'principles' (species, genus, *ens commune*) that constitute his essence here below. In order to become 'deiform', the human being must 'be transformed into the same image' (thus II Corinthians 3:18) by which Christ is the Son of God. The same 'image' both made of Christ a Son of God by nature and lends to the 'just and deiform man' his 'quality of son of God by adoption'.[110] And this is only possible if the Word is truly born in us.

Despite Eckhart's seeming lack of interest in the hypostatic union whose ontology so fascinated many of his contemporaries, Lossky is at pains to stress that he adhered to the doctrine formulated in the wake of the Councils of Nicaea and Ephesus by the Chalcedonian definition. 'If human persons are univocal to the Son of God (=The Just One) as to the humanity he had assumed, they are not so in regard to his divinity.'[111] Lossky dwells on the moment in the creation of man that makes him 'naturally supernatural, so to say', not only because the faculty of understanding gives the human being the possibility of transcending the natural being of the universe but above all because intellectual beings are made to receive the 'second grace' which is 'properly supernatural'.[112] (Here we do find Lossky recognizing the importance of the twofold order of nature and grace.) By renouncing his own nature, the man created in God's image becomes by the grace of filial adoption what Christ is by his divine nature, i.e. the Father's Son.

Using the Sirach text 'my flowers are my fruits' (Ecclesiasticus 24:23), Eckhart speaks of the interior work of God which is the formation of the image as a work always new, since no interval transpires between the principle and the end. The Son is engendered eternally. His continual birth is now also, since the Incarnation, the uniquely divine *esse* of the humanity assumed by Christ. And since his human nature is common with ours, the 'same eternal birth of the Son will also be [in Lossky's paraphrase of Eckhart's teaching] a divine *quo est* for deified men': it will be, in other words, an instrument for their deification.[113]

> This birth which procures for men the divine virtues of the Son can only be instantaneous, thus intemporal—which gives it the character of a continuous action in time by relation to the soul who receives it without cease.[114]

The birth of the Word in us will be how we actually return to the divine 'ground'. Lossky's decision to make this theme the climax of his study chimes with the findings of exemplary readers of the Eckhartian corpus since Lossky's time. Bernard McGinn, doyen of historians of mediaeval mysticism in the English-speaking world, has declared *geburt* ('birth') to be the 'focus' of Eckhart's preaching,[115] while Hans Urs von Balthasar wrote memorably in the metaphysics volume of his theological aesthetics, '[Meister Eckhart] melted down the philosophy of every thinker and recast it into the central mystery of divine birth'.[116]

Conclusion

The intellectual generosity with which Lossky investigated Eckhart's teaching is an exemplary act of interpretative charity. But at the same time, as I have occasionally signalled in the course of this chapter, it is impossible to overlook the contrast between Lossky's approach and that of his own contemporary, Sergeï Bulgakov.

The generosity concerned is especially noticeable in the way Lossky deals with Eckhart's assertion of a God beyond the Trinity. What does Eckhart mean, in his German sermons, by opposing 'Deity', *gotheit*, to 'God', *got*? What does he intend by exalting the 'desert of the Deity' above the 'Trinity which manifests Deity'? Lossky admits that the distinction seems 'altogether disquieting and strange'.[117] But he thinks he can give it a benign sense. It can be argued that 'The distinction between God and Deity concerns two aspects—exterior and interior—under which creatures *in via* conceive the same simple reality, by opposing two levels on account of an inevitable optic here below'.[118] Again, in this book Lossky is notably sympathetic to Eckhart's desire to baptize non-Christian philosophers and draw their insights into service in the expression of the patrimony of Tradition. A key passage is prompted by Eckhart's reflections on how creaturely essences are most themselves as living in the Father's Word:

> If the *Vivum intellectuale*, with all the traits of Trinitarian theology it implies, represents for Meister Eckhart the aspect under which being constitutes the proper object of metaphysics, we shall not be looking to the Thuringian mystic for a precise discrimination between natural theology and revealed truths. The perspective in which Eckhart wants to consider being will transform into enunciations of metaphysics the scriptural texts and the theological authorities of the *sancti et doctores nostri*; but it will also lend a character of Trinitarian theology to the speculations of the 'philosophers', Greek, Arab, or Jewish. The 'pagan' masters will thereby become witnesses to the mystery of the Christian faith. The definition of Aristotle, which would have it that metaphysics is a science of being qua being, will need to receive for Meister Eckhart a theological *arrière-sens* which attaches itself for him to the *inquantum*,

signifying the 'return of being on itself', the *sum qui sum*, the circular movement of the intellectual monad engendering the monad and 'reflecting' on itself its ardour or love.'[119]

We have seen how Lossky does not fully approve of that 'circular movement' idea. Yet once again the mildness of his attitude to Eckhart's distinctive positions—and to the overall audacity of the Eckhartian project—makes an odd contrast to his severity in the Bulgakov case, where the attempted Christian redeployment of unusual philosophical resources was also at stake.

Just as Lossky's thesis on Eckhart fell short of completion at the time of his death, so likewise he did not live to make, vis-à-vis Bulgakov, what might have transpired in due course: honourable amends. Though no concrete opportunity presented itself to revisit the Bulgakov affair, we can, I think, discern a change of heart in a somewhat surprising source: Lossky's description of the effect on the Russian philosopher and critic Ivan Vasileevich Kireevskiĭ (1806–56) of the teaching of the *startsi* of the Optino monastery, the single most celebrated centre of spiritual teaching in nineteenth-century Russia. Those 'old men', i.e. spiritual fathers, were a topic of consuming interest in the last years of Lossky's life. Lossky cites Kireevsky as writing:

> Our Church has never made of a human system, a theological science, the foundation of its Truth. That is why it has never been opposed to the free development of thought in other systems; it has never persecuted these systems as enemies capable of shaking its foundation.[120]

It is possible that Kireevsky's text put Lossky in mind of the trial or trials of Eckhart,[121] one of the few mediaeval theologians to be formally indicted on a charge of heresy (which carried, at the hands of the State, the capital penalty). But it is also possible that, in choosing to quote these words, Lossky saw implications for the 'Debate about Wisdom' held, with such a legacy of bitterness, so many years before. Schelling—often regarded as the principal, if to a degree transitory, philosophical influence on Bulgakov[122]—had fewer warmer admirers than Kireevsky, whom one historian of Russian culture has gone so far as to call the 'iconographer and master of ceremonies' of a Schelling cult in Russia in the Nicholaevan age' (the reign of Tsar Nicholas I, 1826–55).[123] No suggestion of such philosophical dependence, not to say sycophancy, was ever made in connexion with Bulgakov, Lossky's erstwhile *bête-noire*.

Notes

1   Vladimir Lossky, *Théologie négative et connaissance de Dieu chez Maître Eckhart* (2nd edition, Paris: Vrin, 1998), pp. 12–13.

2   Cited *ibid.*, p. 14.

3   *Ibid.*, p. 15.

4   Augustine, *On Christian Teaching*, I. 6.

5   Lossky, *Théologie négative et connaissance de Dieu chez Maître Eckhart*, p. 16.

6   Augustine, *On the True Religion* , I. 39.

7   Lossky, *Théologie négative et connaissance de Dieu chez Maître Eckhart*, p. 16

8   *Ibid.*, p. 18.

9   *Ibid.*, p. 20.

10   *Ibid.*, p. 21.

11   Thomas Aquinas, *Commentary on the Divine Names*, lectio 3.

12   Thomas Aquinas, *Summa Theologiae*, Ia., q. 12, a. 1, ad iii.

13   Lossky, *Théologie négative et connaissance de Dieu chez Maître Eckhart*, p. 24.

14   *Ibid.*, p. 25.

15   *Ibid.*, p. 27.

16   Josef Koch, 'Augustinische und dionysische Neuplatonismus im Mittelalter', in Werner Beierwaltes (ed.), *Platonismus in der Philosophie des Mittelalters* (Darmstadt: Wissenschaftliche Buchhandlung, 1969), pp. 317–42.

17   Bernard McGinn, *The Mystical Thought of Meister Eckhart* (New York: Herder and Herder, 2001), p. 177.

18   Alain de Libera, *La Mystique rhénane d'Albert le Grand et Maître Eckhart* (Paris: Editions du Seuil, 1994).

19   Lossky, *Théologie négative et connaissance de Dieu chez Maître Eckhart*, p. 32.

20   Chronicled in Ingeborg Degenhardt, *Studien zum Wandel des Eckhartbildes* (Leiden: Brill, 1967). No doubt further ideological readings have accumulated since she wrote.

21   Oliver Davies, *Meister Eckhart. Mystical Theologian* (London: SPCK, 1991), p. 1.

22 *Ibid.*, p. 3.

23 *Ibid.*

24 Lossky, *The Mystical Theology of the Eastern Church*, p. 14.

25 Cited from a manuscript source of Eckhart's *Commentary on John* in Lossky, *Théologie négative et connaissance de Dieu chez Maître Eckhart*, p. 34.

26 Aidan Nichols, *Wisdom from Above. A Primer in the Theology of Father Sergei Bulgakov* (Leominster: Gracewing, 2005), pp. 43–5.

27 Lossky, *Théologie négative et connaissance de Dieu chez Maître Eckhart*, p. 35.

28 *Ibid.*, p. 37.

29 *Ibid.*

30 See the essays collected in Serge-Thomas Bonino, O.P. (ed.), *Surnaturel. A Controversy at the Heart of Twentieth Century Thomistic Thought* (Ave Maria, FL: Sapienta Press, 2009).

31 Lossky, *The Mystical Theology of the Eastern Church*, p. 101.

32 Lossky, *Théologie négative et connaissance de Dieu chez Maître Eckhart*, p. 37.

33 Cited from German Sermon XV, *ibid.*, p. 39.

34 *Ibid.*, p. 38.

35 *Ibid.*, pp. 41–2.

36 *Ibid.*, p. 42.

37 *Ibid.*, p. 43.

38 *Ibid.*, p. 45.

39 *Ibid.*

40 *Ibid.*, p. 48.

41 *Ibid.*, p. 116.

42 *Ibid.*, p. 117.

43 Nichols, *Wisdom from Above*, pp. 33–9.

44 Cited in Arjakovsky, *Essai sur le Père Serge Boulgakov*, p. 80.

45 Lossky, *Théologie négative et connaissance de Dieu chez Maître Eckhart*, p. 55.

46 *Ibid.*, p. 56.

47 *Ibid.*, footnote 57.

48 *Ibid.*

49 *Ibid.*, p. 57.

50 *Ibid.*, p. 59.

51 Eckhart, writes Lossky, 'eliminates all idea of a non-being which could be opposed to divine Being considered in itself, independently of creaturely causality', *ibid.*, p. 74.

52 The debt to Boehme is manifest in his writings, and recognized in his introduction, 'Unground and Freedom', in Jacob Boehme, *Six Theosophic Points and Other Writings* (Ann Arbor, MI: University of Michigan Press, 1958). The notion of 'meonic freedom', quasi-ubiquitous in Berdyaev's books, helped furnish the title for an overall study of his work: Matthew Spinka, *Nicolas Berdiaev, Captive of Freedom* (Philadelphia: Westminster, 1950).

53 Nicolas Berdyaev, *The Destiny of Man* (New York: Harper and Row, 1960), p. 25.

54 Lossky, *Théologie négative et connaissance de Dieu chez Maître Eckhart*, p. 75.

55 *Ibid*.

56 The text of the articles, in Latin, with a French translation, can be found in F. Vernet, 'Eckart', in A. Vacant, E. Mangenot, E. Amann (ed.), *Dictionnaire de théologie catholique* IV.2 (Paris: Letouzey et Ané, 1939), cols. 2062–4. Vernet's entry, acknowledging the need, on the eve of the Second World War, for further textual research, is extremely judicious on the topic of Eckhart's orthodoxy.

57 Lossky, *Théologie négative et connaissance de Dieu chez Maître Eckhart*, p. 98.

58 *Ibid*., p. 125.

59 *Ibid*., p. 131.

60 *Ibid*., p. 287. The whole of Lossky's chapter five, covering pp. 251–337 of his study, is devoted to winkling out the interrelations of analogy, equivocity, and univocity in Eckhart's account: interrelations which follow from his distinctive creation ontology. In McGinn's judgement, Lossky's discussion of such 'dialectized analogy' is the most original of his contributions to modern Eckhart scholarship. See McGinn, *The Mystical Thought of Meister Eckhart*, p. 229, footnote 121.

61 Lossky, *Théologie négative et connaissance de Dieu chez Maître Eckhart*, p. 333.

62 *Ibid*., p. 287.

63 *Ibid*., p. 60.

64 *Ibid*.

65 Cited *ibid*., p. 61.

66 Cf. Dionysius, *On the Divine Names* III, 3.

67 Lossky, *Théologie négative et connaissance de Dieu chez Maître Eckhart*, p. 63. Lossky cites from the *Commentary on the Gospel of St John* the very striking Eckhartian version of John 14:8: 'Show us the One [not, as in the original text of the Gospel, *the Father*] and it suffices us', *ibid*., p. 65.

68 *Ibid*., p. 64.

69 *Ibid*.

70 See Davies, *Meister Eckhart*, pp. 201–7 for a careful discussion of whether Eckhart seeks to go beyond Trinitarianism.

The Latin Master

71 Lossky, *Théologie négative et connaissance de Dieu chez Maître Eckhart*, p. 66.

72 *Ibid.*

73 *Ibid.*, p. 68.

74 *Ibid.*

75 Françoise Hudry (ed.), *Liber Viginti Quattuor Philosophorum*, Corpus Christianorum Continuatio Medievalis 143A (Turnhout: Brepols, 1997).

76 Lossky, *Théologie négative et connaissance de Dieu chez Maître Eckhart*, p. 70.

77 *Ibid.*

78 John of Damascus, *On the Orthodox Faith* I. 7.

79 Augustine, *On the Trinity* IX. 10.

80 Lossky wrote, 'The Orthodox Church would not be what it is of it had not had St. Cyprian, St Augustine and St Gregory the Great', *The Mystical Theology of the Eastern Church*, p. 12. For a survey of opinion see George E. Demacopoulos and Aristotle Papanikolaou (ed.), *Orthodox Readings of Augustine* (Crestwood, NY: St Vladimir's Seminary Press, 2008).

81 Lossky, *Théologie négative et connaissance de Dieu chez Maître Eckhart*, p. 71.

82 *Ibid.*

83 *Ibid.*

84 *Ibid.*

85 *Ibid.*, p. 165.

86 Cited from the first of Eckhart's *Parisian Questions* at *ibid.*, p. 210.

87 *Ibid.*, p. 217.

88 *Ibid.*, p. 166.

89 *Ibid.*

90 *Ibid.*, p. 170.

91 E. I. Watkin speaks of 'Julian's vision of the ground of the soul as outside the time series in the eternal Now of God', *On Julian of Norwich and in Defence of Margery Kempe* (Exeter: University of Exeter Press, 1979), p. 18.

92 Martin Grabmann, *Neuaufgefundene Pariser Quaestionen Meister Eckharts und ihre Stelling in seiner geistigen Entwicklungslage: Untersuchungen und Texte* (Munich: Verlag der bayrischen Akademie der Wissenschaften, 1927).

93 F. Vernet, 'Eckart', in A. Vacant, E. Mangenot, E. Amann (ed.), *Dictionnaire de théologie catholique* IV.2, col. 2064.

94 Quoted in Lossky, *Théologie négative et connaissance de Dieu chez Maître Eckhart*, p. 170.

95 Cited *ibid.*

96 Cited *ibid.*, p. 181.

97 Ibid., p. 182.

98 Ibid., p. 185.

99 Meister Eckhart, Latin Sermons IX.

100 Lossky, The Mystical Theology of the Eastern Church, p. 204.

101 Lossky, Théologie négative et connaissance de Dieu chez Maître Eckhart, p. 188.

102 Jacques Maritain, La Personne et le bien commun (Paris: Desclée de Brouwer, 1947). Over thirty years earlier, Maritain had already identified the distinction between individuality and personhood as a problem insoluble for 'modernity': Trois réformateurs: Luther, Descartes, Rousseau (Paris: Plon, 1925), p. 26.

103 Lossky, The Mystical Theology of the Eastern Church, p. 124.

104 Zenkovsky, History of Russian Philosophy II., pp. 795–7. 'He alone of the sophiological school', judges Lossky, 'remained perfectly orthodox in his theological thought', The Mystical Theology of the Eastern Church, p. 133, note 1.

105 Lossky, Théologie négative et connaissance de Dieu chez Maître Eckhart, p. 190, Lossky cites here Eckhart's Latin Sermons VII and XXII.

106 Ibid., p. 195, citing Meister Eckhart, German Sermons IX.

107 And especially to Daniélou, Platonisme et théologie mystique, pp. 309–26.

108 Lossky,Théologie negative et connaissance de Dieu, citing Meister Eckhart, German Sermons XV.

109 Ibid., pp. 196–7.

110 Phrases Lossky has excerpted from Eckhart's Commentary on John, though the Expositio at this point is cross-referencing to a Pauline text, II Corinthians 3:18, ibid., pp. 358–9.

111 Ibid., p. 360.

112 Ibid., p. 362.

113 Ibid., p. 367.

114 Ibid., p. 368.

115 McGinn, The Mystical Thought of Meister Eckhart, p. 142.

116 Hans Urs von Balthasar, The Glory of the Lord. A Theological Aesthetics. V. The Realm of Metaphysics in the Modern Age (San Francisco: Ignatius, 1991), p. 33.

117 Lossky,Théologie negative et connaissance de Dieu, p. 343.

118 Ibid. In the Essai, however, Lossky suggested that Eckhart's theocentrism which, by implication, would have been fine in the Christian East was, in the circumstances of the West whose Triadology gave priority to the divine nature, in danger of 'becoming an impersonal apophaticism of the divine-nothingness prior to the Trinity', The Mystical Theology of the Eastern Church, p. 65.

119   Lossky, *Théologie negative et connaissance de Dieu*, p. 120.

120   Lossky and Arseniev, *La Paternité spirituelle en Russie au XVIIIème et XIXème siècles*, p. 124.

121   The two sets of hearings in Cologne and at Avignon were one process, inasmuch as the latter was the result of Eckhart's appeal to the Roman curia. See for a detailed discussion Winfred Trusen, *Der Prozess gegen Meister Eckhart. Vorgeschichte, Verlauf und Folgen* (Paderborn: Schöningh, 1988).

122   Thus for Paul Valliere, *Modern Russian Theology: Bukharev, Soloviev, Bulgakov. Orthodox Theology in a New Key* (Grand Rapids, MI: Eerdmans, 2000), pp. 295–6, Bulgakov found in Schelling's 'positive philosophy' the acceptable face of Idealism—itself, in Bulgakov's view, the distinctively modern caste of intellectuality. Schelling's was, however, an influence that diminished over time, as is noted by Jennifer Newsome Martin, *Hans Urs von Balthasar and the Critical Appropriation of Russian Religious Thought* (Notre Dame, IN: University of Notre Dame Press, 2015), p. 214, n. 58.

123   Billington, *The Icon and the Axe*, p. 312.

✢ 4 ✢

A Fundamental Theology

It is time now to present an overview of the wider doctrine for which Vladimir Lossky sought a significantly apophatic articulation in the service of the Gospel of the Kingdom. One obvious question to put at the outset runs, 'Is mystical theology all the theology there is?'

The scope of mystical theology

Lossky's *Essai sur la théologie mystique de l'Église d'Orient*—as its title suggests—gives the interested reader an *entrée* to his view of specifically mystical theology. But in that work he does not claim for mystical theology a total imperium over theology as a whole. It is the single most important mode of practising theology. But it is not necessarily co-terminous with theology as such. It does not of itself furnish the complete story of theology's scope and foundations.

Were we to look in the pages of Lossky's *œuvre* for a 'fundamental theology' in the modern Roman Catholic sense which has generated the phrase—namely, the study of what theology is, and how it is grounded, then there are two obvious places to which to turn. And these are: first, the substantial 'Introduction' to his posthumously published lecture course *Théologie dogmatique*, and, secondly, the lengthy essay on the topic of Tradition in *The Meaning of Icons*—the lavishly illustrated book he co-authored with the iconographer Leonid Ouspensky (1902–87). That is not to say, however, that in either of those sources we should expect a radically different account of theology from what the *Essai* provides.

The basis of theology — and the virtues and gifts it needs

In *Théologie dogmatique* Lossky's opening statement is less concerned with the subjective manner of approaching theology's content and more with that content's objective grounding in divine action. In his own words,

> The foundation of theological teaching is the incarnation of the Word, exactly as with iconography. Since the Word has become incarnate it can be thought and taught, just as it can be painted.[1]

'Incarnation reveals', he will add later, 'and it constitutes revelation itself.'[2] This suggests a broader programme than that of *The Mystical Theology of the Eastern Church*, and a more Christologically concentrated one as well. But then Lossky follows up this statement with another which at once calls to mind the 'mystical' preoccupations of the *Essai*. The Incarnation has 'no other aim than to lead us to the Father, in the Spirit'. And that means, then, that our thinking must always be open to a reality that goes beyond it—which it can only be if it is 'grasped, mortified and vivified' by a faith Lossky terms 'contemplative' in character. Yes, 'science and reasoning' help to define the theologian's calling, but so too do 'charism and silence'. This overall combination—science and 'contemplation' (the latter denoting 'charism and silence', which can also be described as 'gnosis')—enables Lossky to identify theology's setting in life, and the virtues and gifts it requires.[3]

He deals first with the 'gnosis' component. It is under this rubric that he re-presents the role of *apophasis*—and thus of epistemology, and, ultimately, of thinking—in his work, as well as the need to go beyond all of these.

> Theology must lead the mind towards contemplation, towards the pure prayer where thought stops. As thinking beings we need theological thought to go beyond thought towards the ineffable. Theology is thus indispensable for the thinking, conscious Christian.[4]

A Fundamental Theology

Theological thinking is here interpreted eschatologically, as a movement towards a vision for meta-history, since this is what enables Lossky to point up the contrast between the 'gnostic' component in theology and its 'scientific' complement.

'Taught theology, *la théologie enseignée*', however, has inevitably to privilege the scientific element—that duo of rationality and erudition, 'science and reasoning'. It must take into account the point human culture has reached in its development, having to 'adapt to milieux and moments'.[5] But Lossky does not linger on this topic, other than to say that, by sharing in both 'gnosis' and *epistēmē* ('science'), theology at large really belongs to neither. This, presumably, is because the former is too purely contemplative in character and the latter too much a matter of debate and scholarship. His own preference for the 'gnosis' element becomes plain, however, when he writes that, whereas simple 'science' is a temptation for the theologian, to yield to pure 'gnosis' is to rise higher than theological thought.

An attempt to do justice to both of these components—ironically enough considering Lossky's opposition to Sophiology—is found by invoking the term *sophia*. The latter is a divine attribute which also exists humanly. In us it takes the form of a sort of moral skill, which Lossky would link to prudence in the ancient Hellenic sense of that word: *phronēsis*. As he explains:

> Theology as Sophia signifies thus the ability to adapt one's own thought to Revelation, to find able and inspired words to give testimony in the language (but not the limits) of human thought by responding to the needs of the moment.[6]

He says 'not the limits', having already warned his hearers against the enclosure of theology in a system ('always dangerous'[7]). We may recall from Chapter One how this was a source of hesitation in working on a planned, but never written, fully fledged dogmatics.

Lossky's reference to 'revelation' belongs with the introduction of two new subjects in these early pages of *Théologie dogmatique*: the priority of divine initiative, and the baptismal rule of faith. In the life to which theology belongs, God's initiative is always prior in an engagement with human beings whose intended outcome is not only reciprocity but union. Lossky appeals in this connexion, in somewhat airy terms, to the apostolic authority of St Paul and St John. Probably in his mind is the Pauline confession, 'I shall know as I am known' (I Corinthians 13:12), and the Johannine credo 'He loved us first' (I John 4:19), both of which speak of the priority of divine action, in knowledge and love respectively. This antecedent divine initiative can only be grasped by specifically Christian faith, which is where the baptismal rule enters the picture. Adhering to the 'presence which grants certitude' implies the baptismal gift of the Holy Spirit.[8] Lossky has both the divine initiative and the baptismal rule of faith in mind when he writes that 'faith as ontological participation included in a personal encounter, is the first precondition of theological knowledge'.[9] Here we have moved on from epistemology to ontology, from thought to being.

Lossky introduces a fourth Greek term—after gnosis, *epistēmē* and *sophia*—and this is 'the anointing', *chrisma*, as described by St John (again) in his First Letter. The Holy Spirit's unction 'instructs you in all things' (2:27), for which claim Lossky brings to the witness-stand Augustine's homilies on that epistle.[10] Comparing it with the *anamnēsis*, or pre-existent 'memory' of the soul—in the *Dialogues* of Plato, Lossky insists that the anointing cannot, however, just remain latent. It must be actualized—and this is the task of theology, at whatever level of education or vocational demand. An unreflective faith is not enough. 'The faith of the charcoal-burner does not suffice, least of all for a pastor.'[11]

In the service of the personal Absolute

The God around whom the theology of Revelation takes its focus is, says Lossky, the Absolute, but he is also a 'Thou'. This combination—'Absolute-hood' (if the neologism may be allowed) along with personality—is not found outside Judaeo-Christianity. In the case of the gods of polytheistic devotion there may well be personality, but their status prevents us from saying that, in such religious traditions, what is personal is the Absolute. Neo-Platonism has an Absolute in the One, constituted in no respect by anything other than Itself, but here, in Lossky's words, the 'knowledge of the divine nature finds at once its fulfillment and annulment in the impersonality of unknowing',[12] taking place by an intellectual ecstasy. (That said, Lossky has great respect for Plotinus, in particular, pointing out that Neo-Platonist thought will be 'assimilated and utilized by numerous [Church] Fathers', who in so doing press it beyond its own bounds.[13])

The account of God given so far in this Losskeian 'Charter for Theology' assumes the unity of Judaism and Christianity. What has been said is equally true of the Elder Testament and of the New. But now we must note a difference: 'the God of the Jews hides the depths of his nature; he is only manifested by his authority, his Name is itself unpronounceable'.[14] Given this lack of reciprocity in the Judaic approach to the personal Absolute, theology as the Fathers of the Church understand it is simply impossible for Israel.

These observations enable Lossky to work out a rather neat scheme. In Judaism, and later on in Islam, we have a monotheism which affirms the personal character of God but does not know his nature. In the Hellenic world (and beyond) we have a henotheism which surmises the nature of the Absolute but can only access it by dissolving the notion of personality. In the latter case, divine personality is absorbed into the ineffable; in the former, with 'nature drowning the person', a knowledge of God is denied by the divine personality itself, 'the divine person hiding the nature'.[15] We can perhaps see where this leading. The revelation found in Christianity holds, in Blaise Pascal's expression, both ends of the chain. Or, in Lossky's words,

> Christianity frees man from these two limitations by fully revealing at once the personal God and his nature. He thus fulfils the best of Israel and the best of the other religions or metaphysics, not as a cultural synthesis but as a 'dogmatic fact' in Christ and by Christ. In him, indeed, humanity and divinity are united, and the divine nature communicates itself to the human nature in order to deify it: that is the response to Israel. But the Son is consubstantial with the Father and the Spirit: that is the response to the impersonal metaphysics.

> The divine nature is not beyond the person. Rather, its plenitude resides in the total communion of the divine persons amongst themselves, and its communication to man is done also in a personal rapport.[16]

Lossky notes with realism—and with fidelity to Paul's remarks in I Corinthians (1:23) that in both respects the supreme revelation does not only fulfil. It also scandalizes both Jew and Greek alike.

Lossky worries that, in a pejorative sense of the words, 'Greeks' and 'Jews' still remain in the Church: that is, there are would-be theologians who either 'Hellenize' or 'Semitize' excessively. The first lot, by over-intellectualizing revelation, risk losing the 'existential character of the encounter with God which the apparent anthropomorphism of Israel discloses'.[17] This is the temptation of Scholastics in all periods as well as of the 'erudite theologians' of the nineteenth century with their accumulation of positive data about Christian origins and subsequent history. The second lot, who are a more recent phenomenon, over-react to the first by seeking to remake theology in exclusively Hebraic categories.[18] But, Lossky insists, Christian theology must be universal. Divine Providence chose the Fathers from a Greek milieu to 'purify and sanctify the language of philosophers and mystics', so as to express a message which includes that of Israel but also goes beyond it.[19]

The negative and affirmative ways again

Readers of the *Essai* (or of any of the works discussed so far) will not be surprised to hear that the author of this introductory piece cannot resist drawing in at this point the topic of the negative and affirmative ways. But how he sets about it is something of a new departure.

In *Théologie dogmatique* Lossky speaks of revelation as a historically given 'theo-cosmic' relation which is inclusive of ourselves. In more biblical language, we might call it a covenanted extension of the God-world relationship in which human beings function as covenant partners. That is why we cannot stand outside that relation so as to view it 'objectively' (as, probably unwisely, we might wish to put it). That is not feasable because as Christians we find ourselves situated always within the revelation-relation. But precisely through this immanent presence God reveals himself to us as transcendent vis-à-vis his creation as a whole.

At this juncture we may surmise that Lossky is about to drop the apophatic bombshell, and so it is. 'Trying to think God in himself reduces us to silence, since neither thought nor language can imprison the Infinite in concepts which, so as to define it, limit it.'[20] We need, therefore, to recognize the inevitability of apophasis. Yet outside Christianity, the negative way leads to the depersonalization both of God and of the human being who is looking for him. An 'abyss' separates pagan from Christian apophaticism. Why? 'A Gregory of Nyssa or a Dionysius 'do not see in apophaticism Revelation but [only] a necessary condition for receiving Revelation: they finish with the personal presence of the hidden God'.[21] In the Liturgy they celebrated and in which the Orthodox faithful participate today, 'one says "Thou" to this unknowable God who surpasses all names'.[22] In this discussion Lossky seems to accept after all the notion that the apophatic way 'corrects' the cataphatic (to which in the *Essai* he had been allergic). Yet he remains concerned chiefly with what he calls 'the "mystical marriage" of the soul—and the Church—with God'.[23] Apophaticism teaches that the approach to God is a 'limitless flight'—not, however, the 'ineffable fusion' of the Plotinian ecstasy, but the continuing discovery of God as 'other'—interpreted by Lossky to mean 'always new, inexhaustible'.[24] The Incarnation guards us from thinking that this could ever mean absorption in the impersonal. The key terms must be 'encounter' with God and 'communion' with him.[25]

The role of philosophy

One notes the congruity, in this perspective, of Lossky's robustly Christological starting-point for theology. 'For the theologian the departure-point is Christ, and he is also the point of arrival.'[26] But while refusing any other foundation for theology than the Christological (there is no suggestion here, as in Neo-Thomism, for instance, of a necessary rational 'preamble of faith'), Lossky does not for all that dismiss the philosophical tradition as valueless to the life of the Christian mind. The God of revelation may be concrete and personal, but he also 'contains' the God of the philosophers, 'abstract and impersonal' though the latter be. The God of reason is not a 'mirage' but a reflection of reality — albeit only 'in human thought'.[27] Granted that thought's native deficiencies — this is the manifest burden of Lossky's remarks — the only way to salvage philosophy and redeem its value, is to start from faith.

One obvious example of an unredeemed philosophy emerges in Lossky's criticism in this connexion of the notion of the God–world relation in the Platonist tradition. There is, for an insufficiently baptized Platonism, no real ontological *coupure* — no clean cut — between God and the world. But in reality there is in creation a 'total ontological *coupure*'.[28] It is hard to think Lossky does not have Bulgakov in mind in this exaggerated statement. Lossky uses Augustine — but he could also have used Eckhart — to say that beings do not truly have being. Addressing God, 'They are because they are by you; they are not because they are not what you are.'[29] Even so, this assertion does not imply the total break between God and the world Lossky calls on theology (and in its wake philosophy) to acknowledge.

What Lossky expects is that when devoting itself to ultimate questions a philosophy that knows its proper business will end with a question-mark. And that of course is where the bearers of revelation are meant to enter the picture. 'Theology must respond to [philosophy's] question by replying that transcendence is revealed in the immanence of the Incarnation.'[30] The very idea of revelation implies immanence but it is in this immanence itself that God is revealed as transcendent. The only natural theology acceptable to Lossky, as this chapter of *Théologie dogmatique* draws to its close, is the assertion that God is not defined by opposition to anything, and hence lies beyond the opposition of being and nothingness. Citing Nicholas of Cusa, God is grasped only in non-grasping. Not surprisingly, then, the chapter ends in a paean to apophasis, the place of which seemed somewhat minimized earlier. Lossky reverts to the manner of the *Essai* when he says of apophasis that it must be understood, in the last resort, not as therapy for philosophy but as opening the way to deification.

So far in this text Lossky has offered us a theological epistemology suited to an Incarnation-founded religion that aims at divine union. But he has not done much to show us the sources from which that religion will draw its necessary content. This is more the task of 'Tradition and Traditions', to which I now turn.

Introducing the concept of Tradition

The concept of Tradition can be understood, so Lossky opens his account, in various ways, for in some quarters it has undergone secularization and in others is used with unhelpful vagueness. Two features of the history of the word are, however, worth preserving. One is its connotation of fullness — Lossky uses the New Testament word 'pleroma', and here he is guarding against any subversive secularizing tendencies that might be around. The other is the desire of classical theologians to introduce some precisions into its use, and this is how he intends to deal with the menace of vagueness. 'To distinguish does not always mean to separate, nor even to oppose.'[31] It was a sentiment he could well have taken from Jacques Maritain, who used it as the title of one of his most famous works,[32] and licenses the entry of a certain element of 'Orthodox Scholasticism' into Lossky's corpus. But Lossky's immediate target is what he calls 'the polemicists of the Counter-Reformation' who, he thinks, wrong-footed themselves precisely by opposing Tradition to Scripture — that is, treating Tradition as 'an external principle in relation to Scripture', rather than the 'living breath' that gives the Scriptures their 'fundamental coherence'.[33] For Lossky issues such as the primacy of Scripture (or of Tradition), the partial difference of their contents, and their respective authority are all examples of 'false problems'.[34] Both Scripture and Tradition are, to coin a word, 'pleromatic'. Yet there can hardly be two 'pleromas'. There can only be 'two modalities of one and the same fullness of the Revelation communicated to the Church'.[35]

The Council of Trent, to whom it fell to adjudicate some of these matters in the sixteenth-century debate, used a plural term: *traditiones*. For Lossky that usage follows inevitably from separating Tradition from Scripture. Once that separation in thought has taken place what is left is only the identification as Tradition of the—multiple—'written and oral testimonies which are added to the Holy Scripture, accompanying or following it'. For such testimonies may arise contemporaneously with the New Testament Scriptures (thus accompanying), or at some later date (thus following, though presumably still within the apostolic era).

An advance on a view of Tradition which, like the one ascribed to Trent, is both separating and quantitative is found when the distinction between Bible and Tradition is expressed in terms, rather, of a contrast between the written and the oral. These are, at any rate, two modes rather than (as yet) two contents. The preaching of the apostles, and their successors, will now be juxtaposed to all written forms of revelation beginning with the Holy Scriptures. Were we to adopt this perspective, Lossky has no hesitation is saying that we should be obliged to grant Tradition primacy over Scripture since the apostles' kerygmatic activity surely preceded their scribal work. But this distinction between oral and written still remains, in his view, somewhat superficial.

More satisfactory, in his judgement, is St Basil's distinction between, on the one hand, that which is kept in secret and hence is not the subject of writing, and, on the other, that which, since it has been publicly declared, can appropriately by written down. The classic reference is from Basil's treatise *On the Holy Spirit*, and the discussion is reminiscent of John Henry Newman (1801–90) in his early Anglican writings.[36] It is not a matter of a secret apostolic tradition known esoterically only to a few within the Christian body (that is, rather, a Gnostic stratagem). In St Basil's words, the 'teaching (*didaskalia*), unpublished and secret, that our fathers kept in silence, free from disquiet and curiosity well knowing that in being silent one safeguards the sacred character of the mysteries'[37] is known to all the sacramentally initiated, and it can, moreover, become public preaching if some necessity obliges the Church so to decree. The emergence of a heresy is Lossky's predictable example as, when writing *The Arians of the Fourth Century*, it had been Newman's.[38] Basil's own examples, contrastingly, have to do with the sacramental and liturgical life. They are traditions that 'point to the "mysterial character" of Christian knowledge'.[39] Through sacramental initiation one comes to share in the revealed mystery—here Lossky makes glad acknowledgement of the work of the monk of Maria Laach, Dom Odo Casel (1886–1948), in his influential statement of a 'theology of the Mysteries', *Das christliche Kultusmysterium*.[40] But this is still not enough. For in the upshot, Basil's view anticipates that of Trent. The secret Tradition consists of many *traditiones*, and hence is quantitative (and even separate!) after all.

Lossky's own solution

So now Lossky approaches his own solution. The 'horizontal' line of the traditions, as received from the apostles if not from Christ himself, is insufficient if taken alone. It must be intersected by a 'vertical' line—and this (here we come to Lossky's distinctive view) is 'the communication of the Holy Spirit, which opens to members of the Church an infinite perspective of mystery in each word of the revealed Truth'.[41] Whether oral or written, whether preserved in secret or publicly proclaimed to pagans, both Tradition and Scripture are—without this 'vertical' intervention—a matter of sheer words, of verbal expression. And indeed in patristic usage the term *logia* (a Greek version of the English 'words') can equally mean the Scriptures or the 'Symbol of Faith', the Creed, which is of course an articulation of Tradition. All that expresses the Incarnation of the Word becomes in some manner 'scripture' (with a lower case initial), alongside Holy Scripture. Lossky brings even iconography under this heading, since it is expression of the Inexpressible—like the Bible as read in the Church. The Orthodox speak about 'writing' rather than 'painting' icons, so this is not as bizarre as it might seem. But Lossky's point is that all these embodiments of Revelation are to be contrasted with the action of the Spirit that renders them vehicles of the divine self-disclosure—and this is the distinct reality for which he would like to preserve the name 'Tradition'.

Lossky goes so far in his stress on non-verbal 'verticality' as to take seriously the possibility that Tradition is Silence—appealing to the two modes in which Ignatius of Antioch says Jesus may be 'heard' in his Letter to the Ephesians (by his speech, yes, but also by his silence).[42] As Lossky puts it, 'The words of Revelation have then a margin of silence which cannot be picked up by the ears of those who are outside'.[43] Admittedly, that is true of Scripture as well, citing St Basil once more. 'There is also a form of silence namely the obscurity used by the Scripture, in order it make it difficult to gain understanding of the teaching, for the profit of readers.'[44] But that simply underscores the point that so as to receive the revealed mystery in its fullness there must be a 'conversion towards the vertical plane', so as to comprehend 'with all the saints' its breadth, length, height, depth, citing now another writer to the Ephesians—St Paul.[45]

So Lossky's position is becoming clearer. The Scriptures and all the other words the Church can produce (some of them visual!) are modes of *expressing* the Truth. Tradition, by contrasting, is the one and only mode of *receiving* the Truth.

> It is not the content of Revelation, but the light that receives it; it is not the word, but the living breath which makes the word heard at the same time as the silence from which it came; it is not the Truth, but a communication of the Spirit of Truth, outside of which the Truth cannot be received.[46]

There is, I note in passing, a strong whiff of polemic against Rome in the allied explanatory statement that Tradition 'does not impose on human consciousness by formal guarantees of the truths of faith', i.e. in its further expression as doctrine, through crystallization by the teaching activity of bishops and pope (the 'magisterium').[47]

Lossky's reference to the Holy Spirit in what he evidently hoped might become a distinctive Orthodox view of 'Tradition and traditions' is crucial. So much becomes plain in the very next sentence:

> The pure notion of Tradition can then be defined by saying that it is the life of the Holy Spirit in the Church, communicating to each member of the Body of Christ the faculty of

hearing, of receiving, of knowing the Truth in the Light which belongs to it, and not according to the light of human reason.[48]

Notice there the closing phrase, with a polemic against theological liberalism comparable to the earlier attempt to demarcate a position over against Catholic 'magisterial' practice.

If the Revelation found in the Incarnation is a dispensation of the Word who became flesh—and licensed in so doing all subsequent expressions of himself in words of every kind, then Tradition, as the way of receiving Revelation, must be counted a dispensation of the Holy Spirit. This statement allows Lossky to look more closely at the interrelation of the economies of the Son and the Spirit as the 'two hands' of the Father—a phrase made famous by St Irenaeus of Lyons.[49] In the saving economy, the Spirit is, before the Paschal Mystery, in function to the Word, whereas afterwards the Word is in function to the Spirit—and it is the Spirit who actualizes the Word's saving work in the world. Just as it was by the Spirit that the Virgin was able to mother forth the Word, so too in Revelation, the Spirit 'acts as function of the Word as a power for expressing the Truth in intelligible definitions or sensible images whether or not they belong to its Tradition'.[50]

Some consequences

The most immediate conclusion Lossky draws concerns the Canon. For the historian of religions the unity of the Old Testament within itself is accidental (to the secular eye this little library of books is more or less haphazard), and its unity with the New Testament factitious.

> It is only in the Church that one will be able to recognize in full consciousness the unity of inspiration of the sacred books, because the Church alone possesses the Tradition—the knowledge in the Holy Spirit of the Word Incarnate.[51]

Moreover, the way in which the Church preserves the Canon, which is by no means 'static and inert' but 'dynamic and conscious', is, says Lossky, paradigmatic for her behaviour as a whole.

The conservative attitude is not unconditionally praiseworthy, for heretics are not always innovators. Lossky even goes so far as to say that Tradition is the 'critical spirit of the Church'.[52] But the criterion of this criticism is nothing other than the 'pleroma', the 'undiminished fullness of Revelation'.[53]

Lossky distances himself from a 'traditionalism' that is credulous towards all custom: in a footnote, among the items mentioned are a (not further described) number of 'liturgical monstrosities'. A good example of the critical power of Tradition (as Lossky sees it) is the way the Church sifts the apocryphal books, such as, for instance, the Protoevangelium of James, using them liturgically or iconographically in moderation 'to the extent that they may represent corrupted apostolic traditions'.[54] Sometimes much labour is necessary before a text can be reclaimed as a witness to Tradition: Lossky cites here Maximus the Confessor's reformulation of the teachings of Dionysius.

What of the criterion of Tradition that is the rule put forward by Vincent of Lerins (early fifth century) in his *Commonitorium*: in the celebrated words, *Quod semper, quod ubique, quod ab omnibus* (what has been approved always, everywhere, by everybody)? Lossky does not rate it highly. The *homoousion*, the affirmation that the Son is 'consubstantial' with the Father, could not easily pass Vincent's test, and yet the Church has made it an oracle. Not that fidelity to dogmatic formulae by itself means fidelity to Tradition for the latter requires a 'ceaseless renewing, like all that comes from the Spirit'.[55]

Any idea that Lossky will adopt a version of the modern Catholic theology of doctrinal development is, however, soon scotched. The renewal he has in mind does not consist in the fuller elaboration of the content of Revelation. Before Pentecost one can speak of an increase in knowledge of the divine mysteries, but not after.

> At every moment of its history the Church gives to its members the faculty of knowing the truth in a fullness that the world cannot contain. It is this mode of knowing the living Truth in the Tradition that it defends in creating new dogmatic definitions.[56]

A Fundamental Theology

Knowing in part (compare I Corinthians 13:12) will not be filled out by dogmatic development but by the eschatological actualization of the fullness that is already known—though when Lossky adds in qualification of the latter 'confusedly, but surely' he comes close to conceding that an aspect of that actualization will be clarification, and cannot that be anticipated sometimes now? Lossky's concern that pre-eschatological and eschatological amplitude should never be identified is especially marked when he writes that 'As an expression of truth, a dogma of faith belongs to the Tradition without all the same constituting one of its "parts"'. And he goes on to explain that it is only 'a means, an intelligible instrument, which makes for adherence to the Tradition of the Church; it is a witness of Tradition, its external limit, or rather the narrow door which leads to knowledge of Truth in the Tradition'.[57] Lossky would appear, then, to be among those who reject anything resembling what has become in Roman Catholicism a modern classic, Newman's *Essay on the Development of Christian Doctrine*, whose first edition coincides with his 1845 abandonment of the Church of England and reception into the Church of Rome.[58]

Where Lossky does speak of increasing knowledge is in regard to the individual believer, where it will be, he thinks, closely correlated with growth in holiness. Paul's prayer for his converts in the opening chapter of Colossians suggests as much. 'Our prayer is, that you may be filled with that closer knowledge of God's will which brings all wisdom and all spiritual insight with it' (Colossians 1:9b).

And yet Lossky has in a way conceded the principal point: namely, that owing to theological errors the Church may amplify her doctrinal statements. In fact he allows the term 'dogmatic development' if only in a restricted sense. What the Church does is to 'extend the rule of faith, whilst remaining, in her new definitions, in conformity with the dogmas already received by all'.[59] What he is dead against is all talk of enriching Tradition: only on the horizontal level of the traditions could one speak of augmentation here. The Tradition and the dogmatic tradition which the Church establishes through the teaching ministry are not to be separated but neither are they to be confused.

Like Scripture, dogmas *live* in the Tradition, with this difference that the scriptural Canon forms a determinate body which excludes all possibility of further increase, whilst the 'dogmatic tradition', in keeping its stability as the 'rule of faith', from which nothing can be cut off, can be increased by receiving, to the extent that may be necessary, new expressions of revealed Truth, formulated by the Church.[60]

And since his essay was written to introduce a study of 'The Meaning of Icons', Lossky ends appropriately enough by returning to that topic. Icons are not hieroglyphs of dogma. If their intelligibility coincides with that of the dogmas that is because and insofar as the two traditions, iconographic and dogmatic, 'express, each by its proper means, the same revealed reality'.[61]

Notes

1 Vladimir Lossky, *Théologie dogmatique* (Paris: Cerf, 2012), p. 16.
2 *Ibid.*, p. 21.
3 *Ibid.*
4 *Ibid.*
5 *Ibid.*
6 *Ibid.*, pp. 19–20.
7 *Ibid.*, p. 18.
8 *Ibid.*, p. 19.
9 *Ibid.*
10 Augustine, *Homilies on the First Letter of John* III. 13.
11 Lossky, *Théologie dogmatique*, p. 21.
12 *Ibid.*, p. 23.
13 *Ibid.*
14 *Ibid.*, pp. 23–4.
15 *Ibid.*, p. 24.
16 *Ibid.*, pp. 24–5.
17 *Ibid.*, p. 25.
18 *Ibid.*
19 *Ibid.*, p. 26.

20 *Ibid.*, p. 27.

21 *Ibid.*

22 *Ibid.*, p. 28.

23 *Ibid.*, citing Gregory of Nyssa's *Homilies on the Song of Songs*.

24 *Ibid.*, p. 29.

25 *Ibid.*, p. 30.

26 *Ibid.*, p. 31.

27 *Ibid.*, p. 33.

28 *Ibid.*, p. 35.

29 Augustine, *Confessions* VII. 11, 17, cited *ibid.*, p. 36.

30 *Ibid.*, p. 34.

31 'Tradition and Traditions' in Vladimir Lossky and Leonid Ouspensky, *The Meaning of Icons* (Crestwood, NY: Saint Vladimir's Seminary Press, 1982), p. 11.

32 Jacques Maritain, *Distinguer pour unir ou les Degrés du savoir* (Paris: Desclée de Brouwer, 1932).

33 Lossky, 'Tradition and Traditions', p. 11.

34 *Ibid.*

35 *Ibid.*

36 Robin C. Selby, *The Principle of Reserve in the Writings of John Henry Cardinal Newman* (Oxford: Oxford University Press, 1975), pp. 1–43.

37 Basil, *On the Holy Spirit*, 27.

38 Lossky, 'Tradition and Traditions', pp. 12–13. Compare John Henry Newman, *The Arians of the Fourth Century* (3rd edition, London: Lumley, 1871), p. 57 and the comments thereon by Stephen Thomas, *Newman and Heresy: The Anglican Years* (Cambridge: Cambridge University Press, 1991), pp. 180–1.

39 Lossky, 'Tradition and Traditions', p. 13.

40 Odo Casel, *Das christliche Kultusmysterium* (Regensburg: Pustet, 1932).

41 Lossky and Ouspensky, *The Meaning of Icons*, p. 13.

42 Ignatius, *To the Ephesians* 15, 2.

43 Lossky and Ouspensky, *The Meaning of Icons*, p. 15.

44 Basil, *On the Holy Spirit*, 27.

45 Lossky and Ouspensky, *The Meaning of Icons*, p. 15, citing Ephesians 3:18.

46 *Ibid.*

47 *Ibid.*

48 *Ibid.*

49 Irenaeus, *Against the Heresies* IV, Preface; V. 6, 1.

50 Lossky and Ouspensky, *The Meaning of Icons*, p. 16.

51 *Ibid.*, p. 17.

52 *Ibid.*

53 *Ibid.*

54 *Ibid.*, p. 18.

55 *Ibid.*, p. 19.

56 *Ibid.*

57 *Ibid.*, pp. 18–19.

58 The second, 1878, edition, is, however, the more frequently cited, as in the American republication at the end of the 1980s (Notre Dame, IN: University of Notre Dame Press, 1989). For a discussion of the views of Lossky, and other Orthodox theologians, in the light of Newman's *Essay* see Daniel J. Lattier, 'The Orthodox Rejection of Doctrinal Development', *Pro Ecclesia* XX. 4 (2012), pp. 389–410.

59 Lossky and Ouspensky, *The Meaning of Icons*, p. 21.

60 *Ibid.*

61 *Ibid.*, p. 22.

✥ 5 ✥

The Trinity and Creation

Lossky's 'Triadology', his theological presentation of the Holy Trinity, is sophisticated—but it is also at times markedly anti-Latin in tone, and this tonality, more than his positive prescriptions, is how he is chiefly remembered, unfortunately, in the theological academy in the West.

Incarnation implies Trinity

Lossky's starting-point is clear. As attested in the Gospels and elsewhere in the New Testament writings, Incarnation implies Trinity. In *Théologie dogmatique* Lossky stresses the evangelical roots of Orthodox Triadology, privileging here the work of St John the Divine (Gospel and First Letter). In fact, he gives this evangelist's making of the Incarnation/Trinity connexion as the reason for John's title in the Greek East: *ho theologos*, 'the theologian', *par excellence*.[1]

The opening verses of the Johannine Prologue assert both identity and otherness in God. The temptation to rationalize this state of affairs leads to either Unitarianism or Tritheism, both of them incompatible with the Gospel revelation. In the Great Church, 'Unitarianism' has taken the form, historically speaking, of an absolute 'Monarchianism', where Son and Spirit are seen as emanatory modes of the Father, reabsorbed into his being when their economies are completed. 'Tritheism', belief in three Gods, is too absurd ever to have been explicitly taught. Yet, observes Lossky, one 'often observes a certain enfeeblement of Trinitarian reciprocity' in discourse about the Three.[2] In the ancient Church this was sometimes owed to the influence of that later development of Plato's thought known as

'Middle Platonism'. People identified the Father with the One, the supreme Unity, and were left, almost inevitably, with a Subordinationist view of the Son as instrument of the Father, and of the Spirit as instrument of the Son. (We noted, however, in the third chapter of this book, that Meister Eckhart manages an account of the Father as the One and a full-blooded Trinitarianism — at any rate, Lossky absolved him of all charges to the contrary.) In the patristic Church, the triumph of Trinitarian orthodoxy was the result, says Lossky — beautifully — of a 'saturation of thought by a mystery which . . . is an inexhaustible light'.[3] The transcendence, stability, and plenitude of the triune God are fully maintained in the Orthodox dogma, for which the Son and the Spirit who are 'with' the Father — the first by generation, the second by procession, each of which relations indicates both diversity and communion — enter the world so as to bring it into relation with the Father, the source of the divine nature as communicated to the other Two.

Where Lossky adds his own theological opinion to that dogma is in the statement — found more thoroughly developed in the *Essai* — that the Son's mission is to 'unite to himself and regenerate our nature', whereas that of the Spirit is to 'revivify our personal freedom'.[4] This is probably not the best way of distinguishing the aim of their economies, granted that it leaves out of count much relevant New Testament material both in relation to Christ and to the Holy Spirit. It is too obviously indebted to Lossky's enthusiasm for the nature/person distinction as key to what human beings are — something we shall be looking at in the context of his theological anthropology in Chapter Eight. It does, however, satisfy Lossky's requirement that the functional interrelation of their economies should be plainly set forth.

Trinitarian terminology

Lossky deals elegantly with the topic of Trinitarian terminology, which entailed a transformation of both philosophical and ordinary language. He had already explained the principles involved in *Essai sur la théologie mystique de l'Église d'Orient*.

The mystery of the Trinity only becomes accessible to that ignorance which rises above all that can be contained within the language of the philosophers. Yet this *ignorantia*, not only *docta* ['learned'] but charitable also, redescends again upon these concepts that it may mould them; that it may transform the expressions of human wisdom into instruments of that Wisdom of God which is to the Greeks foolishness.[5]

Ousia, the word chosen for the divine being in common to Father, Son, and Spirit, was well placed as an ontological signifier, owing to its relation to the verb *einai*, to be. It indicated identity—but in its qualified form as *homoousios*, 'of the same substance', declared that identity to be the case with a twosome who, however, as Father and Son, are also irreducibly different. To signify such difference in identity for Father, Son, and Spirit (a revolutionary undertaking, since ancient Hellenic thought ascribed supreme value to identity and treated difference as a 'disagregation of being'[6]), the Fathers remodelled an additional word to make it fit for usage for the Persons. This word was 'hypostasis', which in the English language now occupies a recognized niche of its own in theological dictionaries, suitably naturalized (for theological students, that is!) in the tongue of Shakespeare and Milton. In a lucid summary of the philosophical background, Lossky wrote:

> In the language of everyday [hypostasis] designated subsistence; but, among certain of the Stoics, it had taken on the sense of distinct substance, of an individual. Taken overall, *ousia* and hypostasis were near-synonyms, both in relation to being, the former noting more the essence, the second the singularity, without one being able, moreover, to press the divergence (in Aristotle, indeed, the 'first *ousiai*' designated individual subsistences, and [the word] *hypostasis*, as St John Damascene was to note later, sometimes simply signified existence. This relative equivalence favoured the elaboration of Christian language; no pre-existing context could break the equilibrium of the two terms whose equal dignity the Fathers intended to underline; one escaped the danger of giving the preponderance to the personal essence.[7]

The fact that at the start *ousia* and hypostasis were almost synonyms had, however, the disadvantage (though Lossky does not advert to this) that they could be confused. But it also meant that the doctors of the patristic age were able to 'root being in the person and [therefore] personalize ontology'.[8] Here Lossky—as a man of his own age—is not only playing the part of a historian. He is also responding, in a way he hopes will gain sympathy, to a preoccupation of his own time.

Substance and person

Lossky warns against some common misunderstandings of the substance–person distinction in the Holy Trinity. Trinitarian discourse is no bare declaration that a common nature is shared by three individuals. He remarks, first of all, that the concept of the divine *ousia*, as handled by the Fathers, draws from the apophatic background of Greek patristic theology the 'profound meta-logic of an unknowable transcendence'.[9] In the late (1953) essay 'Apophasis and Trinitarian Theology', reprinted in the posthumous collection *In the Image and Likeness of God*, Lossky had identified Dionysius, the master of apophasis, as for this reason a master in Triadology as well. The substance of this essay has already been surveyed in the second chapter of this book in the context of Lossky's apophaticism as quest for the vision of God. So here it will suffice to state his—highly Dionysian—conclusion in which he lauds the unknown patristic author for his charter for right thinking about the triune God. The interplay of cataphasis and apophasis, he notes, was vital to such thinking precisely because

> The dialectic of affirmations and non-opposed negations, applied to Trinitarian dogma, makes it necessary to go beyond the One opposed to the Other. It is not the impersonal Monad, but the 'superessential and more-than-divine Triad' that the author of the *Mystical Theology* [i.e. Dionysius] invokes at the beginning of his treatise, in order that It direct 'even beyond unknowing' and towards the way of union with triune Divinity, the theologian in search of the God of Christian revelation, who transcends the opposition between

the transcendent and the immanent, since He is beyond all affirmation and negation.[10]

In *Théologie dogmatique*, after noticing once more this apophatic dimension, Lossky goes on to argue there is, in the tradition of the Fathers, nothing individualist (in his lexicon, a highly pejorative term) about a Trinitarian Person. Normally, of course, the individual is part of the species which he, she, or it helps to divide up by their existence. But there is nothing like this with the Persons of the Trinity. In God, each hypostasis 'assumes in its plenitude the divine nature'.[11]

> The hypostases ... are infinitely one and infinitely other: they *are* the divine nature, but none possesses it or breaks it to have it for himself; it is precisely because each opens himself to the others, because they partake of the nature without restriction that the nature is not divided.[12]

Their unity is the 'fecund tension of an irreducible diversity'.[13]

Lossky joins hands with Latin theologians when he says that the only way of distinguishing the Persons is their relations—and notably their relations with the Father (generation for the Second and procession for the Third)—which in each case enable us to tell them apart from the First in his 'innascibility' or unbegotten-ness. More specifically Losskian is the further statement that the relations 'designate' the hypostatic diversity but do not found it, and the additional anti-Latin comment that they are not relations of opposition but 'simple relations of diversity', whose 'ternary' character means they can never be brought back to a mere dyad, to the duality that the term 'opposition' entails.[14] Here Lossky follows Mark of Ephesus (Mark Eugenikos, d. 1444), the rebel bishop who set in operation the deconstruction of the consensus agreed at the Council of Florence—and thus gained in the East the laudatory description 'the conscience of Orthodoxy'. For Mark, the Trinitarian relations are diverse, not oppositional—even if the price of saying so is the inability to establish what might be the positive character of the procession of the Spirit as distinct from the generation of the Son.[15] Elsewhere Lossky had spoken of the word 'procession' as, in the Spirit's case, 'confront[ing] us with the mystery of an anonymous person, whose hypostatic character is presented to us negatively: it is not generation, it is other than that of the Son'.[16] That citation comes from the 1948 essay 'The Procession of the Holy Spirit in Orthodox Trinitarian Doctrine' where he underlines his dislike of the notion of 'relative opposites' as developed by, especially, St Thomas Aquinas.

> [T]he absolute diversity of the three cannot be based on their relations of opposition without admitting, implicitly or explicitly, the primacy of the essence over the hypostases, by assuming a relative (and therefore secondary) basis for personal diversity, in contrast to natural identity. But that is precisely what Orthodox theology cannot admit.[17]

And, combining apophaticism with personalism, Lossky adds that

> To follow here the positive approach, and to envisage the relations of origin otherwise than as signs of the inexpressible diversity of the persons, is to suppress the absolute quality of this personal diversity, i.e. to relativize the Trinity and in some sense to depersonalize it.[18]

Evidently, there is at work, once more, an apophatic factor in this insistence on not going beyond the affirmation of diversity among the Persons. But in the footsteps of St Basil and St Maximus, Lossky also offers, in pursuit of his stress on the sheer three-in-oneness of God, a little exercise in what he terms 'meta-mathematics' — and this is scarcely (we might reasonably feel) an apophatic enterprise. There must be, he says, a surpassing of the monad, because 'the Father *is* the gift of his divinity to the Son and the Spirit'.[19] But surely, one might think, the Father is by definition Father-of-the-Son. Is it necessary to invoke a threesome rather than a twosome to understand his hypostatic Name? Lossky's response is crisp.

> The monad being open, the personal plenitude of God cannot be stabilised on the dyad for the two implies opposition and reciprocal limitation; the two would divide the divine nature and would situate in the infinite the root of the indefinite, the first polarity of a creation which would become, as in the Gnostic systems, manifestation. The divine reality is thus unthinkable in two persons. The surpassing of the

two, that is to say of number, is done in the three: not by return to the origin but by the expansion, *épanouissement*, of personal existence.[20]

Here we meet again, at any rate subjacently, the 'litmus test' for Triadology supplied by St Gregory the Theologian with reference to which Lossky ventured to impress Meister Eckhart's doctrine of the Three-in-One. The Three who are 'beyond all calculation, beyond all opposition' are the ones who 'inaugurate the absolute diversity'.[21] Here faith takes thinking beyond itself into a sphere of contemplation the goal of which is our divinization. We recall from the discussion of Lossky's fundamental theology how for him Christian 'gnosis', in its contemplative character, goes beyond theological thought as such. Lossky will shortly say, *à propos* of Gregory of Nazianzus again, that *poetry* is best for speaking of the Trinity since poetry celebrates, rather than explains, as analyses of concepts do. In the *Essai* he had already accepted the description of Gregory of Nazianzus as 'the minstrel of the Holy Trinity'.[22]

This Trinitarian discussion had, in Christianity, a most salutary rebound effect on anthropology. The Fathers understood that 'person is liberty in regard to nature', from which there must follow the uniqueness and indefinability of each (human) person.[23] An irreducible residue remains once the human nature of this or that person is affirmed, and for that residue, unique in each one's case, apophasis, with its de-conceptualizing mission, is altogether necessary. The 'residue' can only be apprehended in personal relationships that bear within themselves some analogy to those of the Triune Persons. I shall return to this in Chapter Eight, on theological anthropology, to be explored in imperfect obedience to Alexander Pope's celebrated dictum, 'The proper study of mankind is man'.

The divine nature, then, is at once common to the Trinitarian Persons and yet proper to each of the Three in their uniqueness: 'the Father as source, the Son as engendered, the Spirit as proceeding from the Father'.[24] As with all Orthodox theologians, indebted as these are to the Cappadocian Fathers of the fourth century, the 'monarchy' of the Father—the Father's fontal role seen in fullness—is all-important for Lossky. Does it not imply, though, a subordination of Son and Spirit? He answers, No, and the reason for saying as much is profound. A principle 'cannot be perfect unless it is the principle of a reality equal to itself'.[25] It is, one might comment, just the kind of metaphysical axiom, appealing to enlightened common sense, that Latin Scholastics put forward in the mediaeval and early modern West.

Be that as it may, all the divine Names which indicate what is common to the *ousia* of God, and so the 'life common to the Three', come to us from those co-equal persons: the Father being the Source, the Son the Manifestation and the Spirit the Power that makes manifest.[26] In the 1948 essay, conscious, no doubt, that his stress on the absolute diversity of the Persons could be regarded as tilting the balance so far away from Unitarianism as to invite criticisms of Tritheism, he made haste to emphasize that the doctrine he commends (Photian Monopatrism) does not ignore the importance of the common *ousia*.

> [S]ince consubstantiality is the non-hypostatic identity of the Three, in that they have (or rather *are*) a common essence, the unity of the three hypostases is inconceivable apart from the monarchy of the Father, who is the *principle* of the same one essence.[27]

Another look at the Energies

Mediaeval Byzantine theology calls the Names that typify the common *ousia* in its outreach from the Persons the 'energies' of God—and, as we have seen, when examining his apophaticism in Chapter Two above, Lossky likes the word. It communicates— better than the term 'attributes', more frequent in Scholastic theology, and better even than Dionysius' term 'powers'—what, in a highpoint of religious rhetoric, Lossky calls *ces jaillissements, ces débordements* ('these cascadings, these overflowings') of the divine Glory.[28]

For Lossky, the Names of God are indeed above all Names of God's glory. The energies are the glorious manifestation of the inexhaustible divine nature and as such they do not begin with the economy, in view of creation and salvation. Rather are they eternally active. Flowing as they do from the common *ousia* they are not for all that impersonal. Indeed, they manifest Father, Son, and Spirit and do so as the Persons communicate not only with ourselves but with each other. Here Lossky finds an exalted place in his theology for the category of manifestation with which Bulgakov sought to replace that of causal origin (or even relation) in thinking about the Trinity.[29]

There is an advance here on what he had to say in the 1948 essay on the procession of the Spirit. In that essay, when treating the 'manifesting and energetic aspect of the Trinity', he saw that aspect as, rather, the 'energetic manifestation of the content common to the Three', i.e. the content that is the divine nature, without further reference to the specificity of the Persons.[30] The Son, he had written then, shows forth not so much *who* as *what* the Father is, and the Spirit likewise shows forth not so much *who* as *what* the Son is.[31] It sufficed to say that the energetic manifestation concerns the unity of the divine *ousia* and hence the common 'Glory', the 'eternal splendor of the divine nature' as such.[32]

The *Filioque* question past — and future

Something more must be said about Lossky's attitude to the *Filioque*, the claim of doctrine in the Latin Church that the Spirit proceeds not only from the Father but from the Son as well. Lossky's reputation is as an Orthodox 'hard-liner' on this issue. Its invasion of the ecumenical Creed was indefensible. In *Sept jours sur les routes de France* he had laid the blame squarely at the door of the Carolingian court, a 'court grouped around the imperial "Chapel", gripped by theological fervour, seeking to assure the triumph of a new doctrine on the procession of the Holy Spirit'.[33] As to the actual substance (rather than the credal form) given to the teaching on the *Filioque*, Lossky went further than almost any Orthodox theologian before him in tracing to the conventional understanding of the dual procession almost all the woes of Western Christendom.[34] Already before the schism, it was, he thought, 'From the religious point of view . . . the sole issue of importance in the chain of events which terminated in the separation'.³⁵ In the *Essai*, he had declared the combination of Filioquism and the concept of the Holy Spirit as 'bond' between Father and Son a recipe for disaster—the disaster of sub-personalist essentialism.

> The hypostatic characteristics (paternity, generation, procession) find themselves more or less swallowed up in the nature or essence which, differentiated by relationships—to the Son as Father, to the Holy Spirit as Father and Son—becomes the principle of unity within the Trinity.³⁶

This is why the East, so he writes in that work, has 'always defended the ineffable, apophatic character of the procession of the Holy Spirit from the Father', against what he frankly admits is the 'more rational doctrine' of the West which, however, by treating Father and Son as common origin of the Spirit 'places the common nature above the persons'.³⁷

His full position is, however, more nuanced than this. We see this at once when we note how in 'The Procession of the Holy Spirit in Orthodox Trinitarian Doctrine', Lossky disagrees with those Orthodox 'polemicists' (his word) for whom the *per Filium* or 'through the Son' formula of a number of the Fathers must not be allowed to refer to anything more than the purely temporal mission of the Holy Spirit in the post-Ascension economy, for fear that otherwise it will open the door to Filioquism.³⁸ True, 'Latinizing Greeks' sought foolishly, in Lossky's opinion, to reconcile the Triadologies of East and West by pressing the claims of the formula 'through the Son' for the eternal procession of the Holy Spirit. But that does not mean the Byzantine Unionists were wrong in supposing ancient writers necessarily had in mind in using these words both the eternal manifestation (in Greek, *ekphansis*) of the Holy Spirit and also the very subsistence of his person by procession (in Greek, *ekporeusis*).³⁹ But if the *Filioque* is understood only of the eternal manifestation of the Holy Spirit, then it can, in Lossky's opinion, be fully Orthodox—even for a Photian Monopatrist! The latter—and Lossky certainly counted himself such—is only concerned to affirm subsistence by procession as 'from the Father alone'. Perhaps, muses Lossky, the Spanish

The Trinity and Creation

Filioquist theologians of the late patristic period will turn out to fall into the category of manifestation-theologians, in which case their credal orthodoxy will turn out to be perfectly secure.[40] Even Augustine might fit here—though Lossky prefers to await a full exegesis from the Eastern standpoint of the latter's *On the Trinity* before saying more. But alas, so benign a view cannot include the 'dual procession' taught by the Reunion Councils (in the Roman Catholic list of ecumenical assemblies, Lyons II and Ferrara-Florence) whose doctrine, accordingly, must be laid aside.

That corresponds to Lossky's position in *Théologie dogmatique* as well. In *Théologie dogmatique* he concedes that there can be an Orthodox understanding of the *Filioque*—and restricts himself to saying that the formulation of the Second Council of Lyons (the first of the 'Reunion Councils', held in 1274) is not it. Nor in *Théologie dogmatique* is he an anti-Augustinian, seeing Augustine's Trinitarian thought as 'complex' and including formulae that are not Filioquist at all.[41]

More on rivals

In his Trinitarian theology in *Théologie dogmatique* Lossky adds two further critiques to those of the Anselmian-Thomist view mainstream in Latin theology (on which he also makes a concluding animadversion). The first critique concerns Bulgakov's Sophiology, found guilty of an excessive personalism in the doctrine of God and an unhappy necessitarianism in regard to the act of creation.

In the 1948 essay on the Spirit's procession Lossky does not at first name Bulgakov but he surely has him in mind when in this study he defends the language of causality as applied to the Father as source.

> It is worthwhile to recall here what we have said before about the negative approach characteristic of Orthodox thought—an approach which radically changes the value of philosophical terms applied to God . . . causality is nothing but a somewhat defective image, which tries to express the personal unity which determines the origin of the Son and the Holy Spirit

> ... The Father is the cause of the other hypostases in that He is not His essence, i.e. in that He does not have His essence for Himself alone.[42]

Bulgakov's proposal in 'The Comforter'—which was his treatise on the place of the Holy Spirit in the Trinity and the economy of salvation—that 'manifestation' might be a better term than 'causation' for the eternal processions (corresponding, as we have seen, to the Greek *ekporeusis* and not only *ekphansis*, for which 'manifestation' is the literal translation) does not at all meet with Lossky's approval. It would, he thinks, confuse two 'planes of thought', the existence of the Trinity in and of Itself and Its existence as declared to the creation in the radiance of the divine Glory.[43] But no such confusion would arise—one might propose on Bulgakov's behalf—if one were to introduce a simple distinction: hypostatic manifestation (made known in the eternal communion of divine persons) is one thing, energetic manifestation (made known in history to human persons in Israel and the Church) is another. That would, however, require the theologian to restrict the use of energy language to the God–world relationship.

Lossky's second critique where distortions of Trinitarian believing are concerned takes as its target what he terms a 'mediaeval Augustinianism for which Augustine is not responsible'—a phrase eloquent of Lossky's desire to exempt the North African doctor from the strictures to which many modern Orthodox have subjected him.[44] Here the problem is with a 'monad that redoubles itself and then recloses on itself' in the generation of the Word and the resultant dyad's spiration of the Holy Spirit as the *nexus amoris* or 'bond of love' between Son and Father.[45] (We have noted how in the *Essai* it is precisely the combination of the 'bond' idea with that of Filioquism that aroused Lossky's ire.) In the context of *Théologie dogmatique* Lossky objects to—as he puts it—the 'imagery' involved. How can a Person be a mere 'nexus'? How can It—or rather He—be simply the unity between Father and Son? It was, he thinks, an unfortunate image for Latins to select from the *embarras de richesses* laid before them in Augustine's corpus. Lossky was seemingly unaware that the characterization of the Spirit as bond of love is also found in the supreme Byzantine theologian, St Gregory Palamas. And he did not seem to object to it—not obviously at least—when it recurred in the work of Meister Eckhart, to whom half a lifetime of theological effort was devoted.

There remains that concluding observation on 'Anselmian-Thomism', the staple Trinitarianism of the post-mediaeval Latin Church. What Lossky thinks of as the 'Anselmian-Thomist view' is, to his mind, an unfortunate extrapolation from comments of St Augustine that were never intended to provide a systematic Triadology of a comprehensive sort. The drawing of an analogy for the Holy Trinity from a 'mind' (compare the Father) whence proceeds, by knowing itself, a 'word' (compare the Son), which thereby breaks forth in 'love' (compare the Holy Spirit) is

> a philosophical anthropomorphism having nothing in common with Biblical anthropomorphism; for the Biblical theophanies, while showing us in human guise the acts and manifestations of a personal God in the history of the world, also place us face to face with the mystery of His unknowable Being[46]

And Lossky warns sternly that, 'for us' (he means for the Orthodox), 'the Trinity remains the *Deus absconditus*, the Holy of Holies of divine existence, where no "strange fire" may be introduced'.[47]

Creation

The Holy Trinity is of course active not only in salvation but in creation. Lossky's doctrine of creation in *Théologie dogmatique* opens—and here we may well see a further reminiscence of the sophiological controversy—with a ringing declaration of the 'otherness' of creation to God. Stretching grammar to its uttermost: creation, for II Maccabees (7:28), is from 'the not-beings'—that is, it is from absolutely nothing! It has, in other words, no pre-existing substrate, least of all an uncreated substrate that would render it an emanation of God. There is nothing on which creatures are founded except the will of God. The sermons of Philaret of Moscow (Vasili Mikhaĭlovich Drozdov, 1782–1867), a bishop-theologian admired by Lossky for his continuance of the ethos of the Fathers, offered him at this point a suitably illustrative citation:

> All creatures are balanced upon the creative word of God, as if upon a bridge of diamond; above them is the abyss of the divine infinitude, below them that of their own nothingness.[48]

Indeed, in the *Essai*, where these words are cited, belief in creation is said to require a kind of 'reverse apophaticism' in that the conviction that there is something other than God, a 'totally new subject' besides God, requires no less strenuous a faith, if one of a very different kind, from the *credenda* that set us on our way into the divine mystery.[49] Greek sages could envisage a divine ordering of the cosmos (the 'demiurge' in Plato's dialogue *Timaeus* is obviously in Lossky's mind), but ancient philosophy knew nothing of a free divine act that serves as 'the sole foundation for the existence of all beings'.[50]

Utterly gratuitous as it is, the 'moral' motivations sometimes suggested for the creative act are to Lossky's mind 'unimportant platitudes'.[51] In no sense does the God who is the source need another than himself, since in the circumincession of the Trinitarian hypostases he already has an uncreated Other—a point more fully developed by the Swiss dogmatician Hans Urs von Balthasar who sees the otherness of the Word to the Father as the ground of possibility for the created 'other' that is the world.[52] If we dislike the notion that God created in utter freedom, that is because we are confusing the free with the arbitrary. By the order, purposiveness, and love it contains we can tell that the world God freely made has nothing of the arbitrary about it. In a word, if we think defectively in this way what we are doing is merely projecting our own 'disordered pseudo-liberty' onto God.[53]

The creative act makes the new stand forth, and its apogee is the coming forth of another liberty, namely, the liberty of spiritual beings such as ourselves. Another liberty? That must mean for God, writes Lossky, a 'supreme risk'.[54] The remark is surely intended as an allusion to Fall and Redemption, topics to which all the succeeding chapters of this book will be pertinent. Lossky's soteriology will be laid out in them from various angles, if most formally in the concluding chapter on 'The Pattern of Salvation'. But we can at least note that, for Lossky, the aim of creation was always deification—like the revisionist Scholastics of French Catholicism in the years when he was writing, he cannot envisage creation ever having a 'natural beatitude' as its goal.[55]

Lossky now wants to look at the doctrine of 'creation from nothing' over again, this time in the light of two further themes. And these are: the creative Trinity, which poses no problem for his theology of creation so far, and the 'divine ideas'—a notion readily at home in Christian Platonism and the Russian Sophiologists, but less easily combined with Lossky's stress on the will of God in creating. He affirms, 'the creature only exists in God, in the creative will which, precisely, makes it different from God, that is to say, makes it creature'.[56]

The creative Trinity

That the Holy Trinity is the Creator is the primal confession of the Great Creed, the Creed of Nicaea-Constantinople. The Creed calls the Father 'Creator of heaven and earth'; it says of the Son that 'through him all things were made'; and it terms the Holy Spirit the 'maker of life'. The Three create together, each acting in the way appropriate to his hypostasis.

Here Lossky calls to the witness-stand St Basil the Great, for whom, in his treatise *On the Holy Spirit*, the Father is primordial Cause, the Son operative Cause, the Spirit perfecting Cause.[57] Lossky interprets these terms to mean that the Son (or, better, in this context, *le Verbe*, 'the Word') enacts the will of the Father, calling the creature by conferring on it 'ontological density', so as to lead it to the Father, while the Spirit fulfils it in goodness and beauty, helping it respond to the Word's appeal and in so doing communicating perfection.[58]

The divine ideas

But what of those divine ideas—the archetypes, in the mind of God, of all created realities? When we mention this topic, the ghost of Christian Platonism, and indeed of Sophiology, returns to haunt us. Despite his disapproval of these currents of thought, Lossky must inevitably make some concession here. The theme of the *logoi* or creative 'words' of God, which constitute the foundation of the intelligibility of things in God's own eternal Logos, is too well represented in the Greek patristic corpus safely to be denied. In fact, it underlies Lossky's own affirmation that the Word confers that 'ontological density' on things as he actualizes in them the Father's creative will. A *logos* (lower case 'l') always represents the norm of something's existence and, more than that, its programme or destiny, its 'way of transfiguration'.[59]

Without disputing the Platonic resonances of the notion, Lossky argues that, as the Greek Fathers make use of it, the *logos* concept is really more biblical than it is Hellenic. For the Fathers, both Greek and Latin, the 'ideas of all things are contained in [the divine] will and wisdom, and not in the divine essence'.[60] Augustine, towards the end of his life, felt he had gone too far in the direction of exemplarism, as if there were two worlds, one in God and one outside him.[61] But the idea of the exemplary causes of things contained in the divine *ousia* would have a long future ahead of it in the West, especially in the 'Thomist systematization'.[62] Taking upon himself the mantle of spokesman for Orthodoxy, Lossky calls this a depreciation of the originality of the creation, and thus an undervaluing of the Creator.

In the Greek patristic tradition, the 'ideas' are living words suited to the—biblically so called—'living God'. With its restrained yet, for the adverted reader, unmistakeable undertones of hostility to Sophiology, this had been Lossky's starting-point in the chapter on creation in the *Essai*. Both there and in the lectures on Orthodox dogmatics he cites the same Damascene text from John's *On the Orthodox Faith* concerning the 'volitional thoughts' of the Creator God.[63] No doubt God 'thought' the world from eternity (as Bulgakov had stressed in his own, sophiologically inflected, cosmology). But he thought it only in view of its willed beginning in time. The ideas are an instrument for creation, they are not creation's 'beyond'.[64]

Time and eternity

The interrelated topics of time and eternity clearly require some attention in this context. The Prologue of St John's Gospel speaks of a beginning, and so does the Book of Genesis. Lossky points out that the two—the origin of the Word, and the origin of the world—are by no means the same. The Word has his birth, but not his creation. His origination is anterior to that of the world made through him. The two beginnings are not identical, then, yet Lossky does not deny they are related. And here his teaching has considerable overlap with that of Bulgakov. The two beginnings, one eternal and the other the occasion of the arousal of time, cannot be wholly alien to each other if 'we remember the intentional character of the divine ideas, of the Wisdom at once eternal and turned towards this 'other' that must, in the proper sense, begin'.[65] And he cites what is for a sophiological creation account the crucial text of Scripture: Proverbs 8:22: 'The Lord had me as the first fruits of his ways, as prelude of his works, from evermore'.

How then are time and eternity related? Lossky dismisses two approaches, one of them philosophically rationalist and the other biblicist. A philosophical rationalization of the symbolism of the Bible will not serve, for 'true theology surpasses and transfigures metaphysics'.[66] Yet a human being must have the courage to think. It will not suffice, with the Swiss Protestant theologian of Scripture Oscar Cullmann (1902–99), in his study *Christus und die Zeit*, to refuse all help from philosophical culture.[67] That will only expose one to philosophical howlers, such as Cullmann is guilty of when he compares eternity to an infinite line of which time is one finite segment. Cullmann not only forgets that infinite and finite are incommensurable. He also undermines the very idea of transcendence.

By contrast, the Fathers avoided both rationalism and pious platitude. How did they manage it? Taking St Basil as his point of reference, Lossky argues that the first moment of time is not itself within time. That 'moment' cannot in fact be thought. It can only be conceptualized as a 'limit' between eternity and time, itself without duration, or again as 'an instantaneity in itself non-temporal but whose creative explosion arouses time'.[68]

That is protology, an approach to the first things. But this discussion also requires some account of eschatology, the last things. Since time is a form of created being, whereas eternity is God's, Lossky can only understand the eschatological abolition of time as time's transformation into an ever-renewed *epektasis* — the 'stretching forward' which Basil's fellow-Cappadocian Gregory of Nyssa considered to be the hall-mark of human life in the vision of God. At the weekly celebration of Sunday, the first and eighth day, both creation and recreation are at stake.

Lossky insists that temporal categories must not be applied to God's eternity save in the sense of biblical metaphors that speak of its vitality. As to counter-temporal categories suggestive of a static changelessness they are even less helpful. 'If God lives in eternity this living eternity must go beyond the opposition of mobile time and immobile eternity.'[69] Temporal and eternal are a binary that God transcends. Whereas Balthasar, already mentioned in the context of Lossky's doctrine of creation, would not only agree but use the opportunity to launch a robustly cataphatic doctrine of the Trinity's 'super-time', the *Überzeit* of the triune God,[70] Lossky is more reticent. Here, as elsewhere, apophasis must close our mouths. (And, it may be added, the question is, philosophically, a notoriously difficult one. Plato, for instance, allows two possible, but mutually exclusive, interpretations of eternity — timelessness, and everlasting duration — to 'stand side by side . . . without offering a solution'.[71])

Lossky on Genesis

The Genesis creation accounts, which have been, with II Maccabees and John, Lossky's principal source, introduce us to a cosmic order. His last port of call under the heading 'created being' in *Théologie dogmatique* is a consideration of the character of the order in question.

The Trinity and Creation

With the Fathers, he finds the 'heavens' of the primordial creation to be the angelic realm—we hear little more of them in Scripture because it is too difficult to situate our world within 'these spiritual immensities'.[72] The creation account concentrates on 'earth'. It is, in fact, spiritually geocentric because the earth is the 'body of man' who inhabits both sensuous and intelligible spheres. When the Bible speaks of the angels it is always in connexion with their role in the divine economy *on earth*, in relation to human beings.

Lossky takes us, with the author of Genesis 1:3–31, through the six days of God's active creative work. The 'day' and the 'night' whose bringing into existence on the first day occurs after the divine command 'Let there be light!' require some sophisticated interpretation. Lossky understands 'day' (a reflection of 'light') as referring to created being in its actuality as sprung in perfection from the Word, whereas 'night' stands for the mere potentiality of created being. And yet 'night' here is a positive darkness; it represents 'the uterine mystery of fertility', by which things continue to come to be.[73]

The separation of the waters below the firmament on the second day is, for Lossky, the definitive distinction of the earth from the world of the angels, while the further separation that introduces the third day, this time of dry land from water, lays the foundation for the first life-forms, which are vegetable in nature. The fourth day, to which belong the stars and their 'regular revolution', is the moment when simultaneity becomes succession, life requiring the rhythm of daylight and the nocturnal. On the fifth day the Word brings into being fish and birds, both of which orders exist in an element that is 'fluid and humid'.[74] The Bible is not working with a scientific view of phyla but with a different sense of cosmic hierarchies, for which the 'secondary qualities' of life-forms, neglected by science but evident to close human observers, are paramount. (The Liturgy will consider cosmic nature in this way, as do the Orthodox ascetics in the contemplation of creation known as *physikē theōria*.) That day, which culminates in the appearance of the land animals, closes the account of creation insofar as—for the biblical text under consideration in this little commentary—the creative act proceeds in silence.

By contrast, the sixth day will be dedicated to *homo sapiens*, and the biblical writer marks it by having the Holy Trinity take counsel, breaking into speech. 'Let us make man to our image and likeness' (Genesis 1:26). At this juncture simply commanding the earth to produce is not good enough. Now, in man, a personal being will enter existence who will serve, in the temple of the cosmos, as the image of the triune Creator.

The peculiar place of humankind is underlined in the second of the two creation accounts (Genesis 2:4–25) — which is there not just by literary-historical happenstance but for a Spirit-inspired purpose. The second account, unlike the first, does not present man among the other earthly animals, even if he is also the highest individual product of God's creative work. Instead, so Lossky would have it, the second account makes man creation's very 'principle', with the world brought into being as his environment.[75] The Breath of God makes man a 'living soul' (verse 8) — which Lossky interprets to mean that Adamic man receives not only life but grace, i.e. uncreated Grace. The animals are then brought to Adam to be named in a language which corresponds to their paradisal being, a language formed on the lips of Adam who is the 'poet' to whom it is given to know the 'inner secret' of the beasts.[76] Occultists have sought to find that lost speech, but, says Lossky, they will never succeed. It is only to be discovered, citing the ancient Nestorian author Isaac the Syrian (*c.* 613–*c.* 700), by charitable hearts inflamed with love for all creation.

A few words about the creation of Eve rounds off the account. She is taken from the side of man, near to the heart, while Adam is in an 'ecstatic sleep'.[77] The quasi-cardiac symbolism speaks of intimate consubstantiality which is why the Fathers sometimes compare the emergence of Eve to the procession of the Holy Spirit — and that, remarks Lossky, shows the equality in dignity of woman and man. It is, of course, an aside that speaks of his own characteristically twentieth-century preoccupations — not least those of a convinced personalist. The distinction between nature and person that is at personalism's heart will inevitably recur once again in Lossky's Christology.

The Trinity and Creation

Notes

1. Lossky, *Théologie dogmatique*, p. 39.
2. *Ibid.*, p. 40.
3. *Ibid.*, p. 41.
4. *Ibid.*, p. 42.
5. Lossky, *The Mystical Theology of the Eastern Church*, pp. 49–50.
6. Lossky, *Théologie dogmatique*, p. 44.
7. *Ibid.*
8. *Ibid.*, p. 45.
9. *Ibid.*
10. Lossky, *In the Image and Likeness of God*, p. 29.
11. Lossky, *Théologie dogmatique*, p. 45.
12. *Ibid.*
13. *Ibid.*
14. *Ibid.*, p. 46.
15. Lossky will refer to Mark's *Syllogistic Chapters against the Latins*, 24, *ibid.*, p. 57, footnote 1.
16. Lossky, *In the Image and Likeness of God*, p. 75.
17. *Ibid.*, p. 78.
18. *Ibid.*, p. 79.
19. *Ibid.*, p. 47. Italics original.
20. *Ibid.*, p. 48.
21. *Ibid.* Compare Lossky, *In the Image and Likeness of God*, pp. 84–5 where the same argument is rehearsed. 'The procession of the Holy Spirit is an infinite passage beyond the dyad, which consecrates the absolute (as opposed to relative) diversity of persons. This passage is not an infinite series of persons but the infinity of the procession of the Third Person: the Triad suffices to denote the Living God of revelation.'
22. Lossky, *The Mystical Theology of the Eastern Church*, p. 44.
23. Lossky, *Théologie dogmatique*, p. 49.
24. *Ibid.*, p. 50.
25. *Ibid.*, p. 51.
26. *Ibid.*, p. 52.
27. Lossky, *In the Image and Likeness of God*, p. 81.

28 Lossky, *Théologie dogmatique*, p. 53.

29 Nichols, *Wisdom from Above*, pp. 159–63.

30 Lossky, *In the Image and Likeness of God*, p. 92.

31 *Ibid.*

32 *Ibid.*, p. 93.

33 Lossky, *Sept jours sur les routes de France*, p. 45.

34 I write 'almost', conscious of how the 'condemnation of the *Filioque* as symptomatic of the West's degeneration' is anticipated in such early-nineteenth-century Russian writers as Ivan Kireevskiĭ and Alexeĭ Khomyakov, as well as in Lossky's own teacher at St Petersburg, Lev Karsavin: see Williams, 'The Theology of Vladimir Nikolayevich Lossky', pp. 207, 252.

35 Lossky, *The Mystical Theology of the Eastern Church*, p. 13.

36 *Ibid.*, p. 57.

37 *Ibid.*, p. 62.

38 Lossky, *In the Image and Likeness of God*, p. 94.

39 *Ibid.*, p. 95. He gives as one example the 'pneumatological formula of the Synodicon of St Tarasius read at the Seventh Ecumenical Council' (787).

40 *Ibid.*, p. 73, especially footnote 3.

41 Lossky, *Théologie dogmatique*, p. 59. On the other hand, in this work Lossky takes Maximus Confessor's *Letter to Marinus* not to be the statement of a possible Orthodox understanding of the *Filioque* in a benign sense but, rather, the restriction of Filioquism to the economy, not the eternal processions. He approves the Trinitarian theology of the Cistercians while blaming the overly philosophical account of Anselm, inherited by Aquinas, *ibid.*, pp. 61–2.

42 *Ibid.*, p. 82.

43 *Ibid.*, p. 91. Lossky cites the French translation, *Le Paraclet* (Paris: Aubier, 1946), pp. 69–75.

44 Lossky, *Théologie dogmatique*, p. 67.

45 *Ibid.*

46 Lossky, *In the Image and Likeness of God*, pp. 86–7.

47 *Ibid.*

48 Cited in Lossky, *The Mystical Theology of the Eastern Church*, p. 92, from Georges Florovsky, *Puti russkago bogosloviya* (Paris: YMCA Press, 1937), p. 180.

49 Lossky, *The Mystical Theology of the Eastern Church*, p. 91.

50 *Ibid.*, p. 93.

51 Lossky, *Théologie dogmatique*, p. 77.

52 'If there must exist within God himself (in order that he can be called "love") a One and an Other and their Union, then it is "very good" that the other exists, then the world is not, as in the rest of the monotheisms, a fall from the One', Hans Urs von Balthasar, *Credo. Meditations on the Apostles' Creed* (San Francisco: Ignatius, 1990), pp. 38–9.

53 Lossky, *Théologie dogmatique*, p. 77.

54 *Ibid.*, p. 78.

55 Lossky, *The Mystical Theology of the Eastern Church*, p. 101.

56 Lossky, *Théologie dogmatique*, p. 79.

57 Basil the Great, *On the Holy Spirit*, 16.

58 Lossky, *Théologie dogmatique*, p. 80.

59 *Ibid.*, p. 84.

60 *Ibid.*, p. 82.

61 Augustine, *Retractations* II. 3, 2.

62 Lossky, *Théologie dogmatique*, p. 82.

63 John of Damascus, *On the Orthodox Faith*, II. 2, cited *ibid.*, p. 83. Compare Lossky, *The Mystical Theology of the Eastern Church*, pp. 94–5.

64 Lossky, *Théologie dogmatique*, p. 84.

65 *Ibid.*, p. 85.

66 *Ibid.*

67 Oscar Cullman, *Christus und die Zeit* (Zollikon and Zurich: Evangelischer Verlag, 1946).

68 Lossky, *Théologie dogmatique*, p. 88.

69 *Ibid.*, p. 89.

70 See Gerard F. O'Hanlon, *The Immutability of God in the Theology of Hans Urs von Balthasar* (Cambridge: Cambridge University Press, 1990), pp. 90–6.

71 Richard Sorabji, *Time, Creation and the Continuum* (London: Duckworth, 1983), p. 111.

72 Lossky, *Théologie dogmatique*, p. 90.

73 *Ibid.*, p. 92.

74 *Ibid.*, p. 93.

75 *Ibid.*, p. 95.

76 *Ibid.*, p. 96.

77 *Ibid.*, p. 97.

✢ 6 ✢

A Christology, and the Life of the Incarnate Word

The 'triple barrier'

Lossky's *Théologie dogmatique* is obviously a good place to look for his Christology, where it appears with the thoroughly Chalcedonian title 'Christ, true God and true Man'. Despite the Trinitarian symbols, ambiguous enough as they are, in certain Old Testament texts—and, more strikingly, the conviction of many of the Fathers that the Lord who manifested himself to patriarchs and the prophets was the everlasting Word—Lossky states in plain words that the economy of the Son begins with the Incarnation.[1] Like so many before and after him, he comments as fully as he can on that key formula from the Fourth Gospel, 'The Word became flesh' (John 1:14).

In this enormously influential affirmation, 'flesh' means, in Lossky's reading, the totality of human nature, while 'became' means that, astonishing as this is to the metaphysician, something was added to the plenitude of God the Word. This 'becoming' goes beyond the categories proper to the divine nature which is changeless. That is ontologically possible because because the person of the Word is not his nature. As Lossky's Triadology has insisted and his anthropology (when we reach it) will confirm, nature and hypostasis are different things. Only the Person of the Word became flesh, not the entire Trinity in their self-identical nature. True, the triune God has only one will, but that single will was exercised in the Incarnation with hypostatic diversity: the Father sending, the Son obeying, the Holy Spirit accompanying and assisting. Lossky has a marvellous passage of condensed theological thought spelling out the implications of this assertion for Christ's humanity—the Christ in whom

> there was not only divine will but human will, and [therefore] something like a separation was introduced between the Father and the Son. The accord of the two wills in Christ seals the obedience of the Son to the Father, and the mystery of this obedience is that of our salvation.[2]

Among other things, this reminds us how, in the Word's Incarnation, a saving purpose was at work. The Word became human so as to make possible the union of humankind with God. For this to be achieved, a 'triple barrier' had to be overcome, a trio of hurdles surmounted. The first obstacle—our ontological separation from God—was already overcome in the moment of the Incarnation itself. Nature is the first 'barrier' that needs to be cleared away, and it was. But there remained two other obstacles, closely tied in with man's specifically fallen nature. These were sin and death. The aim of Christ was to 'banish their necessity from the earthly cosmos',[3] which Lossky explains as to render death inoffensive, and sin curable.

As the Incarnation in its *déroulement* makes plain, this would come about through the submission of One who is God to death and to Hell. The death of Christ will remove the obstacle that is sin, his Resurrection the sting that is death. In *The Mystical Theology of the Eastern Church* Lossky had made excellent use in this connexion of a passage from *Life in Christ*, a treatise on the sacraments by the late Byzantine theologian Nicholas Cabasilas (c. 1320–c. 1390), citing from a translation made in the 1930s by monks of Amay in a supplement to their journal *Irénikon*.

> The Lord allowed men, separated from God by the triple barrier of nature, sin and death, to be fully possessed of Him and to be directly united to Him by the fact He has set aside each barrier in turn: that of nature by His incarnation, of sin by His death, and of death by His resurrection.[4]

In the destruction of the 'triple barrier', the ultimate intended outcome is our deification. Lossky remarks in *Théologie dogmatique,*

A Christology

'God descends towards the abysses of non-being which, through the sin of Adam, had opened in creation, so that man can climb up towards divinity.'[5] It is the theme first explicitly formulated, so he believed, by St Irenaeus in *Against the Heresies* and subsequently re-affirmed by St Athanasius in *On the Incarnation of the Word*.[6] Nature transformed by grace: for the patristic reading of Scripture this is the crucial vision of redeemed humanity, at once metaphysical and physical.

Co-involved in Incarnation: the Holy Spirit and the Mother of God

Still focusing on the Incarnation itself, Lossky considers the role of the Holy Spirit in the Fleshtaking. He dislikes the idea of the Spirit as 'Spouse' of Mary—though when, in the moment of the Annunciation, an ovum is provided by the Virgin, its fertilization by the Holy Spirit, that partnership in procreation almost inevitably suggests a comparison with a human husband. In symbolic mode, argues Lossky, and to the degree that Mary represents the Church, she is spouse not of the Spirit but, rather, of her Son. (In the Western tradition, that notion is represented by her title as *socia Redemptoris*, the 'companion of the Redeemer', with roots in the early patristic idea of the 'New Eve'.) The Spirit's task in regard to Mary of Nazareth is not, for Lossky, to espouse her but, instead, to give her the 'most total virginity', a 'purity of entire being'.[7] And this coincides with the coming to be of her divine motherhood.

In *Théologie dogmatique* this purification at the Annunciation moment is not presented as a denial of the Catholic doctrine of her 'immaculate' conception, so much as an immediate preparation of Mary for the Incarnation itself, for what Lossky calls the 'power of receiving and giving birth to the Word'.[8] In the *Essai* he had been more Mariologically focused than this in his account of the Incarnation—but he had also used the opportunity to state (mildly enough, it is true) an objection to the Latin doctrine.

Using a rather arcane source—a Byzantine manuscript from a fourteenth-century patriarch preserved in the Moscow library of the Holy Synod of the post-Petrine tsardom and translated into Russian at Novgorod in 1898—Lossky spoke in that earlier work of how the 'hypostatic Wisdom of the Father "built himself a house"—the most pure flesh of the Virgin assumed by the Word'.[9] That signalled the plenary realization of of the Economy where, thanks to their shared willing, Father, Son, and Holy Spirit have hitherto administered the creation, drawing it towards its goal. This text from Philotheus of Constantinople gives Lossky the opportunity for an excursus on Mary's importance for Christology, not omitting to cite at its outset the highly pertinent affirmation of John of Damascus, that 'the name of the Mother of God (*Theotokos*) contains the whole history of the divine economy in the world'.[10]

Those references to the Economy as a whole are germane to Lossky's case in the *Essai*. Since successive elections of the Old Covenant can be thought of as not only cumulative but also developmental with, at their climax, the preparation of a virgin mother for the humanized Word, he is inclined, like nearly all post-mediaeval Orthodox writers, not to favour the notion of the Immaculate Conception, at least as commonly understood, with its suggestion of a supernaturally sudden intervention in the historical process. But what he dislikes in the Latin theology of this subject is chiefly the idea of a 'privilege of exemption' withdrawing Mary from the common lot of humankind. In *Sept jours sur les routes de France*, Lossky had showed himself perfectly willing to accept not only the authenticity of the appearance of the Blessed Virgin Mary to St Bernadette (the most popular Marian visionary of modern Roman Catholicism) but even the occurrence of the crucial words, on the lips of the Mother of God, 'I am the Immaculate Conception'.[11] What he objected to was 'an abstract dogma of juridical character, that of the privilege accorded to the Virgin in view of the future merit of her Son' which 'disfigured' these simple words.[12] In particular, as he made clear in the *Essai*, Lossky objected to any sundering of Mary of Nazareth from 'the ancestors'.[13] And here he could make good use of a homily by Gregory Palamas on Mary's Presentation in the Temple. Palamas had spoken of her indebtedness to the purifications undergone by her forebears as well as of her own cleansing from all stain at her conception.

Lossky does not doubt, however, that in her total freedom from the consequences of the Fall the Mother of God *was* unlike the rest of mankind. '[S]he has been kept from all taint of sin though without any impairment of her liberty.'[14] His quarrel, or so it seems to this reader of the *Essai*, is only with the Latin terminology for the difference in question. I look further into the question of Lossky's Mariology in Chapter Nine of this book.

The metaphysics of the union

Both in the *Essai* and in *Théologie dogmatique* Lossky is concerned with ontological exactitude. He refines his account of the hypostatic union between the divine and human natures along the following lines. Not only is there no coming together of the divine Person and a human person in Christ (that would be Nestorianism). There is also no addition of an independent (albeit non-personalized) human nature to the Person of God the Word. As with the mature position of St Thomas Aquinas in his *Summa Theologiae*,[15] Lossky holds that the humanity of Christ came into existence within the hypostasis of God the Son. In the words of *Théologie dogmatique*, '[the humanity] never existed outside the person of the Son; it was he who created it within his hypostasis, not *ex nihilo* . . . but from the Virgin, purified by the Holy Spirit'.[16] In the *Essai* this appears as 'in the one and the same act the Word assumed human nature, gave it its existence, and deified it'.[17] It would not be correct to say, underlines Lossky, that an example of human nature was first brought into being and then 'entered into union with God'—not even (we may add) if the 'then' in question is temporally instantaneous, or indeed only logical in force.[18] This insistence on his part will please more rigorous Thomists, if ever they read Lossky, in the Roman Catholic Church.

I described Lossky's chapter heading in *Théologie dogmatique* as robustly Chalcedonian, and indeed everything said so far coheres with the Chalcedonian definition. But now Lossky turns to consider that dogma directly. In Lossky's neat reformulation of the definition, 'there are two consubstantialities [with the Father and with ourselves] but a sole consubstantial one, a sole person'.[19] The formula avoids the mere humanism of the West (contrast the Nestorians), and it escapes likewise the 'cosmic illusionism and pure interiority of the ancient East' (contrast the Monophysites).[20] The celebrated quartet of adverbs chosen by the Fathers of Chalcedon to describe the union of natures—'without mixture' and 'without change' (over against the Monophysites), 'without division' and 'without separation' (over against the Nestorians)—describe apophatically the mystery of the Incarnation, discouraging us from any attempt to imagine how the union worked. In the reiterated—also apophatic!—refusal to venture an account of how the union was both possible and functional, readers of Bulgakov might suppose Lossky has the celebrated sophiologist in mind. Famously, Bulgakov had sought to exhibit the positive presupposition of the union, namely, that relation between the uncreated Wisdom of God and created wisdom which suggests how an Incarnation might be feasible.[21] But no. Lossky's target in *Théologie dogmatique* is would-be 'lives'—i.e. biographies—of Jesus, and hypothetical reconstructions of the psychology of his 'states'. It has been said of Newman that, granted the conviction that the divine Word constitutes the unity of Christ's make-up, he was 'not . . . interested in the reconstructed psychological experiences of a supposedly historical Jesus'.[22] These words could have been written of Lossky too.

The *perikhōrēsis* of the natures and the two wills

But Lossky is at least willing to say about 'how it all worked' that the natures personalized by the Word evidently enjoy an interchange, in which they can compenetrate. Up to a point, on this issue of the (unconfused) compenetration, Lossky, if anything, echoes Bulgakov.[23] The transforming influence of the divinity on the humanity is reciprocated in the form of a certain 'penetration' of the humanity into the divinity. This is Lossky's understanding of what the Greek Fathers call the *perikhōrēsis* of the natures, or what in the Latin language emerges as the *communicatio idiomatum*. The

A Christology

latter, he insists, is not simply a linguistic rule about how to speak of divinity and humanity in Christ (so long as one understands the convention, one can say, on account of the 'communication of the idioms', such things as 'God died' or 'a man is God'). Rather, the *communicatio idiomatum* proclaims an ontological event.

In the *Essai*, Lossky had understood St John of Damascus to be hinting at a certain 'penetration' from the human into the divine even though *perikhōrēsis* must chiefly be understood as operating in the opposite direction.

> This *perichoresis*, or permeating, for St John Damascene, is on the whole unilateral: comes from the divine side, and not from the fleshly side. However, the Divinity, having once penetrated the flesh, gives to it an ineffable faculty of penetrating the Divinity.[24]

Lossky cites here John of Damascus's *On the Orthodox Faith*: the 'flesh became the Word without having lost what it had, though it was identified with the Word in the hypostasis'. It is a claim St John regarded as licensing his cry, 'When adoring my King and my God I adore at the same time the porphyry of His body'.[25] Porphyry was of course the colour of robes dyed with the costly purple reserved to the emperors. There must be—however discreetly expressed—that 'certain penetration' by the humanity of the divinity if Christ's bodily integument truly is the flesh of God.

Lossky's account of the teaching of Chalcedon is offered in the light of its own doctrinal development at the Third Council of Constantinople (681). In the steps of St Maximus Confessor, one of Lossky's favourite patristic sources, that Council, the Sixth Ecumenical, had defined the existence of two wills, human and divine respectively, in the Redeemer Jesus Christ. The God-man wills in ways both divine and human. Since Christ acts in and by both of his two natures he has of course two sets of operations. That, undoubtedly, is what the Fathers of the Sixth Ecumenical Council intended to teach, and yet, cautions Lossky, we must not overstate the duality, for he who thus wills is himself one.

In both the *Essai* and in *Théologie dogmatique* Lossky's discussion of *perikhōrēsis* leads into an account of those two wills—and how it is that they create no schism in Christ's existence. Indebted as he is not only to John of Damascus but also to St Maximus, his analysis shows great finesse. Expounding in *Théologie dogmatique* the latter's teaching, Lossky explains that in Christ there are two 'natural' wills, the divine and the human, but no freedom of indifference or (in Maximus' term) 'gnomic' will by which, in the case of fallen humanity, I either accept, reject, or turn to some other end, my natural will. That is pertinent to the lack of schizophrenia in the Word incarnate, for the 'natural' will, in the Maximian conception, is will that, of itself, tends towards the 'good of reason', which in the last resort must mean, for a human being, will that *tends towards God*. In Jesus there is no natural hypostasis which must constantly choose, in potentially counter-natural 'gnomic' fashion, between good and evil.

The Son's divine will is in any case identical to that of the Father, but the same cannot be said of his human will. It was by his specifically human liberty that Jesus elected what the divine will sought. So it is fortunate for us that the human will of the Redeemer was in full integrity natural will: namely, that it was non-gnomic will. 'Fortunate for us' since in his willing as man the same object that the Trinity wills as God there 'resides the entire mystery of our salvation'.[26] Here the scenario presented by the Gospels on the occasion of the Agony in the Garden is immensely instructive for Lossky, just as it was for his master, St Maximus.

> The proper will of the Word, [which is] his human will, submits itself to the Father, showing by human means, which are not oscillations between yes and no but yes, even via the no of horror and revulsion, the adherence of the New Adam to his God.[27]

The Redemption

In a passage of some complexity the Lossky of *Théologie dogmatique* moves from the theme of Incarnation—an Incarnation kenotic precisely in taking on human 'implenitude'—to the neighbour theme of the Redemption. He writes: '[Christ] alone could measure all the measure of the agony since death took hold (*s'emparait*) from outside his being'. From outside, yes, because, thanks to the hypostatic union, his humanity was already deified.[28] Death for him was not, as it is for fallen men, the expected fate of a 'being [that is] mingled with non-being'; our being as fallen humans is, in Lossky's graphic phrase, inwardly 'corrupted by malady and time'.[29] Untouched by moral and metaphysical delinquency, the incarnate Word in the moment of his human dying could grasp in completeness what it is the negative powers at work in the world are and do. In his 'alone measured death', sin, by 'contact with the all-powerful divinity', then 'consumes itself in the personal unity of Christ', who is at once fully human — and thus in solidarity with all human beings, the 'New Adam', as Lossky has already put it, and also fully divine — and thus empowered with every resource.[30]

Expressed in language that is cooler, less mythopoeic and yet not uninformative about reality (here the description '*onto*-mythological' may be preferred by some): 'the redemption is nothing other than the opening to the ultimate separation of man and God of the One who remained inseparably man and God'.[31] Lossky's further discussion of the Redemption teases out the meaning of this epigrammatic sentence. From the Incarnation, he proposes, there arises what he terms an '*espacement*' between Father and Son, an empty 'space' in which the free (i.e. human) submission of the Word is feasible. This space is the location of the redemptive act. A wholly Innocent One substitutes himself by both 'dereliction' and 'malediction' for those justly condemned. The language here anticipates the powerful 'theological dramatics' of Lossky's Maximus-mentor Hans Urs von Balthasar, behind whom stands the Swiss mystic of the Atonement Adrienne von Speyr (1902–67).[32] In vicarious — representatively substitutionary — sacrifice, Christ becomes the Lamb who 'takes upon himself' the sin of the world. *Prend sur lui*, the French original of the words just quoted, belongs to Lossky's translation of John 1:29, more customarily rendered in English as 'takes away [the world's sin]'. (The translator has interpreted the Greek of St John's Gospel in the light of Hebrew texts from the Book of Isaiah, notably Isaiah 53:7 and 12.[33]) The entire sacrificial tradition of Israel — including that important focus of rabbinic attention the 'Binding' of Isaac (Genesis 22:1–19) — and the promise to the prophets of the liberation of a 'remnant', culminates here in the Passion and death of the divine-human Redeemer.

Deification and the 'syntheses'

Climactic it may be, but Lossky insists that a theology of redemption must never lose sight of the wider contours of the divine plan. The Fall does not change that plan. God's aim remains the deification of man and, through man, the transfiguration of the cosmos. Again the comparison with Newman strikes the eye. Owing to the influence of the Fathers of the Eastern Church, so one late-twentieth-century commentator has observed, Newman's eyes, when considering the God-man, were 'fixed upon a vision of the glorification and deification of humanity'.[34] Yet for Lossky the *means* to that glorious, deified end change drastically in the new post-lapsarian situation.

> [I]t is needful to cure this wound and recapitulate the history-gone-awry of humanity, for the sake of a new beginning: these are the goals of the redemption.[35]

Redemption, *rachat*, is, then, a goal of sorts, but it is not an ultimate goal, which is why it can also be described as a means. Seen in the full perspective of the plan of God, it is only a means — to theosis, of course. 'What would it matter, being saved from death and hell, except that one should lose oneself in God?'[36]

In *Théologie dogmatique* Lossky abandons — possibly having discovered it was too arcane for readers to follow easily — a more strictly Maximian account in the *Essai* of the redemptive Incarnation as the Mediator's overcoming of a series of divisions in the cosmos.[37] *Essai sur la théologie mystique de l'Église d'Orient* makes a good deal of the scheme of cosmic soteriology, centering on the New Adam, which Hans Urs von Balthasar had just laid out for readers of German in *Kosmische Liturgie* — cited by Lossky in his footnotes.[38] Lossky points out that St Maximus was not a Scotist *avant la lettre*. That is to say, unlike the mediaeval Franciscan theologian John Duns Scotus, he did not believe that the Incarnation would have transpired even without the Fall of man. Care must be taken here for not all Maximian scholars agree with this judgement.[39] At any rate on Lossky's reading of the great Greek Father, the Incarnation was to resume a work of unifying 'divisions' in the cosmos which Adam, owing to the Fall, had originally been called to perform but had failed to achieve.[40] Deification was always the plan of God, yes, but not Incarnation. Referring notably to one of Maximus' chief treatises, *On the Ambiguities* (ostensibly a study of difficult passages in the writing of St Gregory the Theologian, hence its title), Lossky explains in the *Essai* how the Word incarnate, from the Nativity to the Parousia, succeeds in overcoming key divisions within the world — and between the world and God.

> By his birth of the Virgin He suppressed the division of human nature into male and female. On the cross He unites paradise, the dwelling place of the first men before the fall, with the terrestrial reality where the fallen descendants of the first Adam now dwell; indeed, He says to the good thief, 'today thou shalt be with Me in paradise', yet He nevertheless continues to hold converse with His disciples during His sojourn on earth after the resurrection. At His ascension, first of all, He unites the earth to the heavenly spheres, that is to the sensible heaven; then He penetrates into the empyreum, passes through the angelic hierarchies and unites the spiritual heaven, the world of mind, with the sensible world. Finally, like a new cosmic Adam, He presents to the Father the totality of the universe restored to unity in Him, by uniting the created to the uncreated.[41]

It is a powerful vision of cosmic reunification but not an especially accessible one — even in a period such as our own where cosmology, scientific and otherwise, has enjoyed something of a renaissance.

Polyvalence on the Cross

Because the Redemption removes various obstacles to the union of God and man, it comprises different 'moments' of increasing openness to the fullness of the divine presence. No one motif can do it justice, no single metaphor capture it. Lossky, like, for instance,

St Thomas before him, believes in a polyvalent theology of the redemption.[42] But the question arises, how are the metaphors, or, it may be, more-than-metaphors, arranged? The Pauline themes of ransom and atonement (at-one-ment) by the Cross, commonplace as they are in the Fathers, should not be 'hardened' into a pure philosophy of legal right.[43] Contextualizing them in the wider metaphorical setting helps to prevent this. Arising from the Gospels there is the theme of the Good Shepherd gone in search of his own, and from the Byzantine Liturgy the motif of the victorious Warrior. The Fathers speak also of the Physician healing the wounds of the race, and of his 'Sacrifice'—the one sub-theme of which Lossky says it is 'much more than a metaphor', and completes whatever is lacking in juridical symbolism of whatever sort.[44] That alerts us to the likelihood of a fuller account. And so it is.

Lossky's theology of the Sacrifice consists in two parts: the negative aspect of its execution by the Son, and the positive aspect of its acceptance by the Father. On the execution of the Sacrifice, Lossky's sources are John Chrysostom, the two Cappadocians Gregory of Nyssa and Gregory of Nazianzus, and Maximus. But the composition of the picture is his own. He emphasizes the dereliction on the Cross, 'God distances himself from the cursed one, the one all abandon'.[45] Christ identifies himself with those who die in the ruptured condition of our nature—though die 'religiously' in that condition (thereby excluding those who die in despair or revolt against God). But in the Word who is consubstantial with the Father there is 'neither rupture nor tragedy' which is why when rupture and tragedy 'penetrate into Christ' they meet their end. 'Disabled from exercise in the person of the Son of God, malediction becomes benediction; through the Cross all the conditions of sin become conditions of salvation.'[46] Lossky finds merit in the notions, above all when combined, of both paying a debt to God and paying a debt to Satan (the twofold indebtedness corresponds, presumably, to the just mentioned 'conditions of sin'). Revulsion at these images is a sign, he thinks, that the 'cosmological perspective' on the work of Christ has been lost to view.[47] The Sacrifice's acceptance by the Father is, in brief, nothing other than Christ's Resurrection.

A Christology

The Resurrection

In the Resurrection the Father accepts the Son's Sacrifice. But that is not all the Resurrection means. We recall that for Lossky the Redemption has a goal beyond itself. The Incarnation of the Word aims not only at our pardon but at our deification, and Christ's Resurrection is the insertion of 'total life' into 'humanity's dry tree'.[48] Hence Lossky can say, in tones reminiscent of the Liturgy, that 'on the Cross, death is swallowed up by life'.[49]

Looking at the Sacrifice in the mode of acceptance, Lossky can complete his account of how it fulfils the Old Testament prefigurations. The new Melchizedek, our Great High Priest, finishes in heaven the work he began on earth. There is a new Passover, suited to a New Covenant, and an Exodus that far exceeds the great escape of old. Yes, the Sacrifice is expiation, but it is also a sacramental act of unlimited power, the 'offering of the cosmos as a receptacle for grace'.[50] And as to humanity, the New Adam is head of the Church, and consequently no 'adverse power' can now 'separate man definitively from grace'.[51] 'In Christ the life of a man can always recommence, however loaded with sin it is; a man can always abandon his life to Christ so that the latter can return it to him free and intact.'[52] The Parousia begins now in the 'souls of the saints'.[53]

Kenoticism

One last comment on Lossky's foundational Christology may be allowed. Despite the attack in *Spor o sofii* on Bulgakov's kenoticism as a patent borrowing from modern Protestantism, unhallowed by any precedent in the Fathers, there are definite touches of kenoticism in Lossky's own account in the *Essai* of the 'Economy of the Son'. The distinctive thing to note about Lossky's own kenoticism in this work is to see just how bound up it is with his personalism. He writes:

> As we have said many times, the perfection of the person consists in self-abandonment: the person expresses itself most truly in that it renounces to exist for itself.[54]

And he continues, making plain that he finds a supreme exemplification of this notion in the Incarnation of the Word, and a confirmation of this claim in — no less — one of the greatest of the Fathers:

> It is the self-emptying of the Person of the Son, the Divine *kenosis*. 'The entire mystery of economy' — said St Cyril of Alexandria — consists in the self-emptying and abasement of the Son of God.[55]

Lossky's kenoticism is of the hypostasis, not of the divine *ousia* as personalized by the Word. That does not prevent its being emphatic. Lossky stresses that the entire mode of existence of the second Trinitarian Person is subject to the kenosis, so much so that kenosis becomes that mode of existence itself.

> The *kenosis* is the mode of existence of the Divine Person who was sent into the world, the Person in whom was accomplished the common will of the Trinity whose source is the Father.[56]

The Son's self-emptying, however, brings about a greater manifestation of the deity of the Son for all who can see — for all, that is, who can 'recognize greatness in abasement, wealth in spoliation, liberty in obedience'.[57] This must presumably be true *a fortiori* of the climax of the Passion, where Lossky interprets the last cry from the Cross in thoroughgoingly kenotic terms.[58] But that will be, once again, a kenosis that simultaneously hides glory and expresses glory. Orthodoxy never separates the sacred humanity from the divine Person of the Word — as Lossky will go on to show by rehearsing hymnic texts from Pascha, and climactically the day called in the West 'Holy Saturday' and in the East 'Great Saturday', the Vigil of Easter. That is when 'the repose in the tomb, the final culmination of divine self-limitation, brings us suddenly into the mysterious repose of the Creator: the work of redemption is identified with the work of creation'.[59]

A Christology

Iconic Christology
and the life of the Incarnate Word

Lossky's Christology also appears in his comments on the holy icons. Just as in the *Essai* he avoids citing the Latin Fathers (despite his appreciation of Augustine elsewhere) or the mediaeval doctors (in spite of his detailed knowledge of the age of Eckhart), and, while mentioning the title of Anselm's treatise *Cur Deus Homo* ('Why did God become man?'), sedulously avoids in his theology of the redemption in *Théologie dogmatique* any reference to the *name* of Anselm himself, so here too, writing jointly with Ouspensky in *The Meaning of Icons*, he is, in his self-confinement to the Eastern tradition, strict and severe.

> In the choice of icons commented on here, whether they be icons of festivals, of Our Lord, of the Virgin or of saints, we have been guided less by their artistic quality than by the orthodoxy of their iconography. In other words, the icons represented here show no trace of any dogmatic deformation, no borrowing from western art, and they transmit the unaltered teaching of the Orthodox Church, in no way infringing the Canon of iconography.[60]

As he remarks, 'The Church, which sees Christ with the eyes of imperturbable faith, will always show, in its liturgical hymns and on its icons, the God-Man preserving His majesty even in humiliation'.[61]

'Liturgical hymns' are relevant because, in his short entry on the 'Icons of Christ' in the book co-authored with Leonid Ouspensky, he begins by citing the Kontakion for the 'Feast of Orthodoxy' (the first Sunday of Lent) which celebrates the Christology implicit in the vindication of visual images in the Byzantine iconoclast controversy of the eighth and ninth centuries. Addressed to the Virgin, the kontakion (a poetic 'stanza' used in the Liturgy) runs:

> The Word of the Father, transcending all determination ['uncircumscribed', *aperigraptos*), determined itself in Its incarnation through Thee, Bearer of God. He made the defiled image as of old, and penetrated it with Divine Beauty.

As Lossky points out, the kontakion establishes not only a Christology but an entire soteriology. The Incarnation means 'not only a perfect theophany, but also the realization of the perfect Man, to which the first Adam was unable to attain.'[62]

But here an important nuance should be added. Christ, the ultimate Adam (I Corinthians 15:45), was the archetype of the first man, and yet in an Economy that was not only manifestation but redemption he took on the likeness of fallen human nature, which means that a certain 'unlikeness' also belongs to the aspect of the 'Suffering Servant' (Isaiah 53:3) who lived among us as the 'Man of Sorrows'. During his earthly life the Saviour held together with the glorious likeness the—very different—kenotic unlikeness. Even the most intimate of his friends were only to glimpse on one occasion the glorious aspect of the deified humanity: namely, at the Transfiguration. The icons show what would not otherwise be apparent from the Gospels taken section by section: the Lord preserved his majesty even in his humiliation.

Lossky illustrates the icons of Christ by two sorts of icon in particular. His first choice falls on a mid-twentieth-century banner-icon, painted by a Russian artist for the church of the Holy Trinity in the Parisian suburb of Vanves. It shows a favoured theme of Russian iconography, the Saviour *Akheiropoiētos* or 'Not Made by Hands'. Lossky does not claim more than legendary status for the Abgar tradition, which ascribes to a king of Edessa either a painted version of the face of Christ or, in the more popular Byzantine account, a miraculously produced image caused by Jesus pressing a piece of linen to his face.[63] It is, of course, the latter image that can be called 'made without hands'—though the same is true of the *keramidia*, impressions subsequently made (by no human means, it was alleged) on the bricks used to secrete the original during a period of persecution in the Syrian city of Edessa itself. What matters for Lossky is not the possible historicity but the dogmatic truth that the legendary narratives express. 'Christian iconography—and above all the possibility of representing Christ—has its foundation in the fact of the Incarnation', for the Word that '"shewed" Itself in "the temple of his body" (John

A Christology

2:21)' was certainly not made by hands.[64] So much is a doctrinal commonplace, but more original is the inference Lossky draws.

> In consequence, the sacred art of icons cannot be an arbitrary creation of artists: just as the theologian expresses by means of thought, so must the iconographer express by his art the living Truth 'made without hands', the Revelation that the Church possesses in her Tradition.[65]

The second sort of Christ-image selected by Lossky is the type called *ho Pantokratōr*, 'the All-Ruler'. In his reading of the facial features of the *Akheiropoiētos* banner-icon Lossky makes much of the 'impassivity of an absolutely pure human nature, which excludes sin, but remains open to all the sorrows of the fallen world'.[66] In the case of the Pantocrator images he distinguishes. The monumental variety, whether frescoed or in mosaic, found in the cupolas of Byzantine churches is indeed formidable, the awful Judge. But the version found where the image is displayed for the veneration of the devout, though retaining the majesty of the macro-icon, has none of its fearfulness. The face while grave is 'full of sweetness; it is the compassionate Lord, come to take on Himself the sins of the world'.[67]

Lossky's examples are all Russian. Understandably, granted the political circumstances (he was writing at the height of the Soviet era), they are held in galleries or found in private collections in the West. The large fifteenth-century icon of Christ Pantocrator now in New York's Metropolitan Museum of Art depicts the Word as Creator 'borne on the Cherubim', his dynamism 'as it were transmitted to the created world, finding its reflecting in the quivering wings of the cherubim, in the variety of their postures and in the movement of the beasts'.[68] The zoomorphic symbols of the evangelists are stretching out, beyond the oval mandorla surrounding the figure of Christ, towards the corners of one of the two curved squares which together make up an octagonal star—symbol of the Age to Come.

An icon of the same subject and comparable in size but a century later in date (at that time in London's Temple Gallery[69]) portrays the Pantocrator carrying, as always, a book open at words of the

Gospel. The text selected is among the most popular for this icon-type: 'Come to me, all you who are weary and are heavy laden, and I will give you rest, for my yoke is easy' (Matthew 11:28 and 30).

The third icon Lossky and Ouspensky chose is nineteenth century, and less technically accomplished (ownership is not indicated so it was probably in private hands). It is included, Lossky explains, so as to show how even in a 'period of decadence' the essential features of the type held their own.[70] Lossky is of course contrasting on the one hand the Westernized icons produced in the early modern period in Russia (except by Old Believers and in village *ateliers* which continued the older style) with, on the other hand, the Russian icons of the high Middle Ages and the sixteenth century. The contrast was particularly striking in that, as the historian of the icon Kurt Weitzmann remarked:

> In Russian icon-painting especially, the dematerialization of the human figures went far beyond the Greek models. Bodies became over elongated, and a loose and fleeting brush technique gave them at times a phantom-like appearance, emphasised by the use of glowing mystical colours.[71]

In the festal cycle

The Christological cycle of feasts in the Byzantine Liturgy enabled Lossky to add more to his comments on the Christ-icons, the *Akheiropoiētos* and the *Pantokratōr*. The Raising of the Cross furnishes a cue for saying something further about the Paschal mystery. He tells us that the Byzantine Church knows three feasts of the Cross (apart of course from the original 'Good Friday'). There is the Adoration, *Proskynēsis*, of the Cross on the third Sunday of Lent, the Procession, *Proodos*, on 1 August, and the Raising, *Hypsōsis*, on 14 September, a date shared with the calendar of the Latins. The annual memorial of the dedication of Constantine's basilica of the Resurrection at Jerusalem—the building known in the Latin Church as 'The Holy Sepulchre'—became associated with the finding of the true Cross by the empress Helena, and eventually was quite overtaken by that happy, if historically unexpected, event. In liturgical act the Cross was literally 'raised', first

A Christology

(at Jerusalem) in its completeness as an object, and then, scattered through the *oikoumenē*, broken up in shards and splinters, for the acclamation of the people.

Lossky distinguishes between a theo-political element in the feast, which is, he says, exclusive to Byzantium, and its wider theo-cosmic significance. Describing the former, he writes: 'the Orthodox people and their *basileus*, the head of Christian civilization, triumph over their enemies by the invincible power of the Cross'.[72] But it is the latter—the Cross, not the Christian emperor—whose significance is eternal, rather than contingent.

> Elevation of the venerable and life-giving Cross has a permanent and essential aspect: that of a cosmic sanctification by the Divine force manifested in the Cross. If Christ is the New Adam, His Cross is the New Tree of Life, giving back to the fallen world the incorruptibility of Paradise.[73]

Beneath the portrayal of the Raising properly so called, Helena is frequently depicted standing at Golgotha with the three crosses she had uncovered from the earth. A modern Russian icon, chosen for purposes of illustration, gives the simplest form of the visual idea. The Jerusalem bishop, assisted by two subdeacons, stands on an ambo holding the Cross with both hands, while to his right are Helena and Constantine and to his left a sick man, assisted by a helper, who has just been miraculously healed by the Cross's power.

The feast of the Presentation of Christ in the Temple, known alternatively in the East as the Meeting (*Hypapantē*)—in other words the encounter of the Holy Family with the prophetic figures of Symeon and Anna (Luke 2:22–38)—also fell to Lossky for comment. Lossky cites texts from Vespers of the feast which bring out its paradoxical character. The Author of the Law carries out what the Law demands: 'He who gave the Law to Moses on Mount Sinai . . . [so as] to observe the Law has himself brought to the Temple'.[74] A Moscow School icon of the early sixteenth century, now in the Casteel Wijenburgh collection (at Echteld, in the Netherlands), enables Lossky to uncover further aspects. The reverence with which the Christ-Child is regarded finds expression in the *maphoria*, voluminous cloths covering the hands, which his mother uses to transfer him to the arms of Symeon. The universality of his significance emerges from the liturgical texts that comment on the two turtle-doves carried by Joseph. The Byzantine Church interpreted them as symbols of the two Testaments, to Israel and the apostolic community respectively, or, again, as, within the New Testament Church, symbols of the *ecclesia ex circumcisione* (the Church of the Jewish Christians) and *ecclesia ex gentibus* (the Church of the Gentiles). Lossky underlines the exalted way in which the Liturgy speaks of Symeon. With greater justice than in the case of Moses he can be called 'he who has seen God, [the] *theoptēs*', since, in Lossky's words, 'to Moses God appeared in darkness, whilst Simeon carried in his arms the eternal incarnate Word'.[75]

Simeon's prophecy, delivered to Mary, pre-announces the Cross of Christ, to which, in the unfolding of the joint commentary with Ouspensky, Lossky now turns. Citing St Gregory of Nazianzus,[76] and, in paraphrase, St Athanasius,[77] Lossky affirms that the Incarnation came about so that the Word should be capable of death, as the 'omnipotent God, who willed to become man and to die as a slave, in order to save His creature'.[78] It was his supreme hour—but it was also the supreme hour of his enemies since only by apparent defeat did real victory come. The iconography must perforce reflect this theological truth. The sixth-century Syrian artists who produced the Rabbula Gospels and, a hundred years or more later, the painters of the Roman fresco at Santa Maria Antiqua, show Christ with open eyes, erect, and clothed with dignity. Lossky thinks that behind both the Syrian and the Roman artefacts lies the Passion narrative of the Fourth Gospel in particular. It was, he speculates, the especial contribution of Byzantine artists to factor in the tradition of the other three Gospels as well, 'completing St. John with elements borrowed from the account of the synoptics: the holy women behind Mary, the centurion with the soldiers, Pharisees and the crowd behind John'.[79] Lossky accepts the suggestion of the French historian of art Gabriel Millet that St John Chrysostom's scene-setting for the Crucifixion in Homily 85 gave Byzantine iconographers the 'programme for a living composition'.⁸⁰ (He was, after all, archbishop of Constantinople; Lossky assumes, possibly wrongly, that most iconographic workshops were in the Empire's capital.⁸¹) The substitution during the eleventh century for the ancient 'Syrian', and, equally, Western, form by a re-imagined Christ figure—nearly naked, its body sagging, its head bowed—shocked and angered the papal legates who in the fateful year 1054 came with their list of complaints to East Rome.⁸² Ironically, it would be the West that, in later iconography, pressed the new naturalism to an extreme.

In Byzantium and Russia, a 'soberness' of composition eventually resulted, not only in overall feeling but also in the restriction of the auxiliary figures to Mary and John, sometimes accompanied, however, by a sample of the holy women and the centurion. This is what is found in a sixteenth-century Russian Crucifixion icon now in the Musée nationale at Paris. Lossky describes the figure of Christ it shows: nude, except for a loin-cloth, the body flexed towards the right with the bowed head and closed eyes that speak of death. And yet, so Lossky continues,

> [Christ's] face, . . . turned towards Mary, preserves a grave expression of majesty in suffering, an expression which makes one think rather of sleep: the body of [the] God-man remained incorruptible in death.⁸³

As a Greek iconographer contemporary with Lossky commented on the Crucifixion icons of Orthodoxy:

> In the Orthodox devotional icon, everything is depicted anagogically, that is, to lift us from the world of the senses to the spiritual realm. In this realm there is nothing from the world of corruption, everything has the comeliness of the incorruptible. Forms and colours do not emit the chilling miasma of death, but the sweet hope of immortality . . . The Lord does not hang on the Cross like some wretched tatter, but rather appears to be supporting the Cross. His hands are not cramped because they are nailed to the wood; instead, he spreads them out serenely in an attitude of supplication, according to the troparion which says, 'Thou hast stretched out thy palms and united what had before been divided, that is, God with man.⁸⁴

Lossky then turns to the ancillary symbolism in this icon. At the foot of the Cross, a cavern stands open. It is a symbol of victory over death and Hell. The Cross itself has eight extremities (Lossky finds at least one Western writer, Pope Innocent III, who considers this the most authentic version of its portrayal). Of the two horizontal cross-pieces, the upper one—the 'phylactery'—would have carried the inscription 'Jesus of Nazareth, king of the Jews', though it is absent on this particular icon. The lower of the two beams replicates the 'stool' or *suppedaneum* to which Christ's feet were nailed. On many icons, but not here, this was placed obliquely, which, according to Lossky, is also a symbolic move on the artists' part. The upward direction to Christ's right represents the justification of the good thief, the downward, to his left, the reprobation of the bad.

The Saviour is shown crucified outside a wall—correct both historically and theologically because the city we seek is not the one here but one that is to come. The upper part of the Cross, however, has the sky as background. For Lossky, crucifixion 'in an open place' signifies the cosmic significance of this death which freed the universe from demonic dominion: a motif in both Athanasius and John Chrsyostom, as he points out.[85]

Lossky's interpretation of the remaining figures—Mary and a holy woman, John and the centurion—is concerned chiefly to underline the role of the blessed Mother. On Lossky's interpretation, her face 'expresses a grief contained, dominated by intrepid faith'—contrasting in this with St John whom Lossky reads as absolutely terrified. By addressing herself in gesture to John the Mother of God 'calls him to contemplate with her the mystery of the salvation which is accomplished in the death of her Son'.[86] That is clearly a possible starting-point for a high theology of Mary's role in the post-Crucifixion Church of which the 'beloved disciple' is the apostolic representative in this scene.

One detail of great spiritual beauty noted by Lossky is the way the iconographer has the centurion hold his hand as if he almost wanted to make the 'sign of the Cross', the ritual act so common in Orthodox as in Catholic worship.

A Christology

A portable cross carved in applewood from the Novgorod school at a slightly earlier date than the icon just described links to the Crucifixion numerous figures from the Communion of Saints, as well as expanding the theological symbolism seen so far. At the top of the cross a portrayal of the 'Old Testament Trinity', the three angels who appeared to Abraham at the oak of Mamre (Genesis 18:1–8), indicates the 'Divine Council presiding over the economy of our salvation which is accomplished on the Cross in the death of the incarnate Son'.[87] Carefully arranged are clusterings of saints: archangels, apostles, doctors of the Church, namely, Basil, Gregory of Nazianzus and John Chrysostom, as well as representatives of the local church of Russia: the great ascetics Sergius of Radonezh (1314–92) and Cyril of Belozersk (1337–1427), and a trio of holy bishops, St Alexis of Moscow (d. 1376), St Peter of Moscow (d. 1326) and St Leontius of Rostov (d. 1073).

The feast of Mid-Pentecost, also Christological (rather than Pneumatological), unknown in the West and rather odd-sounding to the ear of a Latin Christian, is precisely what its name suggests. Situated as it is on the Wednesday of the fourth week of Easter, it marks the mid-point of the 'fifty days' of Paschaltide. The Byzantine Church regards this day as clothed with the splendour of the two solemnities that frame it before and after. Its Gospel is John 7:14–36, which largely consists of a polemical conversation between Jesus and Jewish theologians. The Gospel text opens with the crucial words 'in the midst of the feast Jesus went up to the Temple and taught' (7:14), and while the feast in question, occurring during the public ministry, is Tabernacles rather than Pentecost, the Saviour's use at Tabernacles of the language of 'living water' (a symbol of grace) convinced Byzantine liturgists that an application to Pentecost was perfectly legitimate. Lossky calls it the 'pentecostal transposition of the feast of Tabernacles'.[88]

While the texts of the Liturgy amply explore the 'living water' motif, this has not affected the iconographic tradition which provides for the day a very restrained image: Christ engaged in the activity of teaching as older men wearing headgear (indicative of their status as Jewish doctors) listen to him with varying degrees of astonishment. The particular icon depicted in the Lossky–Ouspensky study is a fifteenth-century work from the Novgorod school. Its youthful Christ, beardless, inevitably reminds the viewer of the Lucan infancy gospel when the parents of Jesus found him in the temple questioning the doctors of the Law (Luke 2:41–52). For Lossky this allusion is intended to suggest the unity of the teaching activity of the Son of God from adolescence to the last year of his life. The kind of depiction chosen acknowledges two dimensions not easily shown together in art: both his time-transcending character as the Logos and also the historical truth whereby, once incarnate, he knew the world from within the experience of childhood and young manhood.

> At all ages of His earthly life, Christ remains this same hypostatical Wisdom of the Father which was made manifest for the first time to the doctors of the Law during His adolescence. The Christ-Emmanuel of the icon of Mid-Pentecost corresponds to the hymns of this festival which speak of 'the Wisdom of God'—*hē Sophia tou Theou*—come into the midst of the festival to promise the water of immortality.[89]

The Transfiguration is the last Christological icon Lossky attempts to interpret. After setting out, briefly enough, the New Testament sources (the Synoptics, and II Peter 1:16–18), Lossky asks the pertinent theological question, 'What was it that the disciples were enabled to contemplate when they saw the Transfiguration phenomenon?' In the sermons of Gregory of Nazianzus, the answer is, quite simply, 'the Divinity', while for John of Damascus, in a formula at once more theologically aesthetic in its terminology yet less ambitious as a piece of speculation, the 'splendour of the divine nature' was what came into view.[90] Lossky makes plain his own opinion, which coheres with his account in his more strictly dogmatic essays. The best understanding to be had comes from Gregory Palamas, and we are familiar with it from Chapter Two above on apophasis and the vision of God. The 'light' in question was neither a literal light sensorily perceived nor a metaphorical light which shone on the mind. Transcending the order of the created, the light is neither material nor immaterial, being the 'ineffable splendor of the one nature of three hypostases'.[91] Christ appeared to the three disciples as a Trinitarian hypostasis who in his Incarnation is not separated from the divine nature common to Father and Holy Spirit as well as to the Word. Making use of the thirty-fifth of Palamas' homilies, Lossky suggests a narrative form for the event that goes beyond the sources without necessarily contradicting them. Lossky paraphrases:

> First Christ showed the glory of His Divinity to the extent that the Apostles could receive the grace of this vision, but afterwards the brilliance of the 'bright cloud' overwhelmed their powers. Christ became invisible and the disciples fell in terror.[92]

Reference to painting from the mediaeval merchant republic, 'Novgorod the Great', is a feature of Lossky's choice of materials in his iconic Christology. An authoritative study by two Soviet era art historians suggests the probable grounds of Lossky's attraction to icons from this background:

> The language of the Novgorod icon is simple, laconic and precise; the composition rests on the opposition of imposing forms; the rhythmic and chromatic structure is tensile and mobile; the design is energetic. An exceptional role is played by the colour engendered by vivid local dyes.[93]

Using as his point of reference another fifteenth-century work from Novgorod, Lossky pauses on each of the actors: Christ; the apostles; and finally, Moses and Elijah. Christ himself stands on the summit of the (stylized) mountain, where a nine-pointed star inscribed in a mandorla represents the biblical 'cloud'. Lossky emphasizes the Trinitarian—and Palamite!—quality of the scene. Three rays pointing down from Christ to the apostles suggest the Trinitarian character of the action—and its uncreated 'energetic' character.

As to the apostles themselves, it was, thinks Lossky, to underline the uncreated nature of the light that, from the fourteenth century on, they are usually depicted falling precipitately down the mountain-side, with Peter and John ending up on their knees and James on his back, looking towards the source of the light but shielding his eyes with his hand. Earlier—and starting in the eleventh century—Peter is represented kneeling, supported on his left hand and raising his right to protect himself from the light, John falling with his back to the light and James either falling likewise or fleeing before it.

What of the two figures from the Old Testament economy? Lossky's account of them is largely occupied with Chrysostom's rich repertoire of interpretations in the fifty-sixth Homily on Matthew. The archbishop of Constantinople found three possibilities. The first is the simplest and, in later tradition, surely the most popular. They stand for the Law (Moses) and the prophets (Elijah). In a second reading: both men enjoyed a secret vision of God, one on Sinai (see Exodus) the other on Mount Carmel (see I Kings). There is also a third option. Perhaps they represent the living and the dead: the living in the person of Elijah, who was taken up to heaven in his lifetime, the dead in the person of Moses, buried on Mount Pisgah. The Byzantine Liturgy, so Lossky reports, favours the last interpretation, which 'underlines the eschatological character of the Transfiguration, Christ appears as the Lord of the quick and the dead, coming in the glory of the future age'.[94]

That glory is unthinkable, however, without the work of the Holy Spirit, so it is to that we must now turn.

Notes

1 Lossky, *Théologie dogmatique*, p. 125.

2 *Ibid.*, p. 127.

3 *Ibid.*

4 Quoted in Lossky, *The Mystical Theology of the Eastern Church*, p. 136, from Nicolas Cabasilas, 'La vie en Christ', III', *Irénikon* IX (1932), Supplement, pp. 89–90.

5 Lossky, *Théologie dogmatique*, p. 127.

6 Irenaeus, *Against the Heresies*, III. 10, 2; III. 16, 3; III. 19, 1; Athanasius, *On the Incarnation of the Word*, 54, 3.

7 Lossky, *Théologie dogmatique*, pp. 128–9.

8 *Ibid.*, p. 129.

9 Lossky, *The Mystical Theology of the Eastern Church*, p. 139, with an internal citation of Proverbs 9:1.

10 John of Damascus, *On the Orthodox Faith*, III.12.

11 Vladimir Lossky, 'La Dogme de l'Immaculée Conception'—'Lourdes', *Messager de l'Exarchat du patriarche russe en Europe occidentale* 20 (1954), pp. 246–51.

12 Lossky, *Sept jours sur les routes de France*, p. 36.

13 Lossky, *The Mystical Theology of the Eastern Church*, p. 140.

14 Ibid., p. 141.

15 The *Summa Theologiae* here records a shift in Thomas's thinking compared with his early master-work, the *Writing on the Sentences*. See Aidan Nichols, *There is no Rose. The Mariology of the Catholic Church* (Minneapolis: Fortress, 2014), pp. 36–42.

16 Vladimir Lossky, *Théologie dogmatique*, op. cit ., p. 129.

17 Lossky, *The Mystical Theology of the Eastern Church*, p. 142.

18 Ibid.

19 Lossky, *Théologie dogmatique*, p. 130.

20 Ibid., p. 132.

21 Nichols, *Wisdom from Above*, pp. 86–8, 90–3.

22 Stephen Thomas, *Newman on Heresy*, p. 130. Thus, in an instance selected by Thomas, whereas from the narratives of the Passion we can tell that Christ had a real human experience of mental suffering, the manner of its happening must be accounted 'inscrutable' since it was 'all along supported by an inherent Divinity', citing John Henry Newman, *Parochial and Plain Sermons* III (London: Rivingtons, 1834), p. 150.

23 Nichols, *Wisdom from Above*, pp. 108–11.

24 Lossky, *The Mystical Theology of the Eastern Church*, pp. 145–6.

25 John of Damascus, *On the Orthodox Faith* III, 8, cited *ibid.*, p. 146.

26 Lossky, *Théologie dogmatique*, p. 135.

27 Ibid., p. 144. See on this François-Marie Léthel, *Théologie de l'agonie du Christ. La liberté humaine et son importance théologique mises en lumière par saint Maxime le Confesseur* (Paris: Beauchesne, 1979).

28 Lossky, *Théologie dogmatique*, p. 147.

29 Ibid.

30 Ibid.

31 Ibid.

32 Hans Urs von Balthasar, *Theo-Drama. Theological Dramatic Theory. Volume 4, The Action* (San Francisco: Ignatius, 1994), and *Mysterium Paschale. The Mystery of Easter* (2nd edition, San Francisco: Ignatius, 2005). His Passiology is summed up in Hans Urs von Balthasar and Adrienne von Speyr, *To the Heart of the Mystery of Redemption* (San Francisco: Ignatius, 2010), pp. 15–42.

33 Lossky, *Théologie dogmatique*, op. cit, p. 147.

34 Stephen Thomas, *Newman on Heresy*, p. 130. See further C. S. Dessain, 'Cardinal Newman and the Eastern Tradition', *Downside Review* 94 (1976), pp. 83–98.

35 Lossky, *Théologie dogmatique*, p. 148.

36 *Ibid.*

37 Lossky, *The Mystical Theology of the Eastern Church*, op cit., pp. 108–10.

38 *Ibid.*, pp. 136–8.

39 See, for instance, Lars Thunberg, *Man and the Cosmos. The Vision of St Maximus the Confessor* (Crestwood, NY: Saint Vladimir's Seminary Press, 1985), p. 55.

40 For the theme of the overcoming of divisions, see *ibid.*, pp. 71–91.

41 Lossky, *The Mystical Theology of the Eastern Church*, pp. 109–10.

42 Aidan Nichols, 'St Thomas Aquinas on the Passion of Christ: A Reading of *Summa Theologiae* IIIa., q. 46', *Scottish Journal of Theology* 43 (1990), pp. 447–59

43 Lossky, *Théologie dogmatique*, op, cit., p. 149.

44 *Ibid.*, p. 150.

45 *Ibid.*

46 *Ibid.*

47 *Ibid.*, p. 152.

48 *Ibid.*, p. 154.

49 *Ibid.*

50 *Ibid.*, p. 155.

51 *Ibid.*, p. 156.

52 *Ibid.*, pp. 156–7.

53 *Ibid.*, p. 157.

54 Lossky, *The Mystical Theology of the Eastern Church*, p. 144.

55 *Ibid.*

56 *Ibid.*, p. 145.

57 *Ibid.*

58 *Ibid.*, pp. 147–8.

59 *Ibid.*, p. 151.

60 Lossky and Ouspensky, *The Meaning of Icons*, p. 145.

61 *Ibid.*, p. 69.

62 *Ibid.*

A Christology

63 Averil Cameron, 'The History of the Image of Edessa: The Telling of a Story', in *Okeanos. Essays Presented to Ihor Ševčenko* (Cambridge, MA: Harvard University Press, 1983), pp. 80–94.

64 Lossky and Ouspensky, *The Meaning of Icons*, p. 72. How the Fathers developed this understanding is brilliantly set forth in Christoph von Schönborn, *L'Icône du Christ. Fondements théologiques élaborés entre le Ier et le IIe Concile de Nicée [325–787]* (Fribourg: Editions universitaires, 1976).

65 Lossky and Ouspensky, *The Meaning of Icons*, p. 72.

66 *Ibid.*

67 *Ibid.*, p. 73.

68 *Ibid.*

69 For the revised edition published by St Vladimir's Seminary Press the Gallery provided, with Ouspensky's approval, photographic reproductions of icons then in their possession that corresponded with Lossky's account. Information provided by Sir Richard Temple in a conversation of 22 January 2016.

70 Lossky and Ouspensky, *The Meaning of Icons*, p. 75.

71 Kurt Weitzmann, 'Introduction: The Origins and Significance of Icons', in Kurt Weitzmann *et al.*, *The Icon* (London: Evans, 1982), p. 9.

72 Lossky and Ouspensky, *The Meaning of Icons*, pp. 148–9.

73 *Ibid.*, p. 149.

74 Cited *ibid.*, p. 168.

75 *Ibid.*, pp. 168–9.

76 Gregory of Nazianzus, *Orations* 45, 28.

77 Athanasius, *On the Incarnation of the Word*, 20.

78 Lossky and Ouspensky, *The Meaning of Icons*, p. 180.

79 *Ibid.*

80 Citing Gabriel Millet, *Recherches sur l'iconographie de l'Evangile aux XIVe, XVe et XVIe siècles: d'après les monuments de Mistra, de la Macédoine et du Mont-Athos* (Paris: Fontemoing, 1916), p. 426.

81 In an authoritative survey Robin Cormack remarks vis-à-vis the Egyptian monastery of St Catherine's, Mount Sinai, 'The evidence of Sinai demonstrates that Byzantine art in the sixth century represents more variety than the art of Constantinople', so the 'art of Constantinople cannot sufficiently document the period', *Byzantine Art* (Oxford; Oxford University Press, 2000), p. 53, while in the same location 'by the twelfth and thirteenth centuries, icons were certainly made on site', *ibid.*, p. 69.

82 See Lodwijk Hermen Grondijs, *Autour de l'iconographie byzantine du Crucifié mort sur la croix* (Leiden: Brill, 1960).

83 Lossky and Ouspensky, *The Meaning of Icons*, p. 181.

84 Photios Kontoglou, in Constantine Cavarnos, *Byzantine Sacred Art* (Belmont, MA: Institute for Byzantine and Modern Greek Studies, 1985 [1957]), p. 119.

85 Athanasius, *On the Incarnation of the Word*, 25; John Chrysostom, *On the Cross and the Thief*, Homily 2.

86 Lossky and Ouspensky, *The Meaning of Icons*, p. 181.

87 *Ibid.*, p. 184.

88 *Ibid.*, p. 193.

89 *Ibid.*

90 Gregory of Nazianzus, *Sermon on the Baptism of Christ*; John of Damascus, *Homily on the Transfiguration*, cited *ibid.*, p. 209.

91 Gregory Palamas, *Homilies* 35, cited *ibid.*, p. 211.

92 *Ibid.*

93 Vera Laourina and Vassili Pouchkariov, 'Les Icônes de Novgorod', in Dimitri Likhatchev, Vera Laourina, and Vassili Pouchkariov, *Les Icônes de Novgorod, XIIe—XVIIe siecles* (Leningrad: Aurore, 1980), p. 21.

94 Lossky and Ouspensky, *The Meaning of Icons*, op. cit ., p. 212.

✟ 7 ✟

Pneumatology and Sanctification

Lossky's Christology is never without some mention of the third Trinitarian Person, whetting his readers' appetite for, hopefully, a substantial treatment of the Holy Spirit. Thus, for example, in the Christological chapter of *Théologie dogmatique* he invokes the Holy Spirit not only as the agent in the Incarnation of Christ but also as the One who by his 'fire' renders the Resurrection of Christ a 'present reality' for humankind in the epoch before the Parousia.[1] The Spirit is crucially involved, then, at both ends of the Economy of the Son. So how will Lossky approach—confining ourselves for the moment to that posthumous publication of his lecture course on dogmatics—this sometimes neglected third Person?

The Spirit's place in the economy of salvation

With the economy of the Son completed by the Session, the world finds itself curiously placed. Considered as the 'body of the First Adam', it remains subservient to 'vanity': that is, to 'separation [from God] and death'. But considered as the body of the Second Adam, its 'first fruits' are to be found 'at the Father's right, in the splendour of divinity'.[2] There are two 'consubstantialities' for humanity now. The first, 'in Adam', is consubstantiality with sin, and by it we are 'delivered up to the "nocturnal" anguish of meonic [i.e. more-or-less-illusory] existence'. The second, 'in Christ', is consubstantiality with God, since we 'share in the new creation where nothing can separate us from him any longer'.[3]

That might sound as though Lossky is about to echo Martin Luther and tell us that we are 'at one and the same time just and sinful': in Luther's famous Latin formula, *simul justus et peccator*. In fact, he does no such thing. Instead it is here that he invokes the Holy Spirit, whose Economy, he thinks, aims precisely at 'reducing this duality', patiently working—this patience is, in this context, the form the Spirit's kenosis takes—in collaboration with our own freedom, all with a view to overcoming the paradox to which Luther prematurely submitted.[4] The Spirit does this by ensuring that we are more and more Christ's just as Christ is for evermore entirely God's. Lossky calls the time of the Church, accordingly, the 'time of the patience of the Spirit'.[5]

The time of the patience of the Spirit

This train of thought leads Lossky into a little disquisition on various views of the nature of time which take further—by a theological deepening—the largely philosophical discussion of the time–eternity relationship we considered in connexion with 'The Trinity and Creation' in Chapter Five. The Christian doctrine of time, so Lossky now argues, turns on the fact that Christ has not only recapitulated human history since the Fall but has brought history to its fulfillment in such a way that the Parousia is already present. Because the Church is Christ's mystical Body, in the Church 'time and eternity are united in a *deified time*'.[6] It is as difficult for a believing historian to write the history of the Church (which in its abiding element is essentially a history of sanctity) as it is impossible for an unbelieving historian to do so.

The concept of time pertinent to the Church embraces and goes beyond two alternative concepts. The first is that of the prophets with their view of time as linear, leading up to a supreme event which would confer meaning on the past by retroaction. The second is that of pre-Christian antiquity for which time was cyclical, with return to a ritually re-enacted paradisal or at least primordial beginning—an 'indefinite return' treated by the author of Ecclesiastes as illusory, the symptom of the sombreness of history.⁷ In the Church, however, the nostalgia for paradise of the ancients is overwhelmed by the Christological recapitulation which actually opens the door to Paradise, while the liturgical repetition is not a vain attempt to return to a lost origin but the very rhythm of the deified time which permits the assimilation by us of the 'theandric plenitude'of the ecclesial body.⁸ Prophetic waiting is no longer what it was under the Old Covenant. Now it is the 'slow maturing of a present already heavy [with significance]'.⁹

But where, the puzzled reader may ask, is the relevance of all this to Pneumatology? Lossky replies, it is by letting the Spirit 'be united with our spirit' that we can inhabit deified time and make it our own.¹⁰ This is what is happening in the process of our sanctification.

The Spirit in our sanctification

The prophecy of Joel is an important text for Lossky's purposes. The prediction that the Lord will 'pour out [his] spirit upon all mankind' (2:28) enables Lossky to argue that already in the Old Testament the messianic age was seen as one of a tremendous effusion of the Spirit of God. This is fulfilled in John 7:38–9 where the evangelist identifies with the Holy Spirit the 'rivers of living Water' the Son describes as set flowing in anyone who believes in him. That shows the conjuncture of the economies of Son and Spirit in the lives of the faithful, reflecting the interrelation of their economies in and of themselves, since it is by the Spirit sent from the Father that the Son is incarnate.

By the Son's Paschal Mystery the Spirit is sent again, this time for the Church's sake at Pentecost. Lossky finds the Roman Catholic tradition somewhat deficient in its grasp of the Pentecost mystery. It stresses, he reports, the significance of the gift of tongues as a sign of the Spirit-borne missionary expansion of the Church, but neglects the way Pentecost entails the restoration to the human person of the grace Adam failed to preserve. The two—Church and person—are linked since each Christian is called to 'hypostasize' the Church in her Christ-renovated nature.

> This personal and nuptial mystery of the Church, not in her Christified body but in her face (*visage*), which is to say the unique face of each Christian: that is the significance of Pentecost.[11]

This is a significance Lossky finds anticipated in the person of the Virgin, the first fully deified human being, who embodies the Church mystery in herself.

The Spirit and diversity of persons

To speak of a Christian only as a member of the Body of Christ might risk submerging him or her in a collectivity (we can perhaps read between the lines and say Lossky finds that the Catholic temptation). That would be to forget the Spirit-anointed 'free hypostasis' where human nature and the uncreated energies of God are united not—as with Christ—in a divine person but in a person who is altogether a creature.

In the Church as in the Trinity unity of nature is manifested in diversity of persons. 'Unity, then, is realized in the Body of Christ, uniqueness in the grace of the Holy Spirit.'[12] Here Lossky anticipates his own ecclesiology.

> The Church as the body of Christ is a sole human nature 'enhypostatized' by a divine person. The Church as spouse of Christ has an absolute diversity of persons enhypostatizing the grace of the Holy Spirit.[13]

There were many tongues of fire in the Upper Room, not just one.

The Giver and the gift

Lossky distinguishes—in line with Thomas Aquinas, criticizing his predecessor in the schools Peter Lombard—between the Spirit as Giver and grace as the gift. This 'secret person' that is the Spirit effaces himself in the gift, for what is given is participation in the common life of the Trinity.

The Holy Spirit's remaining imperceptible in the gift can also be brought under the rubric of his kenosis. His self-emptying enables grace to be the more intimately rooted in our own liberty. The Son by his kenosis revealed a divine person but hid the divine nature. By the kenosis of the Spirit the divine nature is revealed but the Spirit's person hidden. Lossky repeats what might seems the weak point in his theology of the Economy, namely that the Son redeems our nature not our persons while the Spirit 'appropriates to human persons' the divine nature in a work behind which he remains 'effaced.'[14] If the many references to the soteriological work of Son and Spirit in the various theologies within the New Testament corpus could be sorted so simply, it is surprising that this did not occur to the Fathers—or to later theologians in the tradition (until, that is, Lossky).

Further dogmatic considerations

While these materials from *Théologie dogmatique* are rich, they can bear supplementation from Lossky's earlier attempt at a Pneumatology in the chapter 'The Economy of the Holy Spirit' in *The Mystical Theology of the Eastern Church*.

Though in the opening of that chapter Lossky ties Pneumatology closely to ecclesiology, citing a striking text of Irenaeus as to how where the Church is there is the Spirit and vice versa,[15] he is perfectly aware that one cannot really restrict the operation of the Holy Spirit to the post-Paschal economy where the Church is born through the Easter/Pentecost events. The authors of the Creed of Nicaea-Constantinople had professed the 'Spirit of the Lord' who made possible Old Testament prophecy to be none other than the Third Trinitarian Person, and it is with an allusion to their work that Lossky offers a programmatic statement about the wider field of play the Spirit enjoys.

> [T]he Spirit who 'spake by the prophets' was never alien to the divine economy in the world in which the common will of the Trinity was being revealed. He was no less present in the work of creation than in that of redemption.[16]

The difference lies between the Spirit's co-operation with Father and Son in the economy of creation, where there is a common activity between them, and his presence 'considered as Person'.[17] With Easter and Pentecost he comes now not on the basis of his eternal mission from the Father but as sent by the Son in time (again, this must mean 'from the Father', but mediately). So what the Latins hold of the everlasting procession of the Spirit the Greeks believe to be true of his temporal procession. That procession in time is 'through the Son' and indeed 'from the Son' as well. Yet the independence from the hypostasis of the Son of the hypostasis of the Spirit, in the latter's everlasting source in the Father alone, has implications for the temporal mission. What implications? His 'independence' of the Son means that

> the personal advent of the Spirit does not have the character of a work that is subordinate, and in some sense functional, in relation to that of the Son. Pentecost is not a 'continuation' of the Incarnation. It is its sequel, its result.[18]

Indeed, for Lossky—reversing what he takes to be the common Western view—the work of Christ could itself be said to be in function of the work of the Spirit, inasmuch as the acquisition of the Holy Spirit by the redeemed creature is the goal of the Son's economy from start to finish.

Here, however, Lossky enters a caution against a reframing of the events of our salvation in what might be termed a 'Pentecostalist' manner where it is the Spirit, not the Son, who takes centre stage. The Spirit becomes present as Person at Pentecost, yes. But he does not become present as a manifested Person. His hypostasis remains hidden, and so will it stay until the end of time. Here the functionality of the Spirit vis-à-vis the Son, which Lossky has somewhat pooh-poohed as a Latin misconception, returns with a vengeance—but also with an important explanatory clause drawing our attention to the fact that the Son's work is itself altogether functional vis-à-vis the Father. This is what Lossky writes:

> [The Holy Spirit] comes not in His own name, but in the name of the Son, to bear witness to the Son—just as the Son came in the name of the Father, to make the Father known.[19]

Pneumatology and Sanctification

The anonymity of the Spirit

Citing John of Damascus' claim that the Spirit is the image of the Son as the Son of the Father (he spreads Christlikeness abroad), Lossky finds in the absence of any image for the Spirit in another Person (for the Triad never becomes a Quartet) the deepest reason for the peculiar concealedness of the Holy Spirit even in the age of the Spirit, the age of the Church. His are 'apophatic lineaments' as of 'a person at once unknowable and mysterious',[20] something which finds lyrical expression in one of Symeon the New Theologian's ecstatic hymns.

> Come, hidden mystery! Come, treasure
> Without name! Come, unutterable thing!
> Come, unknowable Person. Come, incessant joy![21]

Lossky will call this in the *Essai* the 'kenosis of the Spirit' — not, as will be the case in *Théologie dogmatique*, the Spirit's patience but, rather, his tolerance of his own anonymity. His self-abasement consists in the fact that 'He remains unrevealed, hidden, so to speak, by the gift in order that this gift which He imparts may be fully ours, adapted to our persons'.[22]

Lossky does not fail to quote the important text of St Gregory of Nazianzus on how, developmentally, the accredited witnesses of revelation made progress in their apprehension of the triune life. First they learn of the Godhead of the Father, then of the Godhead of the Son, and finally of the Godhead of the Holy Spirit. But this text from the *Fifth Theological Oration*, which (as he freely admits) attests the incremental growth of doctrine (it is often cited as such in Roman Catholic accounts of the idea of doctrinal development), has in reality less meaning for Lossky than it has for many other writers — including, one would have thought, Gregory of Nazianzus himself. For Lossky's emphasis on the abidingly unknown character of the Holy Spirit deprives Gregory's teaching of some of its force. The Spirit, he stresses, is concealed by the very gift of sanctifying grace that he bestows. Lossky's attraction to apophasis makes him, among modern Orthodox theologians, one of the least sympathetic to ideas of the development of the Church's mind.²³ Though the Spirit is indeed instrumental, in the course of history, in the disclosure of the Persons, including, not least in Gregory of Nazianzus' century, his own Person in self-disclosure, his non-manifest character gives him nevertheless an anonymity that is a hallmark of his Economy and will continue to be so until the Parousia.

For Lossky, that anonymity is accentuated, not diminished, by the 'multiplicity of names' the Spirit receives when Christians transfer to him the language they use for the gift of grace that is his.²⁴ Quoting from Basil's *On the Holy Spirit*, the Third Trinitarian Person is 'the Spirit of truth, the gift of adoption, the pledge of future inheritance, the first-fruits of eternal blessings, the life-giving power, the source of sanctification'.²⁵ This text makes Lossky's point much better than the companion citations from Gregory of Nazianzus and John of Damascus which frame it. Basil does precisely what Lossky says: he names the Third Person from his gifts. Incidentally, Lossky points out that the Latin—and chiefly, in fact, Thomistic—theology of the Seven Gifts of the Holy Spirit which distinguish them from sanctifying grace seems to have no equivalent in Orthodox writing: 'Orthodox theology ... makes no distinction between these gifts and deifying [i.e. sanctifying] grace'.²⁶

The rest of Lossky's account of the economy of the Spirit in *The Mystical Theology of the Eastern Church* falls into two parts: the role of the Spirit in the public life of the Church, and the role of the Spirit in the interior life of Christians.

The Holy Spirit in the public life of the Church

The basic scheme Lossky adumbrates, so far as an ecclesiology of the Spirit is concerned, can be found whenever in his writings he seeks to portray the mystery of the Church. For Lossky, as we have already had occasion to notice, the Church is indebted to the Son for the regeneration of the human *nature* of those who make up her membership; she is indebted to the Holy Spirit for the sanctification of her member's *hypostases*.

> The work of Christ concerns human nature which He recapitulates in His hypostasis. The work of the Holy Spirit on the other hand concerns persons, being applied to each one singly... the one lends His hypostasis to the nature, the other gives His divinity to the persons.[27]

The two economies, though plainly different, are not for all that sundered. On the contrary, they are inseparable. 'Christ creates the unity of His mystical body through the Holy Spirit; the Holy Spirit communicates Himself to human persons through Christ.'[28] Lossky does, however, recognize a certain corporate communication of the Spirit—specifically, in the aftermath of Easter (compare John 20:19–23). This is to the college of the apostles, as a 'bond of unity' and as 'sacerdotal power', the 'last perfection which Christ grants to His Church before He leaves the earth'.[29] But that is not where the emphasis in his pneumatic ecclesiology lies. His stress falls, rather, on the Spirit's gift to individual persons, signified by the division of the tongues of fire of the visible Pentecostal sending—which tongues or flames, according to the Acts of the Apostles, rested on the head of each one present (compare Acts 2:1–5).

The Holy Spirit in the interior lives of Christians

That renders easy the transition to the Spirit's role in the interior lives of Christians. A coming of the Spirit in his own uncreated Person to visit created persons can become the fruiting of the freedom of those persons in a unitive life with God. In Baptism the Holy Spirit unites our nature to the body of Christ thus purifying it, but in Chrismation he deifies our human persons: that is, he lavishes his grace upon them. Here Lossky can once more cite Symeon the New Theologian and, as usual, to good effect.

> We receive the naked fire of the Godhead, the fire of which our Lord said, I am come to cast fire upon the earth'. What is this fire if not the Holy Spirit, consubstantial with the Son by His deity, the Holy Spirit with whom the Father and the Son enter into us and can be contemplated.[30]

Lossky has three comments on this text which will serve to introduce his fuller account of that unitive life in the closing chapters of *The Mystical Theology of the Eastern Church*. He notes firstly how for Symeon the ardent presence of the Holy Spirit must have some resonance in experience, in consciousness. Secondly, although grace is not the Spirit (it is, to Lossky's mind, the energies of God) he is its Giver and in giving 'mysteriously identifies Himself with human persons whilst remaining incommunicable'.[31] Thirdly, this effacing of himself *qua* Person vis-à-vis the human persons 'to whom He appropriates grace' is another way of expressing the Spirit's kenosis.

What now remains is to look at the resultant life of union in and for itself—which is to say, in and for its goal in perfect union in God. Lossky is quite aware that theosis in its maximal sense is not for the here and now.

> The deification or theosis of the creature will be realized in its fullness only in the age to come, after the resurrection of the dead.[32]

But that does not mean it will be in every sense and at every level postponed for posterity. On the contrary, there is here both an obligation that weighs on us to prepare for it in the present, and the gifted provision of the resources we need for it to become ours. As Lossky puts it:

> This deifying union has, nevertheless, to be fulfilled ever more and more in this present life, through the transformation of our corruptible and depraved nature and by its adaptation to eternal life. If God has given us in the Church all the objective conditions, all the means that we need for the attainment of this end, we, on our side, must produce the necessary subjective conditions: for it is in this synergy, this co-operation of man with God, that the union is fulfilled.[33]

Lossky's chapter on 'the way of union' is really his reading of the history of Orthodox spirituality. It is emblematically dominated, as will be his succeeding chapter on 'the divine light', by the figure of St Serafim of Sarov, perhaps the most popular of modern Russian saints. That is owing to Serafim's emphasis on the 'acquisition of the Holy Spirit' to which all other ascetical practices of the Christian life, above all fasting and prayer, are ordered. That is a liberating emphasis for monastics and layfolk who may feel weighed down by the burden of Orthodox ascetic discipline.

Apart from this pneumatological orientation, what are the distinctive features of Lossky's account? A definite self-distancing from the Latin tradition is notable. This concerns, predictably enough, rejection of the Augustinian understanding of how grace and freedom work in the spiritual life, and, more surprisingly, a disagreement with the Carmelite school—not named, but surely intended—on the distinction between active and passive states in the higher reaches of the unitive life. But just as with the Carmelite school (though Lossky would probably not have appreciated this comparison) he too would like to schematize—at any rate, in very broad terms—the development of the spiritual life.

On grace and freedom, Lossky's commendation of synergism does not quite meet its anti-Augustinian target. For Augustinians too (and here Thomists are Augustinians), there is such a thing as a collaborative enterprise between grace and freedom—*gratia cooperans*, 'cooperative grace', the Latins name it. True, there is a difference between the customary Oriental accounts of the relation between grace and freedom where *gratia operans*, 'operative grace', is concerned, but the difference does not lie quite where Lossky would like to put it. For the Augustinian-Thomist tradition, grace in that initiating mode is needed to stimulate human freedom in advance, so the Losskian assertion that 'grace and human freedom are manifested simultaneously' would require some modification to satisfy the theological mainstream of the Latin West.[34] To this extent, Lossky is correct. But the further statement that grace does not 'act upon our liberty as if it were external or foreign to it' fails to hit the mark.[35] Rather is operative grace intimately lodged within our liberty and so effortlessly at home there than it can fructify that liberty from within, doing so without the slightest infringement of freedom's dignity or integrity.[36] Lossky does not do justice to the way that, in the Augustinian-Thomist synthesis, prevenient grace enables human freedom to blossom spontaneously. So much is plain when he writes that Augustine compounded Pelagius's error by transposing spiritual realities onto 'rational ground' where two 'mutually exclusive concepts' (grace and free will) were opposed to each other without 'any possibility that the question could ever be resolved'.[37]

But if Lossky is polemical in this respect, he also draws attention to the great spiritual teachers in the Western Church who bypassed the Augustinian analysis, profound as it is. These include not only Benedict (480–c. 545) and Bernard but also John Cassian (c. 360–435), whose influence, as Lossky rightly says, was pervasive in the monastic tradition of the West—and, one could add, beyond the limits of that tradition, *stricto sensu*, as the example of St Dominic (1170–1221), canon regular and friar-founder, would show. Yet the basic commonality of the two accounts of grace and freedom is exhibited in a fine citation from the nineteenth-century Russian bishop Theophan the Recluse (1815–94). As Lossky reports:

> In the nineteenth century, Bishop Theophanes, a great Russian ascetic writer, asserted that 'the Holy Ghost, acting within us, accomplishes with us our salvation', but he says at the same time that 'being assisted by grace, man accomplishes the work of his salvation'.[38]

As to the 'Carmelite' criticism: Lossky writes that 'the ascetical and mystical tradition of the Eastern Church makes no very clear distinction between active and passive states in the higher reaches of the spiritual life'.[39] And he implies that the characteristically Oriental ascetic concept of 'vigilance' transcends this distinction. With its key features of attention and discernment, that concept is, he thinks, a pointer to 'human nature in a state of wholeness', whereas the active and passive states are 'signs of disintegration'.[40] It would not at all be a good idea to introduce the latter as features of the unitive life as it progresses towards God.

Writing as he is about the mystical theology of the Eastern Church it is hardly surprising that Lossky does not consider the wider Carmelite scheme of development in prayer (perhaps one should write 'schemes', in the plural, for not all commentators seems agreed that John of the Cross and Teresa are entirely at one). He does, however, consider and reject—when treated as a sequence of stages—the distinction between *praktikē* and *theōria* important to the ascetic teaching of Evagrius of Pontus, whom we looked at, through Lossky's eyes, in Chapter Two as a major witness to the apophatic way to God. It is better, says Lossky, to think of growth in virtuous action (the 'practical' life) and growth in contemplative attention (the 'theoretical' life) not as consecutive stages but, rather, as interdependent levels of human development in spiritual living. Lossky retains, however, more or less in its original sense, the Evagrian notion of *apatheia*, an inner freedom where one is no longer swayed by the passions. It is in fact in order to protect *apatheia* as the crown of *praktikē* that Lossky is minded to reject the active–passive distinction found in the mysticism of the sixteenth-century West. 'On the level of the spiritual life, where [*apatheia*] is operative, the opposition between active and passive no longer has any meaning.'[41]

There is, though, one sequence of stages Lossky makes his own, and it is the triadic scheme found in the seventh-century Nestorian bishop Isaac of Nineveh. His spiritual treatises, despite their Christologically flawed origin, had long found a home in the philokalic tradition of Orthodoxy. Isaac's three stages on the way of union are penitence, purification, and perfection—though Lossky immediately qualifies his acceptance of Isaac's picture by saying that repentance is a permanent, quasi-continuous condition of all spiritual progress and can never, actually, be left behind. He links it, in a fine description, to the gift of tears known from the lives of many saints, in both East and West.

> [R]epentance is the fruit of baptismal grace; it is indeed the same grace when it has been acquired, appropriated by the human person, and become in it 'the gift of tears'—the infallible sign that the heart has been overwhelmed by the love of God.[42]

Such 'charismatic' tears are not only the climactic expression of repentance, they are also the beginning of evangelical joy.

Lossky is less clear about the contours of purification, but we can assume that it will include motifs he has touched on already in this chapter—the simplifying concentration of a life turned towards God where the spirit (or the deep mind, the *nous*) is guardian of the faculties, at once intellectual and volitional, of the heart. On 'simplifying concentration' Lossky has a rather unusual understanding of that biblically pejorative phrase (in some, not all, contexts) 'the world'. It is in fact indebted, once again, to Isaac.

> 'The world' signifies here a dispersion, the soul's wandering outside itself, a treason against its real nature. For the soul is not in itself subject to passions, but becomes so when it leaves its interior simplicity and exteriorizes itself. Renunciation of the world is thus a re-entering of the soul into itself, a concentration, a reintegration of the spiritual being in its return to communion with God.[43]

Such reintegration requires the descent of the spirit into the heart—that is, the prevalence of man's faculty for the contemplative seeking of God (*nous*) over his principal activities of knowing and loving at their central point (*kardia*, the heart). In the course of this discussion, Lossky ventures the suggestion that the *nous* is the seat of the hypostasis—the personhood of this or that human individual, and that this is why the major part of the Greek patristic tradition located the divine image in the mind.

In Losskian perspective, that was an attempt, only very partially successful, to conceive of the personal in its relation to nature as the true image—a concept which it took the personalism of the twentieth century, working through Lossky himself (not that Lossky is vain enough to claim the credit!), properly to disengage. The hypostasis (as we shall see in the following chapter of this book, on Lossky's theological anthropology) personalizes spirit, soul and body by uniting these elements in the human composite, and it is the existence of that hypostasis—rather than anything about the composite's nature, though not in total abstraction from its nature—which is the true point of comparison with the triune God.

Fittingly, then, the primacy of person over nature cannot mean that in the movement towards union with God (here we are leaving for the moment theological theory and considering spiritual practice instead), the constituent elements of human nature may be ignored. Our natural powers must be brought into the service of the hypostasis, not least by rightly ordering their own internal relations. As Lossky explains:

> Without the heart, which is the centre of all activity, the spirit is powerless. Without the spirit, the heart remains blind, destitute of direction. It is therefore necessary to attain to a harmonious relationship between the spirit and the heart, in order to develop and build up the personality in the life of grace.[44]

For 'personality' is the concrete form our personhood takes.

The process of purification—to which the factors just described are surely pertinent—must be well under way before the soul can approach what Lossky calls the 'passionlessness which is the frontier of prayer',[45] where (to be more specific) verbal prayers tend to fall mute as the heart lays itself open in silence to God. It is, I think, Lossky's commitment to the Hesychasts (who can forget the relation between the very word 'quiet' and their name?) that governs his account of the higher conditions of the life of prayer. He assumes that petitionary prayers will take a lesser part as time goes on, their place taken by astonishment, wonder, and the 'ravishing of the spirit'.[46] Yet experiences of ecstasy (and here the language of passivity is, he admits, pertinent) are themselves only symptoms of an initial approach to the perfect life. '[T]he soul which progresses in the spiritual life no longer knows ecstasies: instead it has the constant experience of the divine reality in which it lives.'[47] It is sign of the provisional character of this stage that Lossky is willing to agree that 'passivity'—hitherto treated as a negative phenomenon (in contrast to the Carmelites)—is typical of it.[48]

What then of perfection, which subject or stage the latter part of the sentence just quoted at last introduces? The mystical union is accomplished in charity, the love of God, itself, for Lossky, the 'fruit of prayer'.[49] 'For in prayer man meets with God personally. He knows him and he loves him.'[50] In the simplest of teachings, 'Union with God cannot take place outside of prayer, for prayer is a personal relationship with God'.[51] The virtues serve perfection, but they cannot assure it unless the *nous* for which Lossky is willing here to borrow another ancient term and speak of the 'spirit', the *pneuma*, is turned towards God in continual prayer. 'Constant', 'conscious', 'perpetual': these are the adjectives with which he lauds perfect prayer. They encourage him to break off his exposition to situate in history (and in modern scholarship) the Byzantine Hesychasts, his ideal practitioners of prayer. And to his rejection of all conceptualization in the attention to God which corresponds to those adjectival qualifiers he adds also, with a back reference to Evagrius, all imagery for God likewise. Like concepts, images too must be left behind.

This sits uneasily with the practice of prayer before the icons in the Byzantine East as well as with the insistence on the abiding relevance to prayer of the *humanity* of Christ in the Carmelites of the West. Yet Lossky does not intend to eliminate all reference to that humanity since he writes approvingly of the role of the Jesus Prayer in Hesychasm, with its reiterated utterance of the Saviour's name. 'Lord Jesus Christ, Son of God, have mercy on me.'

In such prayer, the grace-love which is the divine energy 'inflames' the soul and 'unites' it to God by the power of the Holy Spirit.[52] Just as Lossky wants to distinguish between gift (grace) and Giver (the Spirit)—and here he is at one with critics of Lombard in the mediaeval West, so he also wants to assert— over against what he takes to be Thomas Aquinas' doctrine—that grace is *uncreated* grace. Aquinas is far from denying that.[53] But St Thomas would wish to emphasize that such uncreated grace has created effects. Hence the term 'created grace', a phrase, be it noted, largely absent from Thomas' corpus, however often it may be used as shorthand by later Scholastics. Creator and creature cannot be conjoined without the uncreated leaving a new form in the created, now newly related as it is to God. There is *both* a created gift and *also* the deifying enjoyment of the divine persons.[54]

Lossky, for his part, is happy to speak, with St Basil, of a 'created disposition' for receiving the grace-love which is the uncreated divine energy whereby man participates in the divine nature.[55] But he evidently thinks that to speak of all three of created disposition, uncreated grace and created grace is excessively to multiply categories. Are not created disposition for grace and uncreated grace categories enough—enough, that is, for establishing how the grace-life is a full-blooded Creator/creature union? Lossky's chapter does not culminate, however, in mere Scholastic-type analysis. His recourse to the testimonies of the saints, and notably Symeon the New Theologian, gives his account of the humanely received divine love enormous warmth. This is despite his avowal, near the very beginning of the *Essai*, that the Eastern tradition deliberately minimizes autobiographical accounts of the spiritual life and any giving of publicity to first-hand experience of the 'way of mystical union' as distinct from its 'fruit' in spiritual teaching.[56] The spirituality of the East, so Lossky observes, is life in Christ rather than the imitation of Christ, a purely Western phenomenon (here a historical sense which sometimes deserts him is once again lacking). Life in Christ here should be understood as life in the 'unity of the body of Christ', his Church-body, wherein are found all the resources necessary (*pace* St Serafim) for the acquisition of the Holy Spirit. (Lossky is very much against anything that smacks of what he terms at the *Essai*'s opening, 'mystical individualism'.[57]) In the Church can be found all the objective conditions for appropriating the grace the Holy Spirit gives, that he might enable the faithful to share the Trinity's life. That includes, very importantly, resources that assist our understanding. Despite his paean to love, Lossky will not have love separated from knowledge. The way of union cannot progress without personal awareness. After all, it is to be illumined by the divine light. We have seen already in Chapter Two of this book what Lossky made of the theme of divine light in *The Mystical Theology of the Eastern Church*.

Lossky's pneumatological reflections there conclude on a high note in the 'feast of the Kingdom'.

> The consciousness of the fullness of the Holy Spirit, given to each member of the Church in that measure which he has attained, banishes the shades of death, the terrors of the Judgement, and the abyss of Hell, in turning our attention solely to the Lord coming in His glory.[58]

Here it is pneumatic plenitude—albeit with a recognition that this 'fullness' is by no means equally available to all—that makes possible real eschatological expectation, as distinct from lip-service to the hope for a Parousia which is going to extend the Resurrection triumph to all Christ's faithful. In fact, the lines from a patristic homily for Easter Matins with which Lossky ends the *Essai*, while certainly illustrating just how full that plenitude can be, do not mention by name the Holy Spirit.[59] But perhaps this is only appropriate for the third Trinitarian Person who is, as Lossky puts it in this closing chapter, 'the Mystagogue of the apophatic way'.[60]

Notes

1 Vladimir Lossky, *Théologie dogmatique*, p. 157.
2 *Ibid.*, p. 159.
3 *Ibid.*, p. 160.
4 *Ibid.*
5 *Ibid.*
6 *Ibid.* Italics original.
7 *Ibid.*, p. 161.
8 *Ibid.*
9 *Ibid.*
10 *Ibid.*, p. 163.
11 *Ibid.*, p. 165.
12 *Ibid.*, p. 166.
13 *Ibid.*
14 *Ibid.*, p. 169.
15 Irenaeus, *Against the Heresies* III. 24, 1.
16 Lossky, *The Mystical Theology of the Eastern Church*, p. 157.
17 *Ibid.*, p. 158.
18 *Ibid.*, p. 159.
19 *Ibid.*
20 *Ibid.*, p. 160.
21 Cited *ibid.*
22 *Ibid.*, p. 168.
23 A major conclusion of Daniel Lattier's 'The Orthodox Rejection of Doctrinal Development'.

24 *Ibid.*, p. 163.

25 Basil the Great, *On the Holy Spirit* 16.

26 Lossky, *The Mystical Theology of the Eastern Church*, p. 162.

27 *Ibid.*, pp. 166, 167.

28 *Ibid.*, p. 167.

29 *Ibid.*

30 Symeon the New Theologian, *Homilies* 45, 9, with an internal quotation of Luke 12:49, cited in Lossky, *The Mystical Theology*, p. 171.

31 *Ibid.*, p. 172. The relation of the doctrine of the energies to Pneumatology is the principal subject of Lison, *L'Ésprit répandu*.

32 Lossky, *The Mystical Theology of the Eastern Church*, p. 196.

33 *Ibid.*

34 *Ibid.*, p. 197.

35 *Ibid.*, p. 198.

36 See Cornelius Ernst, 'Transcendence and Spontaneity in the Metaphysics of Morals', *Dominican Studies* VII (1954), pp. 59–72.

37 Lossky, *The Mystical Theology of the Eastern Church*, p. 198.

38 *Ibid.*, p. 199.

39 *Ibid.*, p. 203.

40 *Ibid.*

41 *Ibid.*

42 *Ibid.*, p. 205.

43 *Ibid.*, p. 200.

44 *Ibid.*, p. 202.

45 *Ibid.*, p. 206.

46 *Ibid.*, p. 209.

47 *Ibid.*, p. 209.

48 *Ibid.*, p. 208.

49 *Ibid.*, p. 207.

50 *Ibid.*

51 *Ibid.*, p. 206.

52 *Ibid.*, p. 212.

53 A comparative study of Gregory Palamas and Thomas Aquinas, as in Anna Williams's *The Ground of Union*, is made difficult by the very different form of their work, a 'pattern of images' for the first, a largely 'linear exposition' (in the great *Summa*) for the second, *ibid.*, p. 103. But she is confident in her

conclusion: 'The ground that Aquinas and Palamas share is vast compared to the points at which they diverge, and considered in context, even their divergences do not reveal diametrical opposition . . . in most respects, to know and affirm the doctrine of deification in one is implicitly to accept the doctrine of the other', *ibid.*, p. 175. The conclusion is warranted if, as she alleges, despite some counter-evidence in Gregory Palamas's writing, notably *Triads in Defence of the Holy Hesychasts*, III. 2. 4, and *The One Hundred and Fifty Chapters* 75, the celebrated Palamite distinction between essence and energies is 'nominal rather than real', *ibid.*, p. 148.

54 Thomas Aquinas, *Summa Theologiae*, Ia., qu. 43, art. 3, ad secundum. '[Thomas] acknowledges that the gift of grace implies not only an effect of grace within the human person . . . but also an assimilation to the Uncreated', Anna Williams, *The Ground of Union*, p. 63.

55 Lossky, *The Mystical Theology of the Eastern Church*, p. 214.

56 *Ibid.*, p. 20.

57 *Ibid.*, p. 21.

58 *Ibid.*, p. 247.

59 *Ibid.*, pp. 247–9.

60 *Ibid.*, p. 239.

✢ 8 ✢

Theological Anthropology

LOSSKY'S THEOLOGICAL ANTHROPOLOGY has already been touched on in connexion with the doctrine of creation. But he also treats this theme for its own sake.

Micro-cosmology or personalism?

Appealing to St Gregory of Nyssa's treatise *On the Making of Man*, which mocks those who think it a privilege to be related to midges and mice,[1] Lossky points out how, for the Greek Fathers, the dignity of man does not lie in his being a *mikrokosmos*, linked to the rest of cosmic forms (this is undeniable, but unremarkable). It consists, rather, in his being in the image and likeness of God. In words of Gregory's homonym and fellow-Cappadocian St Gregory of Nazianzus, 'In my quality as earth I am attached to life here below, but carrying also a divine spark I have in my breast the desire for the future life'.[2] Here immanence gives way to transcendence—but at once a specifically Losskian note is struck when the divine imagehood is construed as being a person.

Lossky did not favour attempts (he calls them 'objectification', or 'naturalisation'—patristically inspired though they are) to identify some aspect of the human being as what makes him or her bearer of the image, precisely because all such attempts deflect attention from the whole person.[3] The task of drawing a fully consistent, or at any rate self-identical, teaching from the patristic corpus is in any case, he thought, an impossible undertaking. In *Essai sur la théologie mystique de l'Église d'Orient* he wrote:

> If we try to find in the Fathers a clear definition of what it is in man which corresponds to the divine image, we run the risk of losing ourselves amidst varying assertions.[4]

While drawing back from describing the Fathers' overall position as self-contradictory, their accounts have, for the most part (he considered) the disadvantage of being partial. Typically, if not everywhere and always, the patristic witnesses seek the image in this or that aspect of the human being. This might be man's soul, or the higher faculties thereof, or, most especially, the faculty of self-determination. Alternatively, the image could be sought in the soul's 'simplicity' or its 'immortality', or in its capacity for knowing God or for living in communion with him.[5] True, Irenaeus of Lyons, along with Gregory of Nyssa and, in a later age, Gregory Palamas, stress the body's participation in imagehood, and this brings one closer to the holistic view Lossky deems desirable. But for a writer who thinks that man is composed of not only soul (or spirit) and body but also of a hypostasis even this, better as it is, will not serve.

So what Lossky takes from the theological anthropology of the Fathers, at least in *The Mystical Theology of the Eastern Church*, is not their attempts to identify the locus of the image. It is their certainty that the making of man was and is a different kind of activity from the making of the rest of creation. For the Book of Genesis, man was created by God's own 'hands'—explained by Irenaeus as a reference to the Father's Word and Spirit, and a divine breath was infused into him. A passage from Gregory of Nazianzus' *Dogmatic Poems* VIII, already excerpted in *Théologie dogmatique*, and now cited in exposition of the 'infusion of the Breath', by ascribing to man a 'divine part' would almost seem to call the soul uncreated. But Lossky explains this language, which (as we have noted) crops up in a somewhat different idiom in Bulgakov's writing, as the 'presence' of 'divine power' in the soul, or a 'participation in the divine energy' that is 'proper to the soul'.[6] For his own part, Lossky would understand such language to denote the soul's creation in grace, a claim that forms one crucial factor in his resolution of the 'image of God' question.

The other key factor is found in his assertion that, if the image (whatever it is) really represents its Archetype, namely God, it must in any case be inherently unknowable. If this be true it explains, of course, the difficulty experienced by the Fathers.

Theological Anthropology

Bringing together the two factors in his analysis, Lossky concludes, 'We can only conceive [the image] through the idea of participation in the infinite goodness of God'.[7] Since, however, freedom is a necessary condition of man's appropriating such 'participation', what we are looking for is what it is about human beings that can be called at once unknowable in depth and yet free in its formal constitution. There can only be one answer: the hypostasis, the person. It is personhood which is the real basis of being 'in the image of God'.

In humanity the world is personalized, and this, not its cosmic structure, is what gives it the affinity to the divine. That affinity *may* allow creation—in dependence on man's conduct and destiny—to become a recipient of God's emancipating and transfiguring grace. Compare Romans 8:19–21:

> If creation is full of expectancy, that is because it is waiting for the sons of God to be made known. Created nature has been condemned to frustratuin; not for some deliberate fault of its own, but for the sake of him who so condemned it, with a hope to look forward to; namely, that nature in its turn will be set free from the tyranny of corruption, to share in the glorious freedom of God's sons.

Contrary to much early-twenty-first-century eco-thinking, Lossky talks not about reintegrating the human species into 'Gaia', or into the cosmic whole, but, contrary-wise, of bringing the cosmos into the 'anthroposphere', as man, through his body, 'hypostatizes' the world of material things.[8] That is the message, in these matters, of *Théologie dogmatique*.

In *Essai sur la théologie mystique de l'Église d'Orient*, in contrast to the lectures on dogmatics, we do not hear so much of this cosmic dimension. But the former insists on an ontology, if not a cosmology, for its anthropology nonetheless. While the divine image is multiplied into a plurality of human hypostases, this should not be regarded as obscuring the unity of the common nature of *homo sapiens*. The 'image' was given in Adam precisely for all human beings who would come to be from his stock. Here Lossky interjects a warning. After the Fall we do not experience, much less conceive, personhood as we should. Instead we confuse it, disastrously so, with mere individuality.

The contrast between personhood and individuality is a major preoccupation of Lossky's as it was for the French Catholic philosophers—including social philosophers—who were his contemporaries (Jacques Maritain, already mentioned in this context, and Emmanuel Mounier (1905–50) are two names that come at once to mind[9]).

> We are in the habit of thinking of these two terms, person and individual, almost as though they were synonyms . . . But, in a certain sense, individual and person mean opposite things, the word individual expressing a certain mixture of the person with elements which belong to the common nature, while person, on the other hand, means that which distinguishes it from nature.[10]

And Lossky puts forward an example, based on a rather pejorative reading of the term 'character'.

> The man who is governed by his nature and acts in the strength of his natural qualities, of his 'character', is the least personal. He sets himself up as an individual, proprietor of his own nature, which he sets against the natures of others and regards as his 'me', thereby confusing person and nature.[11]

This is an 'ego'-ism: what the Byzantine ascetical tradition calls disordered self-love, *philautia*, and the Russian *samost*.

Trinitarian imagehood

One dimension has not yet appeared. Man's being in the image, if it is rooted in his personhood, refers him to the personal God. But does it refer him to the tri-personal God, the Holy Trinity? Lossky does not want to answer with an outright 'No'. In what, then, might our analogically Trinitarian imagehood consist? Considering the idea (to be put into wider circulation by Hans Urs von Balthasar) that such imagehood consists of male, female, and child, he quickly rejects it on two grounds. Firstly, a child is dependent on its two-personed source, but this is not the case with any Trinitarian person, unless we adopt the *Filioque*. Secondly, a child can be replicated at will as more children are planned or at least come along. For Lossky, it is not the nuclear family which reflects the Trinitarian dimension of the image but a human being in-relation-to-his-neighbour-and-to-God. This is slightly odd inasmuch as the third party Lossky substitutes for the claims of child—namely, God—is one on which (*par excellence*!) the two other parties are themselves dependent. And this of course raises, in inverted form, the same objection of non-analogy Lossky had sought to avoid by rejecting the 'family' proposal. The image seen as myself-with-my-neighbour-with God does, however, enjoy one compensating advantage. It enables Lossky to speak about the twofold love command—love of neighbour, love of God—in its unitary or two-in-one character as the key to growth in the image through the life of discipleship as the Gospels and the apostolic Letters depict that life. ('Unitary', or 'two-in-one' because one cannot love the God one has not seen if one does not love the neighbour one has seen.) We note that Lossky does not comment, in *Théologie dogmatique*, on the influential 'psychological' analogy for our Trinitarian imagehood outlined (in various versions) by Augustine in his *De Trinitate*, and this despite his respect for Augustine's theological contribution—something not shared by all Orthodox writers by any manner of means. In Chapter Five, however, we have seen him reject the impoverished version (when compared with Augustine's richly orchestrated discussion in the *De Trinitate*) that emerged as a commonplace in subsequent Western Scholasticism.[12]

In the image and likeness

The posthumous essay collection *In the Image and Likeness of God*, as its overall title indicates, is the fullest place to look for Lossky's reflections on man made in the divine image, a common topos as this is in patristic and mediaeval thought. Arguably, despite the relatively small number of directly pertinent biblical texts, the image doctrine is the foundational teaching of Christian anthropology—as well as being one of the keys to the notion of God's self-manifestation in his Son or Word. Lossky's essay 'The Theology of the Image' does not have to proceed far before we come across the following resounding statement.

> We may say that for a theologian of the catholic tradition in the East and in the West, for one who is true to the main lines of patristic thought, the theme of the image (in its twofold acceptation—the image as the principle of God's self-manifestation and the image as the foundation of a particular relationship of man to God) must belong to the 'essence of Christianity'.[13]

Comparing two German books with the 'essence of Christianity' as their subject and title, Lossky finds in favour of the Catholic Romano Guardini (1885–1968) over against the Lutheran Adolf von Harnack (1851–1930) on this very basis.[14]

Lossky does not deny the comparative paucity of the theme of the image in Scripture—above all in the proto-canonical books. It seems surprising, granted the evident importance of this language to the author of the Genesis creation account, that it does not recur at least at intervals in the prophetic books, or in the Psalter, or in Job, or that highly humane presentation of Mosaic Yahwism we call the Book of Deuteronomy. But so it is. Unlike, say, such giants of twentieth-century Protestant theology as Karl Barth (1886–1968) and Emil Brunner (1889–1966), as well as Anders Nygren, Lossky does not draw the conclusion that the recrudescence of image language in the Greek of the deutero-canonical literature is either irrelevant to the main lines of biblical revelation or an undesirable distortion of those lines by influence from the pagan philosophical schools of Platonism and Stoicism. Lossky's 'take' is quite different:

> One may wonder if this recourse to a new vocabulary, rich in philosophical tradition, was not the answer to an internal need of Revelation itself, which thus received in the last stage of the Old Covenant an increase of light which was to lend new coloring to the sacred books of the Jews.[15]

In view, then, of the imminence of the Incarnation, that would be the crowning of the hope of Israel. Not by accident did the Diaspora, so as to 'keep alive the word of Truth revealed to Israel', give that word this kind of expression, allowing the deutero-canonical authors to 'open up a theology of the image on the eve of the advent of Christianity'.[16]

That is a statement about the theology of the image in the perspective of fundamental theology. Its especial emphasis—to which Lossky will return in the conclusion of his essay—lies on the way this biblical teaching (not in spite of but because of the lateness of much of its date) prepares the way for the appearance of the perfect Image, the God-man Jesus Christ.

But we have not heard anything yet of how Lossky understands the image here in the context of theological anthropology itself. And in fact as the rest of his essay unfolds we discover that his interest in the image theme is above all to do with the theology of God, not of humans. The reason for that—in a patristic perspective—surely astonishing choice will prove to be one we have already touched on: the impossibility of locating any specific dimension of human nature (rationality, say, or language, or the capacity for spiritual love) as the bearer of the image.[17]

Lossky probably concedes too much to critics of the Great Church when he allows that, read in their historical context, the biblical passages on imagehood have 'nothing (or next to nothing) which would permit us to base either a theognosis or a religious anthropology on the notion of the image of God'.[18] Indeed, he almost goes so far as to turn on its head the Genesis teaching about man as the image of God in the temple of the world, allowing that the overall meaning of the passage may be that 'God reveals Himself as transcendent to every image which could make known His nature'.[19] But he makes this concession so as to give the greater force to the remainder of the part-citation just quoted. The same biblical God 'does not refuse personal relationship, living intercourse with men, with a people; He speaks to them and they reply, in a series of concrete situations which unfold as sacred history'.[20] The Hebrew Bible reveals not God's nature but his mysterious design for human beings—and yet the way that design is revealed, which is personal, using (not least in the supreme Old Testament disclosure of the divine

Name at Sinai) the personal pronoun 'I', shows that the Absolute-in-history wishes to be addressed by us as 'Thou', 'intolerable folly to the Greeks' though this is.[21]

The mysterious design of 'I am who I am' culminates in fact in the revelation of God's being or nature in a perfect Image, his Son made man, and the blinding, or, rather, illuminating, light of the Incarnation and Pentecost is the more splendid by contrast with the Old Testament shadows that came before.

> If He excludes images and condemns the curiosity of those who would pry into His transcendent nature, it is because the initiative of revelation belongs to Him alone in the history of the people which He has chosen for the recapitulation, in one unique event, of the whole of history and of the whole nature of the universe ... when God chose to reveal Himself fully to all men, to Jews and to Greeks, by the perfect Image who is of the same nature with Him, and to allow Himself to be known in the Spirit who searches the depths of His nature.[22]

And now Lossky can come clean. So far from being a sympathizer with the radical critics of image theology he holds that with the Incarnation, Christianity's foundational dogma, '"image" and "theology" are linked so closely together that "theology of the image" might almost become a tautology'—even if the proper rendering of such a theology also requires a strenuous intellectual effort, so as to clarify the force and scope of that crucial 'image' term.

If 'theology of the image' is for Lossky a quasi-tautology, then for him all theology has to do with 'the image'. The God-Image, the Son, gives access to the God-Archetype, the Father, without—so Lossky stresses—any implication of the inferiority of image to archetype (as, philosophically speaking, it would be more natural to suppose). In the words of Gregory of Nyssa cited here by Lossky, 'The Son is in the Father as the beauty of the image resides in the archetypal form ... The Father is in the Son as the archetypal beauty remains in its image'.[23] And using that distinction between nature and person inevitable in Christianity once we have accepted the divinity of Christ (as God, he is what the Father is, but not who he is), we must say, with Gregory of Nazianzus, that the Son is the 'concise declaration of the nature of the Father'.[24] He is—this time with St John of Damascus—the Father's 'natural image': 'in everything like the Father, excepting the characteristics of unbegottenness and fatherhood.[25] So likewise the Spirit can be called by the Greek Fathers the image of the Son, inasmuch as he makes manifest the Son's natural qualities as God though not his hypostatic uniqueness. The Trinitarian use of the term 'image', so Lossky sums up, denotes, therefore, 'one divine Person who shows in himself the nature or the natural attributes while referring them to another Hypostasis: the Holy Spirit to the Son, the Son to the Father'.[26] It is the Image of God as manifested in the God-Man that makes him the perfect Icon the New Testament letters declare him to be.

Thus when in Christian anthropology (so at last we return to this!) we say of human beings that they are in the 'image of God', we are not, for Lossky, indicating a relationship of participation, much less a 'kinship'—what the Greeks called *syngeneia*—with God.[27] The *diastēma*, the infinite distance between uncreated and created natures, renders this out of the question. Instead, we are instituting an analogy: in human beings too, we are saying, nature is not personhood, personhood is irreducible to nature, just as it is in God.

The image, then, for this, the most subtle version of Lossky's interpretation of Genesis 1:28, is best thought of as lying in the dialectic between nature and person, or, if one prefers, in the transcendence of person vis-à-vis nature, and not in some aspect of the nature (or, for that matter, of the person). Lossky warns that theologians who insist on looking for some such aspect that makes human beings 'the image' will never free themselves from the error of the Hellenes, in ascribing a natural kinship between man and God. Adoptive filiation, whereby we become sons (and daughters) by grace is something entirely different from such putative kinship. This remained Lossky's steady conviction, as our next section makes plain.

Understanding the 'person'

When writing *ex professo* on the topic of 'The Theological Notion of the Person' in *In the Image and Likeness of God* Lossky confines his discussion to one single issue. If the key to divine personhood is the irreducibility of hypostasis to *ousia*, person to nature (or, if one prefers, to substance, or essence), can we say Christianity has found—before Lossky, he means!—that the same key opens the mystery of human personhood as well? We can at least say that in the case of Jesus Christ, as understood by Chalcedonian orthodoxy, the hypostasis which enhypostatized the human nature of Jesus was irreducible to his human essence, for it was divine. And this cannot but be significant.

> [H]ere the hypostasis of the assumed humanity cannot be reduced to the human substance, to that human individual who was registered with the other subjects of the Roman Empire under Augustus. But at the same time, one can say that it was God who was registered according to His humanity precisely because that individual human, that 'atom' of human nature counted with the others, was not a human 'person'.[28]

It must follow, in fact, that in the case of every human individual, it is possible to distinguish hypostasis from nature. But how?

'A person' is an answer to the question, 'Who?' 'A nature' (or substance, or essence) is an answer to the question, 'What?' Hence Richard of St Victor was right, in Lossky's judgement, to reject as insufficient Boethius' celebrated definition of a person as 'an individual substance of a reasonable nature'. Richard found a good replacement for the Boethian definition in his doctrine of divine persons. But unfortunately he made no attempt to find an alternative formula for human persons.[29] One avenue it might be fruitful to explore is whether 'personhood' denotes the higher, spiritual powers of a human individual, those faculties whose exercise perfect that individual in their being as *homo sapiens*. But we soon find, shows Lossky, that to go down this path brings us ineluctably to the Christological heresy of Apollinarius of Laodicea for whom the divine Logos took the place

Theological Anthropology

of the higher powers of human nature in Jesus's case. (Anxiety that this was the case in Bulgakov's Christology had helped to propel, we may remember from Chapter One, the *ukaz* of Metropolitan Sergeĭ.) To locate human personhood in the higher faculties of man—let us call them compendiously, with the Greek Fathers, *nous*—will mean that we have to amputate them from the humanity of the Jesus who had no human hypostasis and, with the ancient heretic, ascribe the spiritual intelligence of the Word incarnate exclusively to the Logos he embodied. (In the *Essai*, however, despite his difficulties with Bulgakov, Lossky came within hailing distance of his position in treating the *nous* as the 'seat' of the hypostasis.[30]) Lossky finds this example most telling despite its uniqueness—for there has been, of course, only one Incarnation. What it suggests is that, in the case of human personhood universally, we will:

> not find any definable property or attributes which would be foreign to the *phusis* [the nature] and would belong exclusively to the person taken in itself. Under these conditions, it will be impossible for us to form a concept of the human person, and we will have to content ourselves with saying: 'person' signifies the irreducibility of man to his nature—'irreducibility' and not 'something irreducible' precisely because it cannot be here a question of 'something' distinct from 'another nature' but of *someone* who is distinct from his own nature.[31]

And Lossky seeks to explain to the reader that distinctness by writing further of 'someone who goes beyond his nature while still containing it', or again, who 'makes it exist as human nature by this overstepping and yet does not exist in himself beyond the nature which he "enhypostatizes" and which he constantly exceeds'.[32] These somewhat cumbersome expressions are intended to show the difficulty—as well as the possibility—of speaking of the nature/person dialectic, of the only apophatically describable locus of the image.

The theological story of man

Lossky's ontological investigations typically morph at this point into something more like a narrative. Thus in *Théologie dogmatique* the rest of Lossky's theological anthropology tells a story: of Adam and the Fall, of the Old Testament beginnings of salvation, and of their issue in redemptive Incarnation.

On the humanity of Adam Lossky is strongly Maximian. Maximus sees Adam as called to unify—by a series of syntheses made possible through the cooperation of human freedom and God's grace—various divisions found in reality at the primordial beginning of human life. These divisions occur *a.* between the human sexes, *b.* between the earthly paradise and the rest of earth, *c.* between heaven and earth, and *d.* between the created and the uncreated (the most fundamental division of all). Through countervailing syntheses, *a.* in a union of the sexes deeper than the external and thus a reclamation of eros, *b.* by a transforming of the non-paradisal earth into paradise, *c.* through unifying the total environment in spirit and body and entering upon the life of the (heavenly) angels, Adam would *d.* give all creation back to God and receive in return the riches of the divine nature in deification. This was the vocation never achieved, owing to the Fall. It is also the vocation picked up in a new way by the Second Adam, the Word incarnate, who by a new creation will surmount the divisions which since the Fall have been rendered sinful and not just the challenge they were to the First.

How so? In the Incarnation *a.* his Virgin Mother will show forth the two ways of reclaiming eros that are Christian matrimony and monasticism or virginal asceticism. In his Death and Burial *b.* the Incarnate One will, through the contact of his body with the earth of our mortality, make all places into Paradise. In his Resurrection *c.* he will in his glorious risen body unite earth and heaven, and in his Ascension the world below with the realm of the angels. Finally, his Session at the Father's right *d.* takes our humanity into the life of the Trinity as the first-fruits of our deification. And Lossky concludes, 'We can, therefore, re-find the fullness of our Adamic nature only in Christ'.[33]

Theological Anthropology

In two subsidiary discussions, triggered by passages from the Greek Fathers, Lossky opines (disagreeing with Gregory of Nyssa) that the character of 'paradisal sexuality', before the Fall, is 'almost entirely unknown to us',[34] while (agreeing with St Irenaeus) that Adam before the Fall was neither mortal nor immortal, for his nature was 'rich with possibilities' that only his confrontation with the two 'trees'—the Tree of Life, and the Tree of the Knowledge of Good and Evil—could determine.[35] The Tree of Life, i.e. participation in the divine life, was the source of the fruit Adam was offered, but he chose instead to eat of the other Tree, consciously entertaining the thought of evil which, in a paradisal world, should never have entered his mind. Had he nourished himself with the divine presence, the difference between good and evil would not have arisen for him. Still, that there should have been some sort of *testing* (Lossky uses the Greek word *peira*[36]) for human liberty was in itself according to God's will. So much is implied by the sacred writer when he has God communicate the—highly dangerous—information that the Tree of the Knowledge of Good and Evil grows in the paradise garden.

Lossky's account of original sin enables him to offer a little theodicy, opening by pointing out how 'the problem of evil is essentially a Christian problem'.[37] It depends on the claim that the world is inherently good. 'For a lucid atheist, evil is only an aspect of the absurd; for a blind atheist it is the temporary result of a still imperfect organization of society and the universe.'[38] Lossky finds that the privative theory of evil predominant in the Fathers (evil is, literally, nothing—an absence of what should exist) was persuasive for Manichees but not necessarily for moderns who are only too conscious of its terrifying power: probably a reference to political events in the first half of the twentieth century. Lossky applauds the suggestion of the French Oratorian Louis Bouyer (1913–2004) that the better—at any rate, the more concrete (and suitably anguished)—translation of the concluding petition of the Our Father runs 'Deliver us from the Evil One'.[39] Satan embodies the active element in evil, which is revolt against God.

Almost inevitably, that leads Lossky to find a place for an angelology—and not solely an anthropology—in *Théologie dogmatique*.

Despite his report that the Fathers and the Liturgy commonly speak of the angels as pure spirits, Lossky holds to the view that there is an angelic corporeality—to which he can appeal for support to St Bonaventure (1221–74) in the West and Bishop Ignatius Brianchaninov (1807–87) in the East. Though he notes the place of Thomas as one of the gainsayers of this hypothesis, he rallies to Aquinas's angelology in a remarkable manner when he proposes that each angel is a 'nature' (Thomas would say a 'species'), and forms an 'intelligible universe' of its own.[40] The unity of the angelic realm is thus *sui generis*, and Lossky suggests—without following up his own proposal—that music and mathematics may conceivably furnish analogies for it.

The Luciferian sin was the pride that generated revolt against God—so far nothing different from the Latin Fathers and John Milton (1608–74) in *Paradise Lost*. But in adding that the first to fall was the first to be called to deification, Lossky adds a thesis of his own. 'The root of sin is thus the thirst for auto-deification, the hatred of grace.'[41] That turns at once to hatred of the God on whom the archangel depends, and then hatred of being, the primordial medium of the God-angel relation, the consequence of which is the urge to destroy, or at least to disfigure. In the wider sub-angelic world lying open to the Evil One, 'the drama which began in heaven is pursued on earth'.[42]

Lossky describes the upshot of the Fall in terms that are far from minimalist. Man fell into the 'possession' of the Evil One. His nature became 'against nature'. The spirit turned 'parasite' on the soul, the soul on the body, the body on the earthly world.[43] Sin makes nature incapable of receiving grace, whilst death, the other principal 'fruit' of the Fall, renders 'non-being a paradoxical and tragic reality'.[44] Hard, yet a divine pedagogy is at work to prevent total disintegration in the face of evil. Chastizement follows, but mortality at least ensures that man's monstrous condition is not eternalized. A promise is also made (without citing it explicitly Lossky is thinking of the *Protoevangelium* in Genesis 3:15, 'I will establish a feud between thee and the woman, between thy offspring and hers; she is to crush thy head, while thou dost lie in ambush at her heels'). A life-jacket is to be thrown to the shipwrecked, to enable them to resume the journey—for, in keeping with his overall soteriology, Lossky insists that redemption—essentially a rescue operation, from sin and death—is not the goal. The goal is, as from the beginning, deification, namely, union with God.

It is here that for Lossky the message to Israel finds its meaning. Man's condition has become that of a 'dolorous passivity, consisting first and foremost of a tenacious nostalgia for paradise rather than a more and more conscious waiting for salvation'.[45] The Old Testament revelation is intended to shake up that condition. It describes a 'slow progress towards Christ in the course of which the divine "pedagogy" seeks to render possible the fulfillment of the promise made at the moment of the punishment'.[46] Before re-telling the main story-line of the Old Testament (from Cain and Seth to Noah and Babel, from the patriarchs to Moses and the prophets), Lossky offers an overall evaluation of its soteriological status, its standing vis-à-vis the regime of grace. While the Old Testament did not know 'intimate sanctification' it did know holiness in some sense, since grace aroused it 'from without', as an 'effect'.[47] God is electing instruments of his will, which indeed requires certain gifts of grace to bring about the 'obedience and purity' that are needed for these servants of his (the prophets are especially in mind).[48] But the Lord is not yet inaugurating a relationship of the perfect inter-penetration of nature and grace, the happy lot of the Christian saint.

> Holiness as the active sanctification of the whole being and the free assimilation of human nature to God's will not be able to show itself until after the work of Christ, by apprehension of that work.[49]

Especially notable is Lossky's characterization of the overall direction of the Old Testament economy: 'The further God withdraws, the more the prayer of man deepens; the more election becomes limited the more its goal becomes universal: right up to the supreme purity of the Virgin capable of having as her child humanity's Saviour.'[50] It forms a suitable proemium to Mariology.

Notes

1   Cf. Gregory of Nyssa, *On the Making of Man*, 16. Lossky cites the same text in *The Mystical Theology of the Eastern Church*, p. 114.

2   Gregory of Nazianzus, *Dogmatic Poems*, 8.

3   It should be noted, however, that Lossky emphasizes human freedom and responsibility as the principal sign of the image in human persons. The question may well be asked, How does he reconcile the denial that human nature (as distinct from human personhood) is in the image when in his Christology he accepts, with the Sixth Ecumenical Council, that from the two natures of the God-man there follow his two wills? Lossky can say, dismissively, of nature that 'Nature cannot be kept for itself. In abandoning nature one acquires grace', but he adds, however, in the next breath, 'and it is then that nature becomes transparent, resembling [God]', Lossky, *Théologie dogmatique*, p. 105.

4   Lossky, *The Mystical Theology of the Eastern Church*, p. 115.

5   *Ibid.*

6   *Ibid.*, p. 118.

7   *Ibid.*

8   Lossky, *Théologie dogmatique*, p. 100.

9   Emmanuel Mounier, *Le Personnalisme* (Paris: Presses Universitaires de France, 1949).

10   Lossky, *The Mystical Theology of the Eastern Church*, p. 121.

11   *Ibid.*, pp. 121–2.

12   An excellent account of Augustine's free-flowing thought on the matter is given in Edmund Hill, 'Introduction', in Augustine, *The Trinity* (Brooklyn, NY: New City Press, 1991), pp. 18–59.

13   Lossky, *In the Image and Likeness of God*, p. 126.

14   Adolf von Harnack, *Das Wesen des Christentums* (Leipzig: Hinrichs, 1900); Romano Guardini, *Das Wesen des Christentums* (Würzburg: Werkbund Verlag, 1949). As might be expected, the second was a response from the Catholic side to the phenomenal success, in successive printings, of the first.

15   Lossky, *In the Image and Likeness of God*, p. 128.

16   *Ibid.*

17   The diversity is well-evidenced in A.-G. Hamman, *L'Homme, image de Dieu. Essai d'une anthropologie chrétienne dans l'Église des cinq premiers siècles* (Paris: Desclée, 1987).

18   Lossky, *In the Image and Likeness of God*, p. 129.

19   *Ibid.*

20 *Ibid.*

21 *Ibid.*, p. 130.

22 *Ibid.*, p. 133.

23 Gregory of Nyssa, *Against Eunomius* 1.

24 Gregory of Nazianzus, *Theological Orations* 4, 20.

25 John of Damascus, *On the Holy Images* III, 18.

26 Lossky, *In the Image and Likeness of God*, p. 138.

27 *Ibid.*, p. 137.

28 *Ibid.*, p. 118.

29 Lossky is dependent here on M. Bergeron's study, 'La Structure du concept latin de personne', Université de Montréal, Institut des études médiévales, *Études d'histoire littéraire et doctrinale du XIIIe siècle* (Paris and Ottawa: Vrin, 1932).

30 Lossky, *The Mystical Theology of the Eastern Church*, p. 201.

31 Lossky, *In the Image and Likeness of God*, p. 120.

32 *Ibid.*

33 *Ibid.*, p. 107.

34 *Ibid.*, p. 109.

35 *Ibid.*, p. 110.

36 *Ibid.*, p. 115.

37 *Ibid.*, p. 111.

38 *Ibid.*

39 *Ibid.*, p. 112.

40 *Ibid.*, p. 114.

41 *Ibid.*

42 *Ibid.*, p. 115.

43 *Ibid.*, pp. 115–16.

44 *Ibid.*, p. 117.

45 *Ibid.*

46 *Ibid.*, p. 118.

47 *Ibid.*, p. 119.

48 *Ibid.*

49 *Ibid.*

50 *Ibid.*, pp. 119–20.

✢ 9 ✢

The Mother of God and the Saints

IN *The Meaning of Icons*, consulted above for its Christology, Lossky also introduces icons of the Mother of God. Lossky accepts from Catholic Mariology the term 'hyperdulia' as a correct way of denoting the difference between veneration of the Virgin and that of other saints—and indeed of the angels, for Mary is, in the words of a hymn sung at the Byzantine Liturgy, 'exalted above the Cherubim'. As we shall find in Lossky's dogmatic Mariology (not that iconological interpretation would strike him as something different from dogmatics), the divine motherhood is central to his interpretation. When St John of Damascus writes, 'The name of *Theotokos* contains the whole history of the divine economy in the world', he is referring to the pivotal role of Mary's consent to the Incarnation—not an isolated choice but, in Lossky's words, the proper act of a 'creature rendered apt by the Holy Spirit to receive in her womb the Word of the Father come into the world'.[1] The Damascene text just cited was evidently a favourite of Lossky's. It has already appeared in the Christological chapter of the present study, figuring as it does in the discussion of the Economy of the Son in *The Mystical Theology of the Eastern Church*.

Lossky's iconological Mariology

In *The Meaning of Icons* Lossky follows up his short introduction to Marian icons in general by a quartet of contributions on the icon-type known as the Mother of God *Hodegitria*—'she who points the way'. Lossky by no means commits himself to the full-blown legendary account for which the evangelist Luke sent his own painting of the Messianic Child and his Mother to Antioch, and specifically to Theophilus, the recipient of his Gospel book, from which metropolis the fifth-century empress Eudoxia had it transferred to Constantinople.[2] But he notes how, at any rate, 'this history was generally admitted at Byzantium towards the end of the sixth century when the name Hodegitria appears for the first time on seals'.[3] By the ninth century, that name had transferred itself to the entire series of icons that show the Mother of God presenting her Son—who is seated, with back erect, on his mother's left arm, holding a scroll and giving a blessing—presumably to his and her people, the Church of the faithful.

Lossky illustrates the *Hodegitria* type with a trio of icons. These are reproductions of the celebrated miraculous icons of Smolensk (closest to the Byzantine Hodegetria, and thus to the description just given), Tikhvin (here the Child turns somewhat towards his mother, and she towards Him), and Kazan (an even more pronounced inclination of Mary's head towards Jesus). Lossky notes how, 'without looking directly at Her Son, the Mother of God seems to contemplate His mission of Saviour come into the world to suffer the Passion'.[4] On the basis of his pre-Revolutionary experience, Lossky thought the Kazan image 'perhaps the icon of the Mother of God that is most widespread in Russia'.[5]

He was evidently interested by the question of the relation of Mary to the Passion of Christ. Of the remaining seven images of the Theotokos, the Mother-with-her-Son, that are discussed in the Marian section of *The Meaning of Icons*, he left Ouspensky to write all but one. The one in question was 'The Mother of God of the Passion'—in Russian, *Strastnaya*. Disappointingly for anyone seeking to discover how closely (or otherwise) Lossky might approach the Western Catholic theme of Mary's role as *auxiliatrix Passionis* (or even, in the strongest language used, 'co-redemptrix' at the moment of the Atonement), Lossky has little to say about the Marian doctrine encapsulated in this icon-type. He confines himself to interpreting the facial expression of the Mother of God in his exemplar (a triptych from a Parisian private collection). It indicates, he thinks, 'mournful resignation'.[6] Most of the space he devotes to the *Strastnaya* is given over in fact to a presentation of the many other figures on the side panels of the triptych, or to speculating about the possible monastic provenance of the icon in seventeenth-century Russia.

The results of this Mariological enquiry so far may seem a trifle meagre. In part that is a consequence of the division of labour in this dually authored work. But, good to say, there is more to come. The section of *The Meaning of Icons* on the great Marian feasts enabled Lossky to return to the afore-mentioned themes by way of describing the narrative icons that represent the episodes those festivals celebrate. And here the diet he provides is theologically more nourishing.

Lossky's account of the iconography of the Birth of Mary—to begin there—does nothing to fuel Orthodox opposition to the Catholic doctrine of her immaculate conception. 'In the festival of the Nativity of the Mother of God (8 September), the Church celebrates the most holy human birth, whose "fruit most pure" was elect and sanctified from the moment of conception (Conception of St Anna, celebrated 9 December).'[7]

Lossky regards the Protoevangelium of James, the apocryphal source of claims about Mary's background and early life, much drawn-on by iconographers, as itself a composite work, some of which may well be more reliable than the rest. From this, and other early Christian but non-biblical texts, the Church retains, he writes, 'only such data as would throw into relief the scriptural and dogmatic truth: the descent from the race of David and the holy birth of the Virgin, chosen to give human nature to the Word of God'.[8] In one perspective, the ending of the long sterility of Anna is in line with other 'fertilizations' of barren women in the Hebrew Bible, imaginatively considered by Christian writers as 'prefigurations of the Resurrection'.[9] But from another viewpoint, Anna's experience is unique. The 'prefiguration' in question is of a higher order: 'in the person of St. Anna—a woman freed from her sterility to bring into the world a Virgin who would give birth to God incarnate—it is our nature which ceases to be sterile in order to start bearing the fruits of grace'.[10] The icon Lossky chooses here, by a contemporary iconographer, depicts Joachim and Anna, the 'ancestors of God' (the *theopatores*), as of greater stature than the other adult figures shown, with a view to accentuating their dignity. The event constitutes the 'stage that precedes the last decisive act, the Annunciation' when, quoting from Vespers of the feast in the Byzantine rite, Mary becomes the 'King's Palace' where the union of the natures proclaimed at Chalcedon is accomplished.[11] So much for her conception.

The Presentation of the Virgin, sometimes called her 'Entry' into the Temple, is more difficult to write about inasmuch as its historical foundation is, by any ordinary historiographical standards, decidedly unclear. Lossky cannot make a blanket acceptance of all the Protoevangelium of James has to say on this subject but he can pick and choose in the hope of identifying elements that belong to ecclesial memory rather than pious fiction. His key claim runs:

> [T]he Church breaks the silence of the Scriptures and shows us the incomprehensible ways of Providence, which prepare the receptacle of the Word, 'the Mother predetermined before the ages', 'preached by the prophets', now introduced into the Holy of Holies, like a 'Hidden Treasure of the Glory of God'.[12]

So Lossky does accept the historicity of Mary's 'entrance' beyond the court of the women, indeed, beyond the 'second veil', ushered in by Zechariah, the father of the Forerunner, reuniting in his person priestly and prophetic traditions in Israel. This major transgression of the Law (only the Jewish high priest could enter the Holy of Holies) was legitimate inasmuch as Zechariah saw in Mary the new (metaphorical) Ark of the Covenant—for the (literal) Ark, which had been present in the first Temple, was lost by the time of the building of the second. The Byzantine liturgy is clearly aware of the extraordinary nature of this claim, since at Vespers it observes, 'The angels were astonished to see the Virgin enter the Holy of Holies'. The Mary/Ark symbolism—also known in the West where *arca foederis* ('ark of the covenant) is a title used in the Litany of our Lady—lies behind the use of Psalm 131 (verse 8) at Vespers of the Assumption in the Byzantine rite: 'Go up, Lord, to Thy rest: Thou and the ark of Thy holiness', a joint reference, in context, to Christ's Ascension and Mary's Assumption.

In the seventeenth-century Russian icon, now in the Netherlands, which Lossky uses for his commentary, Mary appears twice, once stretching out her hands towards Zechariah as she begins to climb the steps towards the Holy of Holies, and then again, assisted by an angel as she approaches its doorway. Lossky believed that the iconographers were familiar with the exegetical tradition as found in Origen and others whereby the three divisions of the Temple symbolize three stages of spiritual life: purification, illumination, union.

With the Annunciation, a favoured and very ancient theme of Marian art in both East and West (Lossky refers to a second-century fresco of the scene in the Roman catacomb of Priscilla and there are two more, one in the Catacomb of SS Marcellinus and Peter, the other in the Catacomb of the Via Latina, discovered only in 1956), we are on more familiar ground. Lossky's theological reflections are quite elaborate. They turn on the possibility of singling out for special emphasis, or, alternatively, of synthesizing for richness of total effect, three distinct moments within the overall event.

Some icons emphasize the entry of the archangel and Mary's perturbation, shown in dropping the reel of thread she is holding. Others stress her prudence, exhibited in the way she places her hand before her breast with the palm held outwards, a sign of her intellectual perplexity. Others again lay the chief weight on her consent, manifested by the bow of her head. Evidently, the icons are highlighting one or another of three consecutive moments in a temporal sequence. Many icons, however, seek to combine all three phases as Mary turns her hand towards the angel in fear and questioning while also bowing to indicate her submission. Lossky considers this to be a 'synthesis of the psychological state of the Mother of God'.[13]

He is good on the angel, pointing out how, characteristically, Gabriel seems to be running. Holding a staff, the messenger's symbol, in one hand, he gestures towards Mary with the other in what Lossky terms a 'strong movement', which clinches the sense that this is an urgent communication of glad tidings. The Moscow School icon from the seventeenth century, now at Recklinghausen, which accompanies Lossky's text, has a peculiarity of note. The direction of the gaze of Gabriel and Mary is not towards each other. Rather, it converges on a point above their heads. It focuses in fact on a portion of a sphere (symbol of God the Father) from which rays (symbol of the Holy Spirit) are issuing. With this visual evidence Lossky juxtaposes a text from Vespers of the feast: 'The Angel serves the miracle, the virgin womb receives the Son; the Holy Spirit is sent down, the Father sends His favour from on high, and the transformation is made by mutual consent'.[14] As Lossky points out, Mary answers not the messenger but the Sender. That suggests how her consent will entail an active participation in the saving Economy unfolded from the Trinity itself.

The Dormition of the Mother of God is another Losskian choice within the co-authored study. Lossky sounds the beautiful theme, common in Orthodox preaching, of the Easter of summertime.

> This passage from death to life, from life to eternity, from terrestrial condition to celestial beatitude, establishes the Mother of God beyond the general Resurrection and the Last Judgement, beyond the Second Coming which will end the history of the world.[15]

The emphasis on the 'secret first-fruit' and the revelation of this 'secret' to the 'inner consciousness of the Church' is intended to differentiate Orthodoxy at this point from Roman Catholicism which defined Mary's *transitus* as public dogma in 1950.

Lossky does not concern himself with the formidably difficult question of the interrelation of the various *transitus* narratives of the Dormition, although at least in principle a search might identify original elements. He accepts at least three such elements, based notably on the sermon 'Praise on the Dormition' by the early-seventh-century Modestus of Jerusalem. And these are: the presence of the apostles, the appearance of Christ, and the return to life of the Virgin (as distinct from her exemption from dying). It is this trio of elements which defines, by and large, the iconographic representation of the 'falling asleep' in Orthodoxy. As Lossky sums up, 'the Mother of God lying on her deathbed, in the midst of the Apostles, and Christ in glory receiving in His arms the soul of His Mother.'¹⁶ But he also notes that there has also been a desire, if not more than occasionally (it is absent from the sixteenth-century Russian icon in the book), to indicate the bodiliness of Mary's entry into glory: in such cases the artist will depict her enthroned in a mandorla carried upwards by angels. If Jaroslav Pelikan—that learned Lutheran convert to Orthodoxy—is right, even the more customary iconography (he is discussing a twelfth-century example of it) implies Mary's entry into beatitude in both soul and body.

> At the centre of the plaque—in a striking reversal of the roles they took in the conventional icons of Mother and Child—was Christ in majesty with the infant Mary in his arms. And the adult Mary reposed in tranquillity, as she was about to be received into heaven—apparently in body as in soul, as the East and eventually the West came to affirm—where the process by which her humanity was made divine was completed.¹⁷

Finally, Lossky interprets the episode of the hostile Jew, who laid hands on her couch and lost them by an angelic sword, in terms of his theory of the Dormition as secret.

> The presence of this apocryphal detail in the liturgy and in the iconography of the feast is to recall that the end of the life on earth of the Mother of God is an intimate mystery of the Church which must not be exposed to profanation: inaccessible to the view of those without, the glory of the Dormition of Mary can be contemplated only in the inner light of Tradition.¹⁸

The last Marian feast-day treated by Lossky concerns a post-Assumption happening: the tenth-century Constantinopolitan Apparition of Mary to St Andrew the Fool in Christ and his disciple Epiphanius in the church of the Blachernae which gave rise to the festival known as the Protection (or Protecting Veil) of the Mother of God. The fifteenth-century Novgorod icon, at the time of the English-language edition at London's Temple Gallery, shows Mary standing in a posture of intercession above representatives of the faithful. Two angels hold the ends of a billowing veil—in the original legend, the Virgin, though unseen by all but the two visionaries, took off her veil and held it above the people gathered in the church. Below her in a central position stands St Romanos, known from his hymn writing as 'The Melodist'. As Lossky points out, the combination of figures is in no sense historical. Romanos lived three centuries before the event of the Protecting Veil, known in the Slavic lands as the *Pokrov*. He is depicted here because his feast day coincides with that of the Pokrov, and also owing to a Marian privilege all his own. According to his *vita*, he was a choir boy 'despised by his fellows, [who] received from the Mother of God, with the Christmas kontakion, the marvellous gift of hymnography', the ability to write good hymns.[19]

Lossky's dogmatic Mariology

It is convenient that Lossky's account of the Marian icons ends here, with Mary's relation to the Church, since despite the undoubted primacy of the divine motherhood in his Marian writing, that 'ecclesial' relation forms the other great theme of his Mariological reflections.

In the essay 'Panagia' ('The All Holy Woman'), included within *In the Image and Likeness of God*, Lossky makes the claim that 'Based on Christology, the dogma of the Mother of God has a strong Pneumatological accent, and through the double economy of the Son and the Holy Spirit, it is inextricably bound up with ecclesiological reality'.[20] That would suggest, then, that we might find in 'Panagia' two themes: Mary and her Child, the fruit of her Spirit-overshadowed womb, and Mary and the Church, founded by the Son but energized by the Holy Spirit.

The huge differences between the Christian confessions in their assessment of the role of Mary in the New Testament alerts Lossky to the need for some methodological preliminaries. On the one hand, he thinks it possible—up to a point—to defend a high Mariology on internal exegetical grounds. He selects a handful of texts by way of example. Thus for instance, in St Luke's Gospel, the Saviour appears to depreciate his natural mother (and his brethren) in his remark that 'my mother and my brothers are those who hear the word of God and do it' (Luke 8:21). Lossky points out how in the Third Gospel this incident follows immediately after the delivery of the Parable of the Sower where the Lord praises those who 'hearing the word, hold it fast in an honest and good heart' (Luke 8:15). That 'heart' is the faculty which 'elsewhere Christ exalts above the fact of corporeal maternity' (compare Luke 11:28). But, continues Lossky, such a faculty 'the Gospel attributes to no individual except the Mother of the Lord' (compare Luke 2:19).[21] Again, in St Matthew's Gospel (11:11, and there is also a parallel verse in St Luke at 7:28), Jesus says of John the Baptist that he is 'the greatest' of those born of women, excluding then, or so it would seem, any possible competing claim on behalf of Mary of Nazareth. Lossky appeals to the wider promise-fulfilment structure of the Bible to deflect this objection to Marian priority.

> If St. John the Baptist is called 'the greatest' of those before Christ, that is because the greatness of the All-Holy Mother of God belongs not only to the Old Testament, where she was hidden and does not appear, but also to the Church in which she realized her fullness and became manifest, to be glorified by all generations (Luke 1:48).[22]

On the other hand, Lossky is well aware of the methodological insufficiency of *sola scriptura* for any defence of the sort of veneration shown the Mother of the Lord by the Orthodox Church. In the first place, one needs that overall dogmatic determination of New Testament Christianity by which the Great Church defined Jesus Christ to be, on his Godward side, one in substance with the Father. But even that cannot suffice, since Barthians, for instance, accept the Nicene doctrine and its fruits at Ephesus and Chalcedon, yet reject the Marian cultus of Catholicism and Orthodoxy. As Lossky writes:

> This suffices to demonstrate that the Christological dogma of the *Theotókos* taken *in abstracto*, apart from the vital connection between it and the devotion paid by the Church to the Mother of God, would not be enough to justify the unique position, above all created beings, assigned to the Queen of Heaven, to whom the Orthodox liturgy ascribes 'the glory which is appropriate to God' (*hē theoprepēs doxa*).[23]

Without the witness of Church Tradition it would be impossible to justify orthopraxis in Mary's regard, but thanks to that Tradition, 'the holy memory of those who "hear and keep" the words of the revelation', the Church is assured in the rightness of the cultus she pays the Mother of the Lord.[24] In 'Panagia', revisiting for a moment the concept of Tradition, Lossky finds it to be the capacity, granted to the Church by the Holy Spirit, to comprehend the meaning of the Old Testament's fulfilment in the New. In this context, 'The Church's unlimited veneration of the Mother of God which, viewed externally, might seem to be in contradiction with the scriptural data, is spread far and wide in the Tradition of the Church and is the most precious fruit of Tradition'.[25] And as Lossky now goes on to say, not only is it Tradition's fruit it is also its 'germ' and 'stem'—by which he means, Mary is the matrix of Tradition as a whole. Although at the finding in the Temple she, though pondering, did not comprehend, that was only the beginning of an amazing journey.

> Before the consummation of the work of Christ, before the Day of Pentecost, before the Church, even she upon whom the Holy Spirit had come down to fit her for her part in the Incarnation of the Word had not yet attained the fullness which her person was called to realize.[26]

Even so, the 'pondering' already shows the Mother of God keeping and collecting the sayings that issue from the prophetic mind of her Son. That means for Lossky, the connection between the Church's guardianship of Tradition and the assimilating activity of the Virgin is already becoming plain. Just as only the Church can preserve the fullness of revelation, so at the inauguration of the Church's life, only the Mother of Jesus could 'fully realize in her consciousness all the import of the Incarnation of the Word, including the fact of her own divine maternity'.[27] Moreover, Mary does not simply stand comparison with the Church at her own level. She rises to a 'complete consciousness of all that the Holy Spirit says to the Church', in a 'fullness of grace appropriate to the age to come'.[28] This is not thinkable, says Lossky, unless she has been given the greatest possible plenitude of deifying grace.

The Mother of God and the Saints

Despite the exalted language (and concepts) in which Lossky's Mariology is couched, Lossky's Mary never loses touch with the lowly earth of her Israelite genealogy. She is the New Eve, yes. But then the history which joins the first Eve to the second must be crucial to her story. Herein lies Lossky's objection to the Catholic doctrine of the Immaculate Conception, at least in its most 'standard' version.

> She was not, at the moment of the Annunciation, in a state analogous to that of Eve before the Fall... The second Eve... heard and understood the angelic word in the state of fallen humanity. That is why this unique election does not separate her from the rest of humanity, from all her fathers, mothers, brothers, and sisters, whether saints or sinners, whose best part she represents.[29]

That is not, however, meant to keep claims for Mary's unique holiness within suitable bounds. Lossky himself expresses such claims in a deliberately unbounded way:

> [I]f in the person of the Mother of God we see the summit of Old Testament holiness, her own holiness is not limited thereby, for she equally surpassed the highest limits of the New Covenant, realizing the greatest holiness which the Church can attain.[30]

Lossky sees the drama of Mary's life in terms of two Pneumatological events: Annunciation and Pentecost (there is a glaring absence here: the Mother at the Cross). In a somewhat forced manner (acknowledged by the vague if regrettably commonplace adverbial phrase 'in a certain sense'), he sees the two descents of the Spirit upon her as parallel to the two post-Paschal communications of the Spirit to the apostles.[31] In St John's Gospel this takes the form of a conferral of something objective—the power to bind or loose, with which compare the objective gift of the new Life in Mary's womb. In the Acts of the Apostles what the Spirit gives the apostles is (on Lossky's interpretation) the wherewithal to realize Pentecostally personal holiness, with which compare Mary's share in the Cenacle experience when she 'received with the Church the last and only thing she lacked, so that she might grow "to mature manhood, to the measure of the stature of the fullness of Christ" (Eph 4:13)'.[32]

Granted that the suitability of Lossky's comparison does not leap to the eye, he offers a helpful elucidation. In each case, there is complementarity between the functional and the personal. The apostles must strive to attain the holiness without which their Church-task cannot be well served. So, analogously, 'the objective function of her divine maternity, in which [Mary] was placed on the day of the Annunciation will also be the subjective way of her sanctification . . .blessed is she who was not only the Mother of God but also realized in her person the degree of holiness corresponding to that unique function'.[33] Lossky approaches close to Bulgakov's sophiological Mariology when he writes of the Theotokos at the end of her early life that 'the historical development of the church and of the world has already been fulfilled, not only in the uncreated person of the Son but also in the created person of his Mother. This is why St Gregory Palamas calls the Mother of God "the boundary between the uncreated and the created".'[34] Her light must enhance — not extinguish — that of the other saints, to whom, in Lossky's footsteps I now turn.

The Saints

Lossky elected to write accounts of a number of the icons of particular saints: notably, from among the biblical figures discussed in *The Meaning of Icons*, the Archangel Michael (with Ouspensky), St John the Baptist, and the evangelists Luke and John; from the holy men and women of the Church of the patristic age St Demetrius of Thessalonica and St Simon Stylites, and from the mediaeval period St Gregory Palamas, to whose doctrine of grace he was of course strongly committed.

On the Archangel Michael, Lossky notes how seriously the Orthodox Liturgy takes angelic figures.

> The liturgical texts call them 'redoubtable, terrifying': 'let us rid our spirits of all corruptible nature, that our terrestrial lips may sing with fear the praise of the incorporeal forces, which are like fire, like flame, like light'.[35]

Evidently Lossky has no desire to underplay these and similar citations. His own comments, in framing extracts from the liturgical texts, also amplify them.

> Living in the Glory of the 'Triune Sun', the angelic spirits are deified creatures, vehicles of the uncreated glory: 'God-fearing embers, enflamed by the fire of the divine nature. 'Secondary lights', they spread through the universe 'the fire of the inaccessible Divinity, ceaselessly chanting with lips of flame the hymn of the Trinity: Holy, Holy, Holy our God'.[36]

Nevertheless, the exalted condition of the angels notwithstanding, the Economy of the Incarnation was hidden from them. Making his own the teaching of the apostolic letters on this subject, Lossky explains how they learn of it only through the mystery of the Church. In the words of Ephesians, 'The principalities and powers are to see, now, made manifest in the Church, the subtlety of God's wisdom' (3:10), and so, as I Peter puts it (1:12) 'now the angels can satisfy their eager gaze'.

Whatever the process by which knowledge of the Economy of the Incarnation—extending to the Ascension—entered angelic minds, at least we can say that angels are known to us via their 'ministry' as described in Scripture. And where the Archangel Michael is concerned the 'service' in question is military, in the sense, of course, of spiritual warfare. 'The angelic hosts have to defend the creation against the spiritual powers which seek to cast it into ruin.'[37] It is Michael's identification as captain of the host (compare the Apocalypse 12:7–9) that determines his iconography, which a Balkan image of the early seventeenth century, in the Temple Gallery of the early 1980s, exemplifies: the sword in his right hand is his ensign, while in the left he carries an image of Christ. A curious but recurrent feature is found in the ribbons that flow out from Michael's head. On Lossky's reading, they stand for attentive listening to the commands of God.

Lossky draws the reader's attention to the frequency of celebrations involving the holy Forerunner, St John the Baptist, in the Byzantine-rite Church. As always, liturgical prominence is a key to theological priority. Lossky stresses the kenotic aspect of St John's calling. John is the second Elijah but unlike the first, he did no miracle. In fact, he 'remained stripped of every outward sign of his vocation, to be nothing but "the voice of one crying in the wilderness, Make straight the way of the Lord"' (John 1:23).[38] John might seem not only to 'decrease' (John 3:30) but pretty well to disappear from the record. Pentecost reverses any such impression that kenosis means oblivion. 'After the Ascension of the Lord, the Church which will have received from heaven the baptism by the deifying fire of the Holy Ghost (Matthew 3:11) will in the end be able to exalt the Forerunner of Christ.'[39] On the Deisis he will take his place with the Theotokos on either side of the Lord.

Lossky exhibits two icons of John for readers' instruction. The first, in a private collection in France, has been removed from a sixteenth-century Deisis, as the saint's posture indicates. He is holding a scroll carrying the demand for repentance at the heart of his message (it is Matthew's version of his preaching which is cited, at 3:2 and 10). The shaggy locks and beard suggest to Lossky John's further significance as 'prototype of the great Christian anchorites', the monks of the desert.[40] The second icon shown, now in the Netherlands, is Greek, and painted slightly later. It portrays the Forerunner with the wings that allude to his messenger (*angelos*) role, as set out in Malachy 3:1, and echoed in Matthew 11:10. Lossky is able to cite research published in the journal of his erstwhile *alma mater*, the Russian academy at Prague, *Seminarium Kondakovianum*, which finds a Serbian anticipation of this iconography as early as the thirteenth century even though it is only three hundred years later that it becomes at all common.[41]

What does he find to say about images of the Evangelists? On St Luke he is brief. His chosen icon is a Novgorod School work now at Recklinghausen, the renowned German treasury of iconography. Citing the so-called Monarchian Prologue which offers biographical data of some interest, he notes only that the face expresses the 'pious attentiveness' appropriate to a hagiograph engaged in writing down a divinely inspired text.[42] On St John he is rather more forthcoming, as was patristic exegesis of the 'spiritual Gospel' (the phrase comes from a lost work of Clement of Alexandria, of which the relevant fragment is preserved in Eusebius' *Church History*).[43] Lossky not only underwrites Origen

The Mother of God and the Saints

of Alexandria's judgement that the Fourth Gospel is the 'principle' of the rest but finds it the explanation of why John appears first among the evangelists on the developed Byzantine icon-screen. A Moscow school icon of the sixteenth century, in the contemporary period held at the Temple Gallery, shows John listening, Luke-like, to the divine voice while also dictating to a scribe, named as Prochoros (one of the seven deacons mentioned in Acts 6: the identification is followed by 'several authors' for details of whom Lossky refers the reader to the learned researches of the Bollandists[44]). Unlike Western theologians Lossky is unable to make much of the eagle symbolism associated with John's Gospel, because the East, at any rate until the beginning of the early modern period, largely followed St Irenaeus in joining the lion to John and the eagle to Mark, rather than the other way round.[45] Only at the end of the sixteenth century, a generation or so after the icon chosen by Lossky, does the eagle symbol begin to replace the lion in Johannine iconography in Russia.

I turn now to the post-biblical saints, and first of all to two figures from the patristic age, the early-fourth-century Demetrius of Thessalonica and Simon (or Symeon) Stylites (*c.* 390–459). Lossky gives no explanation for his selection of saints but one plausible guess is that he wished to write about one martyr and one monk, the two most prestigious categories (and rightly so) of the time. Demetrius is the martyr, in fact in the Greek-speaking Church he gained the accolade *megalomartys*, 'the Great Martyr', possibly owing to the tradition that he had been named to proconsular rank by the emperor Diocletian before the latter discovered his protégé's religion. Appropriately enough, Lossky illustrates his account with a Greek icon from the mid-fifteenth century preserved in the Benaki Museum in Athens. Demetrius is kitted out in all the apparatus of a soldier (cuirass, buckler, lance, helmet) since, so Lossky argues, the Church does not oppose a Christian 'embracing the career of arms',[46] even if 'Christianity is not a social or political doctrine: its action on the external world is exercised in a realm deeper than that of human institutions'.[47] In the latter statement we can see reflected the careful apoliticism of his stance as a Russian émigré in inter-War Paris.

The Simon Stylites icon is a Russian work of the sixteenth century in France's Musée nationale. As his name implies, St Simon was a pillar saint, utilizing one of the broken remains of ancient masonry that were, presumably, a frequent feature of the long civilized Syrian countryside by the fifth century. The Russian artist shows his pillar as a kind of little tower with a staircase inside, which is not historically probable. Lossky explains the rationale of pillar-habitation. The renowned ascetic wanted to put a certain distance between himself and over-eager visitors. He took up his peculiar dwelling so as 'to preserve his solitude and his peace in prayer, without giving up providing for the needs of his disciples and his innumerable visitors'.[48] According to the *vitae* by the Antiochene theologian and historian Theodoret of Cyr, as well as by his own disciple, the otherwise unknown Anthony, Simon maintained a regular apostolate of teaching, exercised twice daily—one of the ways in which the Latin division of 'contemplative' and 'active' or 'apostolic' can break down when applied to the East. Lossky also mentions something which, as an Orthodox exiled to France, moved him greatly: the discovery that St Genevieve, the patroness of Paris, had received a message from the saint, via merchants travelling to Gaul. It was a miniature of what East–West relations had been—and might be again.

To illustrate the iconography of a bishop and doctor Lossky overleaps the better part of a thousand years to reach St Gregory Palamas, the fourteenth-century Byzantine 'preacher of grace'. For the icon selected the date is indicated, but not the location. It is in fact contemporary with the saint, and Lossky finds this a drawback for too much emphasis is laid on Gregory's appearance. The face 'expresses the fine intelligence of a dialectician, invincible in theological discussions, without allowing one to divine the inner life of a great contemplative'.[49] But while considering the chronological proximity of the iconographer to the subject to be, at least in this case, unfortunate, Lossky also maintains that, where 'Fathers' are concerned time is, in principle, irrelevant.

> Every bishop-theologian who has expressed the truth of the faith, defending it against error, once canonized is

venerated by the Orthodox Church as our father among the saints (*en hagiois patēr hēmōn*), independently of the epoch in which he lived.[50]

The 'patristic epoch', properly understood, has no end. Ecclesial fatherhood is never lacking in the Church. That comment may form a suitable transition to some consideration of Lossky's ecclesiology.

Notes

1 Lossky and Ouspensky, *The Meaning of Icons*, p. 76, citing John of Damascus, *On the Orthodox Faith* III. 12.

2 Gisela Kraut, *Lukas malt die Madonna: Zeugnisse zum künstlerischen Selbstverständnis in der Malerei* (Worms: Wernersche Verlagsgesellschaft, 1986) is an intriguing study stimulated by the legendary account.

3 Lossky and Ouspensky, *The Meaning of Icons*, p. 80.

4 *Ibid.*, p. 88.

5 *Ibid.*.

6 *Ibid.*, p. 102.

7 *Ibid.*, p. 145.

8 *Ibid.*, pp. 145–6.

9 *Ibid.*, p. 146.

10 *Ibid.*

11 Cited *ibid.*

12 *Ibid.*, p. 153, citing extracts from the Troparion for the Presentation of the Holy Virgin in the Temple.

13 *Ibid.*, p. 172.

14 Cited *ibid.*, pp. 172–3.

15 *Ibid.*, p. 213.

16 *Ibid.*, pp. 213–14.

17 Jaroslav Pelikan, *Mary through the Centuries. Her Place in the History of Culture* (New Haven, CT, and London: Yale University Press, 1996), pp. 207–8.

18 Lossky and Ouspensky, *The Meaning of Icons*, p. 214.

19 *Ibid.*, p. 152.

20 Lossky, *In the Image and Likeness of God*, p. 195.

21 *Ibid.*, p. 199.
22 *Ibid.*, p. 201.
23 *Ibid.*, p. 196.
24 *Ibid.*, p. 198.
25 *Ibid.*, pp. 198–9.
26 *Ibid.*, p. 200.
27 *Ibid.*
28 *Ibid.*
29 *Ibid.*, p. 204.
30 *Ibid.*
31 *Ibid.*, p. 206.
32 *Ibid.*
33 *Ibid.*, pp. 206, 207.
34 *Ibid.*, p. 208. For Bulgakov's Mariology, see Nichols, *Wisdom from Above*, pp. 240–53.
35 Lossky and Ouspensky, *The Meaning of Icons*, p. 108.
36 *Ibid.*
37 *Ibid.*
38 *Ibid.*, p. 104.
39 *Ibid.*
40 *Ibid.*
41 Cited *ibid.*, p. 106.
42 *Ibid.*, p. 112.
43 Eusebius, *Ecclesiastical History* VI, 14 cited *ibid.*, p. 113.
44 *Ibid.*
45 Irenaeus, *Against the Heresies* II. 8.
46 Lossky and Ouspensky, *The Meaning of Icons*, p. 133.
47 *Ibid.*
48 *Ibid.*, p. 129.
49 *Ibid.*, p. 119.
50 *Ibid.*

✢ 10 ✢

The Church and her Mysteries

Lossky's discussion of the Church in *Théologie dogmatique* opens by rejecting certain criticisms by the French Dominican Yves Congar (1904–95) in the latter's ground-breaking 1937 charter of Catholic ecumenism, *Chrétiens désunis*.[1] There Congar had suggested that the Orthodox do little in the way of reflection on the Church-organism. Lossky replies that the canonical tradition of Orthodoxy is precisely such reflection in condensed form. Taking the offensive, he wondered whether Catholics did not tend to 'isolate the Church from its spiritual implications to the profit of a sociology'.[2] That question-mark would become an exclamation mark in the aftermath of the Second Vatican Council (1962–5) when discussion of the Church's 'structures' and their possible reform—along with the politicization of her evangelical outreach signalled by that euphemistic phrase 'Justice and Peace'—would thoroughly verify Lossky's modestly expressed claim. Lossky's concentration on the spiritual implications of dogmatics is apparent from this lecture-material on the Church which, moreover, debouches in a miniature study of the sacraments and closes with an eschatological finale.

Church of Son and Spirit

For the Lossky of *Théologie dogmatique*, the Church belongs to the joint economies of Son and Spirit. The Son's continuing work focuses on nature and its unity in God; the Spirit's on personhood and its diversity in the order of grace. The divine person of the Son 'penetrates and renews' the 'recapitulated anthropocosmic nature', engaging in a work of unification (whether of human powers within those who exist in this specific nature, or of the human race is not made clear) by his Incarnation and by Baptism, one of the Church's 'mysteries'. The Spirit bestows 'something of his [the Spirit's] person' on human persons, (further) diversifying them by another of her mysteries, the 'permanent Pentecost of Chrismation'.[3] But just as the economies of Son and Spirit are harmonized—they are the two hands of the Father, so these enterprises must not be thought of as separated in the life of the Church. '[T]he unification cannot be done outside the diversity of persons and their love, nor personal destinies attain their plenitude outside this unity where they lose themselves to find themselves.'[4]

Interconnectedness also emerges when Lossky speaks of the two roles of the Spirit, which concern not only his most distinctive or 'proper' economy: namely, to 'open to each Christian the personal way of holiness', but also a task of 'perfecting the Son's economy' by sanctifying the Church-organism he founded.[5] He contrasts two sendings of the Spirit by the risen Lord, one in the Resurrection appearances in the Gospel of John, the other at the start of the Book of the Acts of the Apostles. The Johannine Pentecost (John 20:22–3) is concerned with a collectivity, endowing with the Spirit those who will be the source of the episcopate, and thus of the ministerial function in the Church; its rationale is the holiness of the Church, not that of persons, with particular reference to the validity of the sacraments. By contrast the Lucan Pentecost (Acts 2:2–3) is concerned with the personal acquisition of grace, the goal—deifying communion with the Trinity—to which the apostolic ministry (and the sacraments) is ultimately directed.

To Lossky's mind, the best example of the co-working of Son and Spirit in the Church is the reception of the Holy Eucharist by a saint. The sacrament, confected in the apostolic succession, belongs with the scope of the Johannine Pentecost, and thus with the Spirit's assistance in the work of the Son. The saint, a particular person, belongs with the scope of the Lucan Pentecost (as interpreted by Lossky, that is) and thus with the Spirit's distinctive and proper economy. 'It is always the same Eucharist'—a little later he calls this 'the perfect unity of the Body of Christ'[6]—'and yet the diversity of the saints is total.'[7] The mediocrity of hagiographers conceals by a thick coating of 'pious conformism' the 'incomparable profusion of grace' in the lives of saints, each of whom had a road of his or her own to holiness. The Church 'is not sociology'—one thinks of his earlier criticism of the Catholic 'temptation' in ecclesiology—'but the revelation of faces'.[8]

The Chalcedonian Church

Christological Nestorianism and Monophysitism, already characterized in the chapter on the Saviour, are not the only variety. These concepts can also be applied to the Church—Congar was doing this too and in roughly the same period when *Théologie dogmatique* received its final version as lectures in 1954–8.[9] Ecclesial Monophysitism fails to realize the Church requires a 'multiform action, a behaviour ever variable according to time and place, allowing the Church to feed the world by her salutary truth'.[10] Ecclesial Nestorianism seeks outside, in human values whether philosophical, social or artistic, the nourishment of the Church. The first, archaizing, confuses the invariable with the variable (Old Calendarists, chides Lossky, are guilty of this failing). The second, modernizing and aspiring to a Kingdom of God in this world, separates, if only unconsciously, a heavenly Church from an earthly, confusing the earthly Church with the world. But, like Christology, ecclesiology must be Chalcedonian, joining inseparably but without confusion two principles—the 'unalterable divine plenitude and the variable human deficiency, *carence*'.[11]

When her existence is thought through in Chalcedonian fashion, the Church will be found to be at once concretely historical yet radically independent of the world. 'Being in the world the Church is not a component part of the world for she contains what the world cannot contain, the plenitude of uncreated grace.'[12] With, surely, the Moscow Patriarchate in mind Lossky speaks of the Church keeping silence before this world's powers yet guarding her supreme freedom. He warns against a temptation on the part of some Orthodox to envy the 'powerful administration' of Rome. But an even worse temptation is to wish to exalt one's own—corporate or individual—interests above the unity of the Church. And here he had in view not just 'patriotisms of all sorts' and convictions about 'social justice' but also the 'defence of "Christian civilization"', a phrase placed, as here, in inverted commas.[13] (Plainly, Lossky entertained a certain scepticism about that concept.)

The Church's 'marks'

Just as Congar made use, in the structuring of ecclesiology, of the four 'marks' or 'notes' of the Church as given in the Great Creed,[14] so too Lossky finds the investigation of the Church's unity, holiness, catholicity and apostolicity to be an obvious manner of advance. Regrettably, he only offers a full account of the third 'mark', in the essay 'Du troisième attribut de l'Église', originally published in the ecumenical journal *Dieu vivant* in 1948,[15] but he uses the opportunity nevertheless to give a glimpse of how he would understand the remaining three.

There is, says Lossky, a definite feeling (among the Orthodox is probably presupposed) that only the 'consensus' of the four attributes ascribed to the Church in the Creed can really express the fullness of her being.[16] Yet people are not that clear about what each mark actually means. Lossky proposes to conduct a short thought-experiment. Let us imagine what the Church would be like if, in turn, one or other of these marks were suppressed. Without unity, he suggests, the other three marks could not subsist. In order to function, they require the undivided Body of which Christ is the Head. Without holiness, the Church would lack the source and goal of her existence in the realized promise of the Holy Spirit. Without apostolicity she would be 'a ghost of the "heavenly Church", disincarnate, useless and abstract',[17] for the power of the Spirit transmitted through the apostles to their successors would not dwell in her. So what shall we say about catholicity? Lossky's answer runs: Without catholicity she would 'lack the mode of knowledge of the Truth proper to the Church, in virtue of which this truth becomes clear to the whole Church, as much to each of her smallest parts as to her totality'.[18] Although the word 'catholic' may be translated 'universal', the catholicity of the truth is, evidently, something different from the geographical universality of the Church which professes that truth. On the one hand, there was nothing geographically universal about the Church in the Cenacle. On the other hand, there is something geographically universal about such non-Christian religions as Islam and Buddhism, both of which have a strong missionary emphasis, while lacking the truth in question. The catholicity in question is not simply a matter of the same doctrinal propositions passed down by the Church's hierarchy (else it would be indistinguishable from her apostolicity), nor is it a matter simply of the personal inspiration of the saints (that would be to confuse it with the Church's holiness). Can we say that catholicity in holding to the truth is a function of how thoroughly integrated one is as a member of the Body of Christ? That would be to risk a further confusion, this time with the unity of the Church.

In order to specify the mode of possession of the truth which catholicity entails Lossky draws on the resources of his wider ecclesiology. It is a mode which will be characterized by a harmony between unity and nature on the one hand (compare the economy of the Son, the Head who recapitulates all humanity in himself) and diversity and persons on the other (compare the economy of the Spirit who distributes gifts as he will). If so, it will bear the sign of the Holy Trinity who is himself perfect unity in consubstantiality of nature together with diversity of persons in a single communion. Lossky calls the Holy Trinity 'the Catholic dogma par excellence, for from it the church receives her catholicity'.[19]

> [I]f the Church possesses catholicity it is because the Son and the Holy Spirit sent by the Father have revealed the Trinity to her, not in an abstract way, as intellectual knowledge, but as the very rule of her life.[20]

When the Church is seen solely through the lens of Christology (at least as Lossky conceives the latter) her catholicity will be skewed by an inappropriate emphasis on external unity. Lossky no doubt has the Roman Catholic Church in view (at any rate as it existed in 1948 when this essay was written) when he speaks here of 'a universal doctrine that absorbs in imposing itself, instead of being a tradition evident to everyone, affirmed by all, at all times and in all places, in an infinite richness of living witness'.[21] But then when the Church is seen through the lens of Pneumatology (again, we should add: as Lossky thinks of it) her catholicity may well also be distorted, this time through internal 'disaggregation'. Here Lossky is surely thinking of the fissiparousness of historic Protestantism where through anarchic multiplication the truth morphs into relativism, and, in stinging words, 'catholicity is replaced by "ecumenism"'.[22] Lossky, it seems, did not share the attraction to the official Ecumenical Movement experienced by Bulgakov—or even, among theologians closer to his own 'neo-patristic' mind-set, by Georges Florovsky, though, as was noted in Chapter One, after the Second World War he put an occasional toe into ecumenical waters. Orthodox catholicity combines Christological unity with Pneumatological diversity and so never falls into either of these traps.

The consciousness of the Church

In the companion essay to this study, 'Catholic Consciousness: Anthropological Implications of the Dogma of the Church', published posthumously in 1963, Lossky is seeking to apply his dialectic of unity and diversity to the topic of the consciousness of the Church—a consciousness for which he often uses the German word, *Bewusstsein*. (Theological concern with this topic derived from German Idealism in the writers of the Catholic Tübingen school with which Lossky was familiar but it was also popular among the Russian Slavophiles.) On that 'consciousness', he would write epigrammatically, 'The Church does not know impersonal collectives any more than she knows individuals in revolt'.[23] Lossky was aware that Orthodoxy has its own temptations to fractiousness—'national churches', to whit. Though Lossky regards the very expression 'national church' as 'erroneous and even heretical', appealing to the condemnation of Ethnophyletism at a synod of the Ecumenical Patriarchate in 1872. However, he knows it is frequently heard—as it is among English Anglicans and Scandinavian Lutherans, and Roman Catholics nostalgic for the glories of the Gallican Church or the Teutonic charms of late-eighteenth-century 'Febronianism'. '[N]o divisive reality', be it of 'sex, race, social class, language, or culture', can, he says, 'enter into the bosom of the *Catholica*'.[24]

> At this point any private consciousness which could link us with any ethnic or political, social or cultural group must disappear, in order to make way for consciousness 'as a whole' (*kath' holon*), a consciousness greater than the consciousness which links us to humanity at large.[25]

Unity in Christ will exceed any other unity since it is the eschatological realization of the unity of our nature as recapitulated in him, the Last Adam, in the new creation.

There are, for the Lossky of 'Concerning the Third Mark of the Church', two lessons to be learned. The first is that someone who gives expression to the catholicity of the Church surpasses mere individuality, since he (or of course she) 'mysteriously identifies himself with the whole and constitutes himself a witness of the Truth in the name of the Church'.[26] A voice may appear to be alone, but here appearances are deceptive. The consciousness of the Church is actualized with different degrees, intensely in this person or that, hardly at all in others. In 'Catholic Consciousness', with its emphatic *Bewusstsein* focus, he would write:

> It is the consciousness of some, free from all subjectivity, which makes Truth triumph in the Church at large—the consciousness of those who speak not in their own name, but in the name of the Church, positing the Church as the unique subject of multiple personal consciousnesses.[27]

A second lesson also concerns the dangers of surface evaluation. A council of the Church may meet all the formal requirements for apostolic authority (one suspects Lossky is thinking of Florence). Yet the canons which 'define its legitimate character as a council' do not suffice of themselves to assure the 'infallibility of its judgement'.[28] It may be only a *conciliabulum*, like so many were during the Arian crisis, and catholicity will 'express itself elsewhere', as 'tradition preserved always and everywhere'. The Church 'always recognizes her own, those who bear the seal of catholicity'.[29] This too was a lesson to which he returned.

> It is very significant that in the course of its liturgical year, the Orthodox Church, on the anniversaries of the great councils, celebrates the memory of the Fathers of the Councils rather than honoring this or that council as a collective group.[30]

An apologia for canon law

Coming from Lossky's study of catholicity and its characteristic 'consciousness', the reader may be surprised by the weight *Théologie dogmatique*, Lossky's continuously revised overall course on dogmatics, gives to canon law. The importance for Lossky of canon law is not so much, however, its role as a guide to catholic truth. It is, rather, the way it acts as a safeguard for the Church's independence of the world. Where that law is held in low regard, there will always be detected a tendency to break down the boundary between her and the surrounding *saeculum*. 'One imposes on her the defence of secular interests, tasks alien to her vocation.'[31] The exalted character of his doctrine of canon law is seen by the fact that he regards canonical authority as conferred on the apostolic 'circle' (a term he prefers to the more Latinate 'college') at the Johannine Pentecost. In Orthodoxy, as is well-known, the lack of a fully functional primacy at the universal level means more leeway for individual bishops or groups of bishops at the local or regional level. This can cause difficulties, and Lossky formulates principles for guidance in these circumstances.

> So long as the canonical acts of a bishop are recognized as such by the apostolic circle, they must be considered as expressing the single power and will of the Church. That is why, before protesting against an unjust sanction by the ecclesiastical authority, one should submit to it, awaiting the judgement of the wider ecclesiastical circle, according to the gravity of the case (metropolitan province, patriarchal synod, accord of the leaders of the autocephalous churches).[32]

Writing those words must have revived memories of the Bulgakov imbroglio.

If defence of the liberty of the Church and the service of its economy towards the world are the two chief aims of the canons, then wrongly constructed canons—'pseudo-canons'—are likely to come in these sizes also. Examples are, for the first, the Bulgarian 'Phyletism' which considered the nation the unit of the Church, and, for the second, the practice of rebaptizing non-Orthodox as in vigour until quite recent times in the Church of Russia. Lossky does not suppose the canonical situation to be altogether happy in his own day. Crimes against the Church's unity have become, if anything, more frequent, and an inappropriate levity regards them as an inevitable if transient evil.

The disdainful attitude of some towards the canons, as mere bureaucracy, shows a false understanding of the Church. Lossky does not hesitate to speak of potential anarchy and actual 'spiritual Protestantism'.[33] The latter means ignoring the concrete character of the Body of Christ except for the Liturgy 'on which one loves to put the accent'.[34] Lossky speaks of provincialism, spiritual laziness, the lack of courage to 'redress the level of the Church's awareness', pushing off the task to future generations.[35]

The sacramental mysteries

It is not necessary to be a pan-liturgist to acknowledge that the Church is in truth a sacramental organism. And this brings Lossky to speak of her sacraments or 'mysteries'. Lossky prefers the latter term as far richer in its associations—not excluding the pagan associations: a participation in the life of a god by the representations of events that took place in the sacral time of the origins. Purified of esotericism and given new depth by an Incarnation that was historically real, the word 'mystery' (and/or, in the West 'sacrament') would have a great future at the hands of the Fathers.

> With the Fathers, the mysteries englobe and surpass the limited reality of our [seven] 'sacraments'. The Church is a single, immense sacrament, and her rites manifest abidingly the mystery of Him who, properly, is the mystery manifesting himself: Christ as the Face of the Father.[36]

There is a depth here that cannot be plumbed: this mystery is 'fully communicated and fully mystery... The more one advances into it, the more it opens itself, and the more it becomes mysterious.'[37] This is Gregory of Nyssa's *epektasis*, 'stretching forward', but now in sacramental mode. Dogmatic manuals may speak of seven sacraments, and seven is typically the number of fullness, but in the past a greater number has been recognized (as indeed has a lesser, too).

Lossky's recommendation here is not to follow Catholics in speaking of mysteric signs beyond the seven as 'the sacramentals', but to rediscover the plenary mystery of which all such signs (including the seven) are aspectual epiphanies. The three sacraments on which Lossky lays himself most emphasis are Baptism, Eucharist, Chrismation, or, as he calls them, the water, the blood, and the fire, linked as they are to the Baptism of Christ, his Death and Resurrection, and Pentecost respectively.

Church and eschaton

Thought of the Church and her mysteries also leads Lossky back to eschatology and that final vision of God from which his mind never wandered far. Lossky defines the 'time of the Church' as *waiting for the Parousia*.[38] Then it is that the Church will fully realize the vocation of all creation. In what is perhaps the most theologically majestic passage in the whole of *The Mystical Theology of the Eastern Church*, Lossky has this to say:

> The world was created from nothing by the sole will of God — this is its origin. It was created in order to participate in the fullness of divine life — this is its vocation. It is called to make this union a reality in liberty, in the free harmony of the created will with the will of God — this is the mystery of the Church inherent in creation. Throughout all the vicissitudes which followed upon the fall of humanity and the destruction of the first Church — the Church of paradise — the creation preserved the idea of its vocation and with it the idea of the Church, which was at length to be fully realized after Golgotha and after Pentecost, as the Church properly so called, the indestructible Church of Christ.[39]

Taking his cue from St Symeon the New Theologian, Lossky affirms that without an effort of transformation by prayer the true life of the Church is imperceptible to us. As with Catholic theologians of his period, Lossky sought to plot the relation between civil history, the special saving history that passes via the Church and the Age to Come. He argues that the world 'moves towards its end as towards a catastrophe', whereas on the line of history that runs through the Church the latter is building a 'time that will be eternalized', a goal already fully realized in the Assumption of the Virgin.[40] Her Assumption is 'the integral deification of a created person, responding to the incarnation of a person who is divine'.[41] She is beyond the judgement, awaiting us in the Kingdom that is our hope. This fully realized condition of glory differentiates her from the other saints and is expressed in the notion of her Queenship.

Is the Christian hope for the final judgement or for a restitution of all things, *apokatastasis*? Lossky does not rule out universal salvation, restricting himself to say it can neither be affirmed nor denied. What he does insist on is that it must not be presented deterministically, as inevitable both for angels and for men—as was done, he believed, by Origen and Bulgakov. A cosmic restoration, the restoration of nature is, however, unproblematic. 'Nature will be restored in its plenitude, but persons will be in grace or out of grace.'[42] As to judgement, it begins now: an incipient disaster for those who are hooked on the world, but for those who 'aspire to Christ' an incipient encounter.[43]

Notes

1 Yves Marie-Jean Congar, *Chrétiens desunis. Principes d'un 'Oecuménisme' catholique* (Paris: Cerf, 1937).

2 Lossky, *Théologie dogmatique*, p. 171.

3 Ibid., pp. 171–2.

4 Ibid., p. 172.

5 Ibid.

6 Ibid., p. 175.

7 Ibid., p. 174.

8 Ibid., p. 175.

9 Yves Marie-Jean Congar, *Le Christ, Marie et l'Église* (Paris: Desclée de Brouwer, 1952).

10 Lossky, *Théologie dogmatique*, pp. 175–6.

11 Ibid., p. 177

12 Ibid.

13 Ibid., p. 179.

14 Yves Marie-Jean Congar, *L'Église une, sainte, catholique et apostolique* (Paris: Cerf, 1970).

15 Vladimir Lossky, 'Du troisième attribut de l'Église', *Dieu vivant* 10 (1948), pp. 78–89.

16 Lossky, *In the Image and Likeness of God*, p. 169.

17 Ibid., p. 172.

18 Ibid., p. 175.

19 Ibid., p. 178.

20 Ibid.

21 Ibid., p. 179.

22 Ibid., p. 179.

23 Ibid., p. 193.

24 Ibid., p. 184.

25 Ibid.

26 Ibid., p. 180.

27 Ibid., pp. 193–4.

28 Ibid., p. 180.

29 Ibid.

30 Ibid., p. 192.

31 Lossky, *Théologie dogmatique*, p. 180.

32 Ibid., p. 181.

33 Ibid., p. 183.

34 Ibid.

35 Ibid.

36 Ibid., p. 186.

37 Ibid.

38 Ibid., p. 191.

39 Lossky, *The Mystical Theology of the Eastern Church*, pp. 112–13.
40 Lossky, *Théologie dogmatique*, p. 192.
41 *Ibid.*
42 *Ibid.*, p. 193.
43 *Ibid.*

✢ 11 ✢

The Pattern of Salvation

LOSSKY'S ARTICLE 'Redemption and Deification', included in the collection *In the Image and Likeness of God* put together shortly before his death, might seem from its title to give the outline we need of how he saw the 'pattern of salvation', the shape of the divine scheme soteriology studies. As we shall see, it requires in fact the supplement of the concluding essay in that collection, 'Dominion and Kingship: an Eschatological Study' or the reader will be deprived of a necessary dimension of Lossky's thought—as of the biblical revelation itself.

Redemption is not enough

Lossky's purpose in writing 'Redemption and Deification' was twofold. In the first place he wanted to insist that redemption, conceived as the rescue of humanity from a negative state of affairs, is by no means the totality of God's saving plan. (This has been a recurring theme in our survey of Lossky's work.) Only a minimalizing, and therefore inadequate, doctrine of salvation would fail to see how redemption forms one moment only, if a crucial one, in a wider scheme. The key term that unlocks that wider scheme is *theōsis*, the 'deification' of the essay's title.

Lossky also had a further, if subsidiary aim. And this was to do more justice than was often done, notably in redemption-centred versions of soteriology, to the economy of the Holy Spirit. The goal of the divine plan is the deification of human nature and the human person by the combined economies of the incarnate Son and the Pentecostal Spirit.

Unlike, however, many theologians, in both East and West, seeking to contextualize the redemption in a wider whole, Lossky is not interested in trying to answer the question, Would there have been an Incarnation if there had been no Fall? Lossky gives short shrift to such a query, robustly dismissing it as 'unreal'.

> [W]e have no knowledge of any condition of the human race except the condition resulting from original sin, in which our deification—the carrying out of the divine purpose for us—has become impossible without the Incarnation of the Son, a fact necessarily having the character of a redemption.[1]

(This would also be the mature view of St Thomas Aquinas.) But while the large space given to the theme of redemption in the soteriology of the Church is justified it must never lead to losing sight of the wider picture—as Lossky thinks it has done, especially in the West and notably among Protestants. For that wider picture there is ample patristic warrant, attested in his pages by a quartet of opening references to Irenaeus, Athanasius, Gregory of Nazianzus and Gregory of Nyssa. All say the same thing: God became man so that man might be divine.[2]

Lossky is inclined to ascribe the narrowing of perspectives to the influence of St Anselm, whose *Cur Deus Homo* not only concentrated unilaterally on the redemption moment but did so by exclusive reference to a metaphor drawn from law or rights. In Lossky's summary of Anselm's text:

> The price of our redemption having been paid in the death of Christ, the resurrection and the ascension are only a glorious happy end of His work, a kind of apotheosis without direct relation to our human destiny.[3]

Lossky contrasts Anselm unfavourably in this respect with Athanasius, who in his treatise *On the Incarnation of the Word* identified in the outcome of Christ's sacrifice not just the restoration of guilty humanity to righteousness but also the creation of the 'first-fruits of the General resurrection with his own incorruptible body'.[4] That text makes plain a further excellence of Athanasius, which is to complement juridical by biological comparisons in the interpretation of the Paschal Mystery. Indeed, Lossky would have wished Athanasius's net to be flung wider still, for the Fathers, taken as a whole, can offer bucolic images of pastoring, medical images of healing, military images of defeating the Enemy, and diplomatic images of outwitting that Enemy by an unsuspected strategy—even if the last of these (for which Lossky looks again to Gregory of Nyssa[5]) has, unlike the rest, no obvious New Testament counterpart. Once again, a cross-reference to Aquinas is not irrelevant: among figures in the tradition he has a quite conscious commitment to a multi-faceted theology of the redemption, using a variety of models and metaphors. We have visited this topic under the rubric of Lossky's Christology in Chapter Six.

A Pneumatological deficit?

Where Lossky cannot applaud Athanasius in this particular passage is in the lack of reference to the Third Trinitarian Person. No account of salvation which omits the Spirit, or thinks of him (as Lossky is inclined to suspect Anselm of doing) as merely 'an auxiliary, an assistant in redemption, causing us to receive Christ's expiating merit' can possibly suffice.[6] As Lossky comments, taking the opportunity to remind the reader of the need for a holistic approach:

> Redemption has our salvation from sin as its immediate aim, but that salvation will be, in its ultimate realization in the age to come, our union with God, the deification of the created beings whom Christ ransomed. But this final realization involves the dispensation of another divine Person, sent into the world after the Son.[7]

Lossky could hardly express surprise if Latin theology did not do justice to the third divine Person since—on his own claims in *The Mystical Theology of the Eastern Church*—the Western tradition had incurred a Pneumatological deficit, rendering the Holy Spirit, in the doctrine of the *Filioque*, a consequence of the generation of the Son. What he does instead is to argue that the Catholic theology of the decades between the two World Wars, in its praiseworthy effort to recover a patristic doctrine of the Church as the 'Mystical Body' of the crucified and risen Son, had re-introduced Pneumatological inferiority in a new form. The 'new' (in fact, ancient) ecclesiology is to be welcomed precisely because of the opening it allows for a full-blooded doctrine of theosis—but it must not be allowed to embed further a deficient account of the Spirit. In Lossky's words:

> What is important at present is to notice that this way of regarding the doctrine of redemption re-opens the way to a wider Christology and a wider ecclesiology, in which the question of our deification, of our union with God, can again be raised. We can now say again what the Fathers said, 'God became man, so that man might become God'. But when one tries to interpret these words solely on a Christological and sacramental basis, in which the part of the Holy Spirit is that of a liaison between the heavenly Head of the Church and His earthly members, we get into grave difficulties and reach insoluble problems.[8]

What difficulties and problems? Lossky does not actually spell them out preferring to refer readers to some pages of the French Oratorian Louis Bouyer's study *Le Mystère pascal*.[9] Holding, as Bouyer does in this work, that the Incarnation of the Son constitutes the sole *raison d'être* of our union with God and the knowledge of God that flows from that union, he can only conclude on the Spirit that—somewhat uninformatively—it is by the Third Person that 'thus union and knowledge are what they ought to be'.[10] (Even vaguer is Bouyer's conclusion on the role of the Paraclete in the High Priestly Prayer of the Fourth Gospel: 'the supreme blessing accorded to human nature in this eulogy which forms the Eucharist's counterpart'.[11])

For his part, Lossky confines himself to describing not so much the problem but the solution—as he sees it. The solution is to distinguish sharply between the redeemed human nature of the members of the Mystical Body of which Christ is Head and their still-to-be-divinized hypostases or persons. It is on this distinction that he will rest his claim for the Holy Spirit's complementary (and not just subsidiary) economy in the work of the Son.

As Lossky puts it, by way of a *captatio benevolentiae*: could a certain totalitarianism creep into the Mystical Body concept unless we take care to preserve in our thinking (and, presumably, acting!)

sufficient space for the diversity of human persons who, after all, are distinct from the Person of Christ as well as from each other? Could there not be a risk of a 'sort of sacramental determinism, in which the organic process of salvation, accomplished in the collective totality of the Church, tends to suppress personal encounter with God?'[12] The questions are rhetorical, expecting the answer 'Yes', and, by way of safeguard against such regrettable developments, a further question then arises which Lossky formulates as follows:

> In what sense are we all one single body in Christ, and in what sense is it true that we are not and cannot be one without ceasing to exist as human persons or hypostases, each of whom is called to realize in his person union with God?[13]

It is of course another opportunity for him to rehearse his theological doctrine of the human person, conceived in the light of Trinitarianism as one who exists for or towards others and rather than exemplifying the common nature of which he or she is a part (as an individual would do) personifies that nature in its wholeness. And here words begin to crack under the burden, for 'each person is an absolutely original and unique aspect of the nature common to all', such that any term we might like to suggest for the diversity of persons will fail to serve.[14]

> Although linked with individual parts of the common nature in created actuality, [persons] potentially contain in themselves, each in his fashion, the whole of nature.[15]

This is still a humanism, not a cosmology, for the 'nature' in question is, I take it, human nature. Lossky's comparative lack of interest in cosmology dissuades him from taking a further step and proposing, in the style of Bulgakov, that each human being hypostatizes in some way the cosmos to which he or she gives a voice.

Empirically scanned, this is, however, a humanism that is only *in fieri* as the Scholastics would say: 'in the process of becoming'. Lossky is quite aware that in everyday experience, particular persons time and again fail to recognize their catholic—universal—

vocation and act for their own individual self-interest, just as the corporate entities to which they belong in the civil sphere (social classes, nation states and the like) do also. But just this is the fallen human condition from which the economy of the Son—and, as we are about to learn, the economy of the Spirit would save us.

A vital conclusion for any account of the 'pattern of salvation' can (Lossky writes 'must') now be drawn.

> [I]f our individual natures are incorporated into the glorious humanity of Christ and enter the unity of His Body by baptism, conforming themselves to the death and resurrection of Christ, our persons need to be confirmed in their personal dignity by the Holy Spirit, so that each may freely realize his own union with the Divinity.[16]

Or to put it in sacramental language, Baptism, the sign of unity in Christ, must be followed by Confirmation—Chrismation, the sign of diversity in the Holy Spirit.

So—this is Lossky's simple and lucid scheme—the Son unifies, the Spirit diversifies. The Son hallows nature, the Spirit persons. But it is not just that we need a divine economy distinct from that of the Son, so as to avoid 'depersonalizing' the Church by submitting hypostatic freedom to the sacramental determinism of an organic body. We need, Lossky goes so far as to say, the economy of another divine person who is essentially 'independent, in his origin, of the Person of the incarnate Son'.[17] We can of course see why, in the perspective of his Triadology, Lossky wants to say this. The Spirit's independence of the Son is the strongest possible statement of anti-Filioquism that could conceivably be made. But in context it strengthens the hint already unavoidable in Lossky's soteriological schema that the economy of the Spirit is needed so as to protect us from the disadvantages the economy of the Son would carry, were it left to follow out its logic to the end. 'Natural unity', the hallmark of the Son's work, would swamp 'personal multiplicity'.[18]

It is perhaps by a recognition, possibly unconscious, of leaving some such impression on readers that Lossky—good theologian as he is—moves at once to neutralize it by stressing the reciprocally supportive action of Spirit and Son. Just as the Son's redeeming work served as the 'indispensable pre-condition' of Pentecost, so without the Spirit there can be no 'full consciousness' by human persons of the divinity of the Son—and hence no adequate appropriation of the redeeming work from which this account set forth. 'The Son has become like us by the incarnation'; we become like him by deification, by 'partaking of the divinity in the Holy Spirit, who communicates the divinity to *each* human person in a particular way'.[19]

Nothing has really been said here about the overall context of such post-Pentecost deification and its eventual outcome when history ends. But 'Redemption and deification' closes on a note that, while concluding the essay, opens a window on these topics. The mystery to be accomplished in each person in the Church 'will be fully revealed in the age to come, when after having reunited all things in Christ, God will become all in all'.[20]

Corporate eschatology

Corporate eschatology is very much the overall perspective of 'Dominion and Kingship', the companion essay—in soteriological perspective—to 'Redemption and Deification' in *À l'image et à la ressemblance de Dieu*. The crucial connecting sentence runs:

> The mystery of deification which is being fulfilled in the Church is eschatology at work, the hidden but entirely new center which is shaping the whole history of the world.[21]

How does Lossky see that history of in biblical perspective? He treats it—with adequate warrant considering the importance in Scripture of 'Kingdom' vocabulary—as a path towards the '*fulfillment* of God's dominion'.[22] Lossky is worried that divine dominion could be seen as a form of necessitarianism. It is true that, extensively speaking, nothing escapes God's power for he is the Creator of all, yet, *intensively* speaking, his dominion is 'changing and dynamic', allowing for the contingency of things and inaugurating a dialogue with his free creation—angelic and human.[23] That for Lossky is the inspired message of the Book of

Job. Lossky gives a high importance to the category of risk when speaking of the specifically divine version of rule. But while he means this to distinguish his thought from the 'abstract' and 'rationalist' theology of omnipotence in the manuals, it does not introduce—not by any manner of means—a sentimental doctrine of God. Rather, he links divine risk-taking in the first place to the wrathfulness of God.

> [T]he God of the Bible reveals Himself by His very wrath as He who undertook the risk of creating a universe whose perfection is continually jeopardized by the freedom of those in whom that perfection ought to reach its highest level.[24]

Only in the second place—in the order of his exposition, I mean—does he see divine risk-taking as the expression of the love of God. When God is all in all, every form of dominion that falls short of the union of divine and human freedoms in love will be obliterated. In final deification there is no place for the master–slave relation.

But the process of aligning the divine and human wills for this end is a demanding one. The Fall of the first Adam entails for him, and the whole earthly cosmos, the frustration of vocation. Before the second Adam can recapitulate humanity, ushering it into the sphere of theosis, there must be a costly realignment, which is how Lossky understands the place in the Bible's historical vision of the Old Testament law. 'Law' means divine dominion as external, and this is a necessary phase, since fallen people must discover the meaning of the sin that they practise: at root, it is revolt against God. But taken by itself such externality would render the Law a caricature of the intended divine-human relationship—which is why the Law can only be seen as, in St Paul's phrase (Galatians 3:24), a 'pedagogue' leading us to Christ inasmuch as it is accompanied by the Promise.

Making good use of Gregory the Great's *Moralia in Job* Lossky proposes that the turbulent nature of the historical process between Fall and deifying 'recapitulation' should not be regarded as counter-evidence for the thesis of divine dominion. What Satan wills by malice God makes use for the purpose of his righteousness.[25]

> The divine economy makes use of the rebel will to fulfill the design of the Creator, in spite of all the obstacles set up by angelic or human free will. If this is so, God's design, which is fixed as to the end in view (the deification of all created beings), must be likened, as to its execution, to a strategy of ever-changing tactics, infinitely rich in possibilities, to a multiform (*polypoikilos*) Wisdom of God in action.[26]

The New Testament revelation of the divine Kingship attests the unexpectedness of this strategy. The 'king' of the messianic Promise is like no other, 'come to earth to undergo death upon the cross', even if John Chrysostom considered it proper to kings to die for their subjects.[27] When he exalts above 'every rule and authority and power and dominion' (Ephesians 1:21) the human nature he has assumed, he demonstrates—for these Pauline terms all embody the dominion concept—how the relation between the Church's members and their glorious Head transcends the dominion idea. Dispossession of the dark powers follows. Even the good angels, guardians of the legal order as they are, no longer serve the same role as before.

> Indeed, all that is dominion halts at the threshold of the Church, the new reality which appears in the world after the Ascension of Christ and the Descent of the Holy Spirit. The sons of the Church are out of reach of the flaming sword of the Angel who closes the gate of paradise to the descendants of the First Adam.[28]

Outwardly, to all appearances, nothing changes. But does that mean that the Eschaton has not in fact begun? Jews and pagans and even some theologians would say so, falsely. They do not realize that 'The End', when the Promise of the Father descends (Acts 1:4–5) is in fact

> the continually renewed beginning of an infinite way of deifying union, in which the dominion of God and the vocation of creation is fulfilled. This realization of the last end, by the grace of the Holy Spirit and by human freedom, is the inner mystery of the Church, a mystery which is accomplished with the angels as wondering witnesses, but which remains impenetrable to those outside[29]

This 'centre', as hidden as it is novel, is what is now shaping world history, its first-fruits realized in the glorification of the Mother of God.

Faithful to his personalist emphasis on hypostatic diversity, Lossky then corrects himself. There is not one centre. There are many of them as the final vocation works itself out in each hypostasis that is moving, if laboriously so, towards theosis. But the final Kingdom concerns more than deified humans. Lossky does not forget to mention the wider creation. The wider material creation will be freed from cyclical repetition. Paraphrasing now the Paul of the Letter to the Romans (8:19–22), that material creation 'will see the beginning of an eternal springtime' when 'all the forces of life , triumphant over death, will come to the fullness of their unfolding'.[30] The destiny of the wider hypostatic creation, namely that of the angels, is treated by Lossky as an open question. '[T]he question of angelic eschatology', he writes, 'remains inaccessible to our theology'.[31] He does not lambast the Nestorian spiritual writer Isaac of Nineveh for praying for the salvation of the devils. But if there is anything in such prayer it is for an aeon beyond ours. For the spiritual warfare in which *we* are involved, 'Satan is the sole enemy, against whom the Church will have to struggle until the end of time'.[32]

The 'true origin' of the ills the human sciences investigate lies beyond them in that cosmic warfare. Even philosophy, though it knows of the concepts of nature and person, cannot reach the level of depth where the eschatological bearings of the aetiology of evils are found. In an astonishing anticipation of the late-twentieth-century English theological movement Radical Orthodoxy, Lossky writes of philosophical discourse: 'The terms which it uses are, for the most part, the result of the decadence and secularization of theological ideas'.[33] And here metaphysics does not suffice, there must be meta-ontology. Philosophy's 'field of vision' falls short of the

> two abysses which theology alone can name, with fear and trembling: the uncreated abyss of the Life of the Trinity and the abyss of hell which opens within the freedom of created persons.[34]

The Pattern of Salvation

The full drama of human existence can only be experienced by those who know of its overall divine plot.

Notes

1 Lossky, *In the Image and Likeness of God*, p. 98.

2 Compare Irenaeus, *Against the Heresies* V, Preface; Athanasius, *On the Incarnation of the Word* 54; Gregory of Nazianzus, *Dogmatic Poems* 10:5–9; Gregory of Nyssa, *Great Catechetical Oration* 25.

3 *Ibid.*, p. 99.

4 Athanasius, *On the Incarnation of the Word* 20, cited *ibid.*, p. 100.

5 Gregory of Nyssa, *Great Catechetical Oration* 22–4.

6 Lossky, *In the Image and Likeness of God*, p. 99.

7 *Ibid.*, p. 103.

8 *Ibid.*, p. 105.

9 L. Bouyer, *Le Mystère pascal (paschale sacramentum): Méditation sur la liturgie des trois derniers jours de la Semaine Sainte* (Paris: Cerf, 1945), pp. 180–94.

10 Citing from the third edition, the only one available to me (Paris: Cerf, 1950), at pp. 211–12.

11 *Ibid.*, pp. 212–13.

12 Lossky, *In the Image and Likeness of God*, p. 105.

13 *Ibid.*

14 *Ibid.*, p. 107.

15 *Ibid.*

16 *Ibid.*, p. 108.

17 *Ibid.*, p. 109.

18 *Ibid.*

19 *Ibid.*

20 *Ibid.*, p. 110.

21 *Ibid.*, p. 224.

22 *Ibid.*, p. 212. Italics original.

23 *Ibid.*, p. 213.

24 *Ibid.*, p. 214.

25 Compare especially Gregory the Great, *Moralia in Job* II, 16–17.

26 Lossky, *In the Image and Likeness of God*, p. 218.

27 *Ibid.*, p. 221.

28 *Ibid.*, pp. 221–2.

29 *Ibid.*, p. 224.

30 *Ibid.*, p. 225.

31 *Ibid.*, p. 227.

32 *Ibid.*

33 *Ibid.*, p. 226. Compare John Milbank, *Theology and Social Theory* (Oxford: Blackwell, 1990).

34 Lossky, *In the Image and Likeness of God*, p. 226.

Conclusion

I HOPE THE READER who has persevered to the end of this study will consider that I have made the case—flagged up in the Preface—for the 'substantial spiritual teaching' available from Lossky's texts. The overall orientation of his doctrine to the vision of God—the only fount of the final flowering of human life—is immensely needed in an age when the horizontalism stemming from a secularized society and its anti-metaphysical culture continues to afflict Church discourse and life. Lossky's emphasis on apophasis reminds us that rational concepts cannot by themselves do justice to the divine mystery to which human life is turned, for that mystery remains always in excess of our speech—even of the language of the poets. The supermatural realism of his doctrine of transfiguration by the divine energies recalls us to the challenge of holiness, to which the mystical saints he cites—a Symeon the New Theologian, a Serafim of Sarov—bore such eloquent witness. In Lossky's case, the 'substantial spiritual teaching' is, of course, married with sophisticated theological reflection: the very distinction between God's essence and his energies, after all, is 'antinomic', entailing an apparent contradiction which, however, is demanded and justified by the goal of the divine plan. The holism of Lossky's basic idea of theology, at once 'mystical' and 'scientific', is admirable, as is his generous notion of Tradition. His theology of the Holy Trinity carries inspiration for Latins as well as for Orientals, going far beyond his famous opposition to Filioquism—and indeed he does not oppose *every* interpretation of that disputed doctrine. His Trinitarianism is in function of what has been called a 'realism of divine-human communion', offering the 'gift of God's very life to that which is "other" than God—the non-divine'.[1] As in all Christian theology, that gift by the Father is communicated by the Son and the Spirit. Lossky's own

Christology maintains a rich polyvalence in its understanding of the redemption, itself contextualized within the wider vocation of theosis, while his Pneumatology sees the Holy Spirit at work anonymously in the Mystical Body of Christ, making to be in God the persons whose nature the Son has redeemed. The personalism of his theological anthropology, so strong as potentially to neutralize interest in the wider cosmos, is in reality balanced by his fascination, owed especially to Maximus Confessor, with the structure of created being at large. His Mariology, while centering on the divine motherhood, learns from the festal icons of the further significance of the Marian narrative as a whole. Lossky's picture of the Church may suffer from systematic overdrive in the rigour of its role-allotments to, respectively, the Son and the Holy Spirit. But it has the merit of holding together the canonical society and the Church-mystery, time and the Parousia, reflecting therein his view of what I have called the 'pattern of salvation' at large, which combines realized with future eschatology.

There is, however, one grumble. Lossky's flagship study, *The Mystical Theology of the Eastern Church*, though entirely deserving of its classic status, is marred by the continuing polemic against Bulgakov, usually expressed either tacitly or by a 'throw-away' line that is unworthy of either its originator or its object. This stands in sharp contrast not only to Lossky's mild treatment of Eckhart (see Chapter Three) but, even more surprisingly—for Eckhart belonged to a time and space far removed from Lossky's own—it contrasts also with the *Essai*'s references to an Orthodox thinker indebted, like Bulgakov, to Russia's Silver Age and its 'new religious consciousness', thoroughly suspect as the latter was in Vladimir Lossky's eyes. I am referring to Father Pavel Florensky (1882–1937).

In a celebrated portrait-in-a-landscape, dating from 1917, by the Russian 'Pre-Raphaelite' Mikhaïl Nesterov (1852–1942), the two men, Florensky and Bulgakov, are pictured walking together in a solidarity of spirit they undoubtedly shared in life. One (Florensky) a mathematician by background, the other (Bulgakov) an economist, they rallied in the turbulent opening years of Russia's twentieth century to the Orthodox Church of which they were

Conclusion

nominal members, taking the decisive step of entering its priesthood: in both cases, at great personal cost. Both can be termed—in a phrase of Lossky *père* not calculated to win the sympathy of Lossky *fils*—'successors of Vladimir Solov'ëv'.[2] Yet the younger Lossky's references to Florensky's writing in the *Essai* are entirely favourable in character,[3] in contrast to the consistently hostile references to Bulgakov's thought.[4] And this despite the fact that, until some of Florensky's posthumous writings came to light in the 1980s, the material produced by this brilliant mathematician-scientist appeared to be almost entirely lacking a Christology,[5] or much attention to the sacraments, the Church's mysteries.[6]

Happy enough with the 'grand lines' of his theology (even if I prefer my own formulation of the essence–energies distinction[7]), I am quite willing to admit Lossky is a surer guide to Orthodoxy than is the Bulgakov he criticized so unremittingly. Bulgakov's speculative audacity generated *theologoumena*—'theological opinions'—that were, indeed, too personal to be universally shared. The admonitions of hierarchs were not without all justification—though there are recent hints of a possible rehabilitation by the Moscow Patriarchate.[8] Still today Bulgakov remains in Russia a controversial figure, both admired and suspect. In this respect, it must be said, the reputation of Florensky among the Orthodox parallels Bulgakov's own.[9] The contrast in Lossky's treatment of these two figures in the *Essai* inclines me to think there was, on his part, a failure of generosity towards a fellow-exile much senior to himself. Lossky had the requisite competence, and the depth of understanding, to recognize the 'ecclesiality' of Bulgakov's intention as well as the sheer scope of the elements in Bulgakov's theological vision that are recuperable for the Church. But somehow he failed to do so.

In any case, the distance between their respective positions was much narrower than Lossky's brusque dismissals allow. I would like to make use of the rest of this brief 'Conclusion' to suggest as much.

Thus, for example, Lossky's suggestion that the hypostasis of the incarnate Word has its seat in the *nous*, the human mind of Christ, is not so different from Bulgakov's view that the Godmanhood of the Word, once expressed kenotically in Incarnation, so unites the uncreated Wisdom of God to the created wisdom in the humanity of Christ, that Jesus acts always as a theandric 'I'.[10] And indeed Lossky's indebtedness to Philaret of Moscow makes him, like Bulgakov, if in less extravagant language, a theologian of kenosis (in different modes) for the entire Trinity of Father, Son, and Spirit, and not just for the divine Son alone.[11]

Again, the 'volitional thoughts' or 'thought-wills' of God which for Lossky serve as the basis for creation are—once considered in their unitary coherence as the foundation of the cosmos—not as different as he liked to think from the divine 'ideas' of Christian Platonism and thence Sophiology. Those ideas in their interrelations reflect the mind of the eternal Logos (and thus the divine Sophia) as well as the basic intelligibility of an ordered world (and thus the creaturely Sophia) which, by final and not just exemplar causality, is called to union with God in his creating and saving plan—itself, of course, the expression of God's will, so volition is far from excluded.

Bulgakov's temptation to soteriological universalism (Dare we hope that all may be saved?) is by no means alien to Lossky who even poses the query, In another aeon, may the fallen angels be redeemable too? Both men had in their minds the seriousness with which Isaac of Nineveh, one of the Fathers represented—despite his Nestorian background—in that great anthology of ascetical and mystical texts the *Philokalia*, had taken, so long ago, that demonic question.[12]

Even the essence–energies distinction (and thus apophaticism) did not altogether divide them. For Bulgakov's Absolute—the Divinity-in-itself about which speech must fall silent, corresponds to Lossky's unknowable divine *ousia*, while Bulgakov's God-turned-towards-creation is none other than the 'energetic' God Lossky found in the Greek Fathers read in the light of Gregory Palamas' teaching.[13]

Not till the end of his life—if we may trust the testimony of Olivier Clément—did Lossky begin to come to terms with the commonalities which joined them together. Both theologians were patristically oriented, moulded by the Byzantine Liturgy,

Conclusion

Christocentric, Trinitarian, and persuaded that the way to transfiguration for the cosmos lies through the Church. They used by way of instrument two different philosophical repertoires in the service of Orthodox theology without for all that having divergent goals.

It is true that Bulgakov's writing sometimes exhibits excessive deference to a historical criticism that is theologically unexamined (on the dominical origin of the sacraments, for instance). And he is not beyond the occasional flight into the bizarre (his ruminations on the angel-nature of St John the Baptist are an example). But Lossky's critique does not touch on these matters. Rather, it focuses centrally on Sophiology as such. Lossky's unhappy memories of Solov'ëv's autobiographical—as well as philosophical-theological—writings inclined him to think of the occurrence of Sophia-language as an infallible indicator of what he termed a 'mystical tradition alien to that of Christianity'.[14]

Contrastingly, Hans Urs von Balthasar, a man not without experience as a spiritual director, had, in his evaluation of Solov'ëv, a wonderment of a different kind. The strange visitations by a female figure, whom Solov'ëv identified as the Lady Wisdom: might these have been, asked Balthasar, moments of encounter with a figure very well known to Orthodoxy? Balthasar wondered whether that 'Lady' could have been, incognito, the Mother of God.[15]

Notes

1 Papanikolaou, *Being with God*, p. 2.

2 Nikolaï Onufriyevich Lossky, 'The Successors of Vladimir Solov'ev', *Slavonic Review* 2 (1924), pp. 92–109.

3 Lossky, *The Mystical Theology of the Eastern Church*, pp. 65, 106.

4 Ibid., pp. 62, 80, 112.

5 In 1904 Florensky wrote out a credo to explain to his family his change of course. The dialogue 'On the Empirical and the Empyrean', with its robust Christological confession, was not published until 1986. See Avril Pyman, *Pavel Florensky. A Quiet Genius* (New York and London: Continuum, 2010), pp. 43–4.

6 Lectures of 1918–28 at the shifting venues where the Moscow Theological Academy took refuge included, however, or even centred on, issues of the philosophy and phenomenology of worship, *ibid.*, pp. 127–8.

7   Aidan Nichols, *Chalice of God. A Systematic Theology in Outline* (Collegeville, MN: Liturgical Press, 2012), p. 95.

8   Arjakovsky, *Le Père Sergii Boulgakov*, p. 79.

9   K. G. Isupov, *P. A. Florensky. Pro et contra. Lichnost' i tvorchestvo Pavla Florenskogo v otsenke russkikh mỳsliteleĭ i issledovateleĭ* (St Petersburg: Russkiĭ Khristianskiĭ Gumanitarnỳĭ Institut, 1996); I. Igor, *S. N. Bulgakov. Pro et contra. Lichnost' i tvorchestvo S. N. Bulgakova v otsenke russkikh mỳsliteleĭ i issledovateleĭ* (St Petersburg: Russkiĭ Khristianskiĭ Gumanitarnỳĭ Institut, 2003).

10 Nichols, *Wisdom from Above*, pp. 88–90.

11 For Bulgakov's doctrine of kenosis, see *ibid.*, pp. 19–21 (Trinity), 96–106 (Christology).

12 *Ibid.*, pp. 234–8. It is, however, the case that Bulgakov's theory of the sophianicity of the created being of the fallen angels inclined him to think that their resistance to God could not in the nature of the case be unending.

13 It is in Bulgakov's early philosophical work *Svet nevechernii* ('The Light Unfailing') (Moscow: Put', 1917), pp. 103–46, that he lays out most fully his notion of how the transcendent Absolute, approachable only apophatically, poses itself as God in creating and revealing, thus making possible cataphatic assertions. But he carried through the idea into his mature dogmatics where it comes across especially clearly in his study of iconology, *Ikona i ikonopochitanie* (Paris: SMCA, 1931): see on the latter Nichols, *Wisdom from Above*, pp. 295–8, and, for the wider picture, Brandon Gallaher, 'The "Sophiological" Origins of Vladimir Lossky's Apophaticism', *Scottish Journal of Theology* 66 (2013), pp. 278–98.

14 Lossky and Arseniev, *La Paternité spirituelle en Russie au XVIIIème et XIXème siecles*, p. 140.

15 H. U. von Balthasar, *The Glory of the Lord. A Theological Aesthetics, III. Studies in Theological Style: Lay Styles* (Edinburgh: Clark, 1986), p. 292.

BIBLIOGRAPHY OF THE WRITINGS OF VLADIMIR LOSSKY

Books

Spor o sofii (Paris: Confrèrie de saint Photios, 1936; reprinted Moscow: Izdatel'stvo Svyato-Vladimirskago Bratstva, 1996)

Essai sur la théologie mystique de l'Église d'Orient (Paris: Aubier, 1944); *The Mystical Theology of the Eastern Church* (London: James Clark, 1957)

Der Sinn der Ikonen (with Leonid Ouspensky) (Berne and Olten: Urs Graf Verlag, 1952); *The Meaning of Icons* (Boston: Boston Book and Art Shop, 1952; 2nd edition, Crestwood, NY: Saint Vladimir's Seminary Press, 1982.

Théologie négative et connaissance de Dieu chez Maître Eckhart (Paris: Vrin, 1960; 2nd edition, Paris: Vrin, 1998).

La Vision de Dieu (Paris: Delachaux et Niestle, 1962); *The Vision of God* (London: Faith Press, 1963).

A l'image et la resemblance de Dieu (Paris: Aubier-Montaigne, 1967; *In the Image and Likeness of God* (Crestwood, NY: Saint Vladimir's Seminary Press, 1974).

La Paternité spirituelle en Russie au XVIIIème et XIXème siècles (with Nicolas Arseniev) (Bellefontaine: Abbaye de Bellefontaine, 1977).

Sept jours sur les routes de France (Paris: Cerf, 1998)

Théologie dogmatique (Paris: Cerf, 2012)

Articles

'Otritsatel'noe bogoslovie v uchenii Dionisiya Areopagita, *Seminarium Kondakovianum* 3 (1929), pp. 133–44

'La Notion des "analogies" chez Denys le Pseudo-Aréopagite', *Archives d'histoire doctrinal et littéraire du Moyen-Age* 5 (1931), pp. 2709–309

'Les Dogmes et les conditions de la vraie connaissance', *Bulletin de la Confrèrie de saint Photios le Confesseur* 1 (1934), pp. 2–9

'Le Théologie négative dans la doctrine de Denys l'Aréopagite', *Revue des sciences philosophiques et théologiques* 28 (1939), pp. 204–21

'Étude sur la terminologie de saint Bernard', *Archivum Latinitatis Medii Aevi* (= Bulletin du Cange] 17 (1942), pp. 79–96

'La théologie de la lumière chez saint Grégoire de Thessalonique', *Dieu vivant* 1 (1945), pp. 94–118

'Redemption and Deification', *Sobornost* 12 (1947), pp. 47–56

'Lichnost' i mỳsl' svyateĭshego patriarkha Sergiya', in *Dukhovnoe nasledstvo patriarkha Sergiya* (Moscow: The Moscow Patriarchate, 1947), pp. 263–70

'Du troisième attribute de l'Église', *Dieu vivant* 10 (1948), pp. 78–89

'Panagia', in E. L. Mascall (ed.), *The Mother of God: A Symposium* (London: Dacre Press, 1949), pp. 24–36

'Soblazni tsekovnogo soznaniya', *Messager de l'Exerchat du patriarche russe en Europe occidentale* 1 (1950), pp. 16–21

'"Ténèbre" et "lumière" dans la connaissance de Dieu', in *Ordre, désordre, lumière* (Paris: Vrin, 1952), pp. 133–43

'Dominion and Kingship: An Eschatological Study', *Sobornost* 14 (1953), pp. 67–9

'Les Éléments de "Théologie negative" dans la pensée de saint Augustin', *Augustinus Magister* 1 (Paris: Éditions des Études augustiniennes, 1954), pp. 575–81

'La Dogme de l'Immaculée Conception—Lourdes', *Messager de l'Exarchat du patriarche russe en Europe occidentale* 20 (1954), pp. 246–51

'La Notion théologique de la Personne humaine', *Messager de l'Exerchat du patriarche russe en Europe occidentale* 24 (1955), pp. 227–35

'Le Problem de la 'Vision face à face' et la Tradition patristique de Byzance', in Kurt Aland and F. L. Cross, *Studia Patristica* 64, 2 (Berlin: Akademie Verlag, 1957)

'The Theology of the Image', *Sobornost* 22 (1957–8), pp. 123–33

'Foi et théologie', *Contacts* 13 (1961), pp. 163–76

'Notes sur la "Credo" de la Messe', *Contacts* 38–9 (1962), pp. 84–6, 88–90

'La Conscience catholique: implications anthropologiqes du dogme de l'Église', *Contacts* 42 (1963), pp. 76–88

www.ingramcontent.com/pod-product-compliance
Lightning Source LLC
Chambersburg PA
CBHW022109150426
43195CB00008B/335